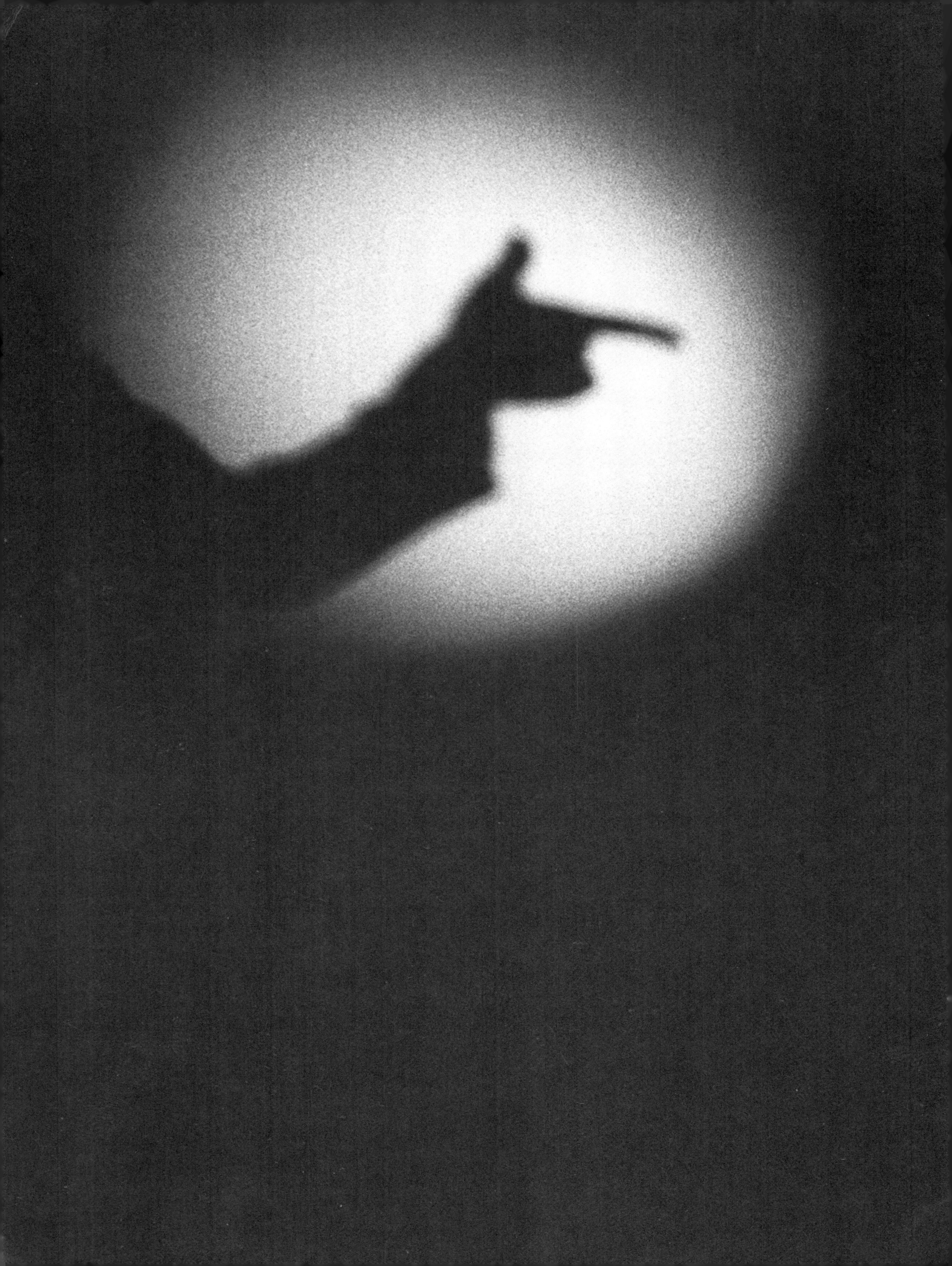

Urban Theater: New York Art in the 1980s

Organized by Michael Auping

With essays by Michael Auping, Andrea Karnes, and Alison Hearst

Skira Rizzoli New York
The Modern

This catalogue is published on the occasion of the exhibition

URBAN THEATER: NEW YORK ART IN THE 1980s

organized by the Modern Art Museum of Fort Worth, on view September 21, 2014–January 4, 2015.

Library of Congress Control Number: 2014940567

ISBN: 978-0-8478-4454-8 (hardcover)
ISBN: 978-0-929865-34-8 (paperback)

First published in the United States of America in 2014 by

Skira Rizzoli Publications, Inc.
300 Park Avenue South
New York, NY 10010
www.rizzoliusa.com

and

Modern Art Museum of Fort Worth
3200 Darnell Street
Fort Worth, TX 76107
www.themodern.org

For Skira Rizzoli Publications, Inc.:
Margaret Rennolds Chace, Associate Publisher

Edited by Leslie Murrell, Modern Art Museum of Fort Worth

Designed by Peter B. Willberg with Judith Brugger

On front jacket: Keith Haring in the New York subway. Keith Haring artwork © Keith Haring Foundation. Photograph © Elinor Vernhes

On back jacket: Palladium nightclub, New York, 1976–97

On case: Keith Haring, *Red* (detail), 1982–84. Gouache and ink on paper. 106¾ × 274 inches. Courtesy Gladstone Gallery, New York and Brussels. Keith Haring artwork © Keith Haring Foundation

Pages 1 and 2: Laurie Anderson, *United States I–IV*, Brooklyn Academy of Music, 1983. Courtesy of the Artist

2014 2015 2016 2017/10 9 8 7 6 5 4 3 2 1

Printed in China

Contents

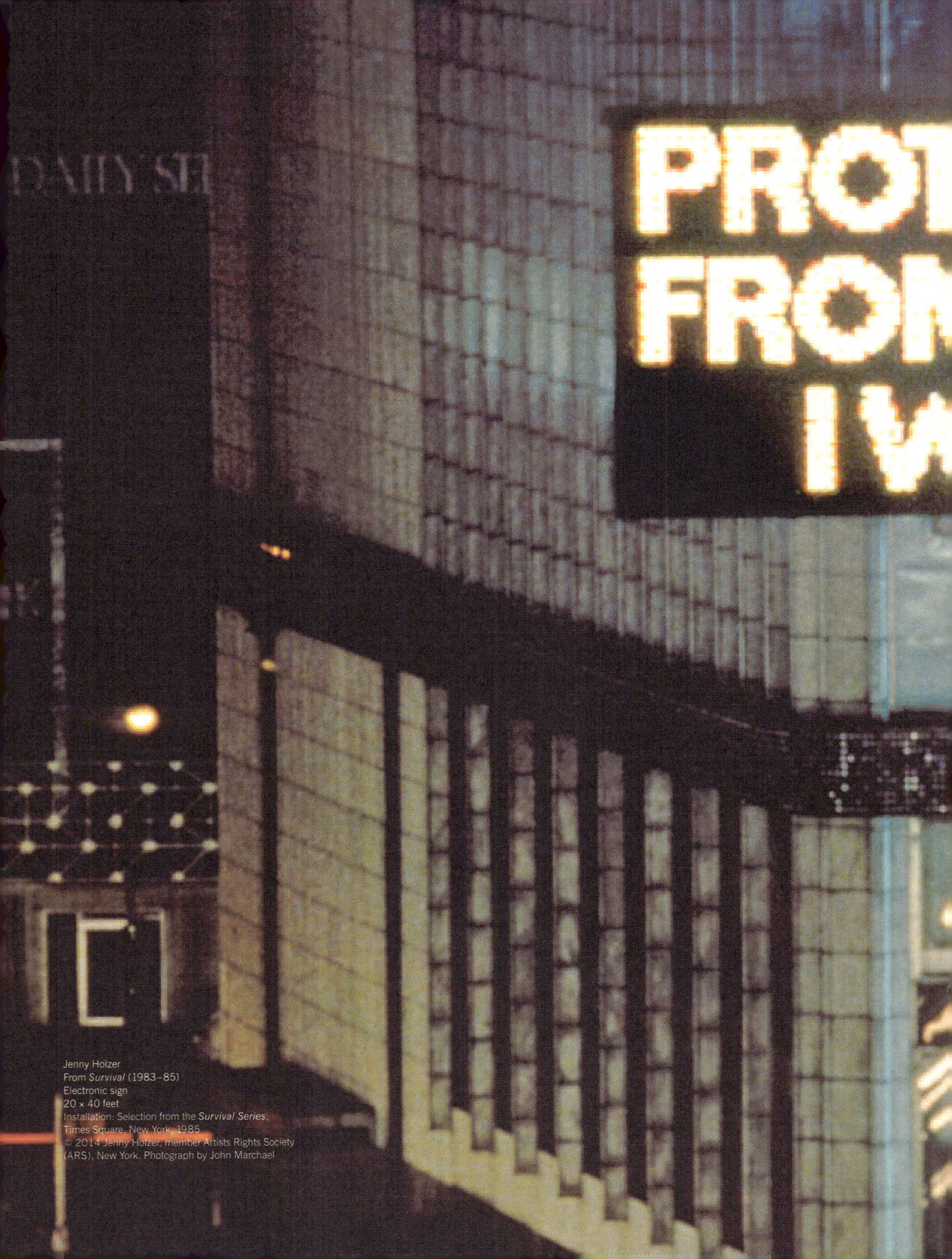

Jenny Holzer
From *Survival* (1983–85)
Electronic sign
20 × 40 feet
Installation: Selection from the *Survival Series*, Times Square, New York, 1985
 Photograph by John Marchael

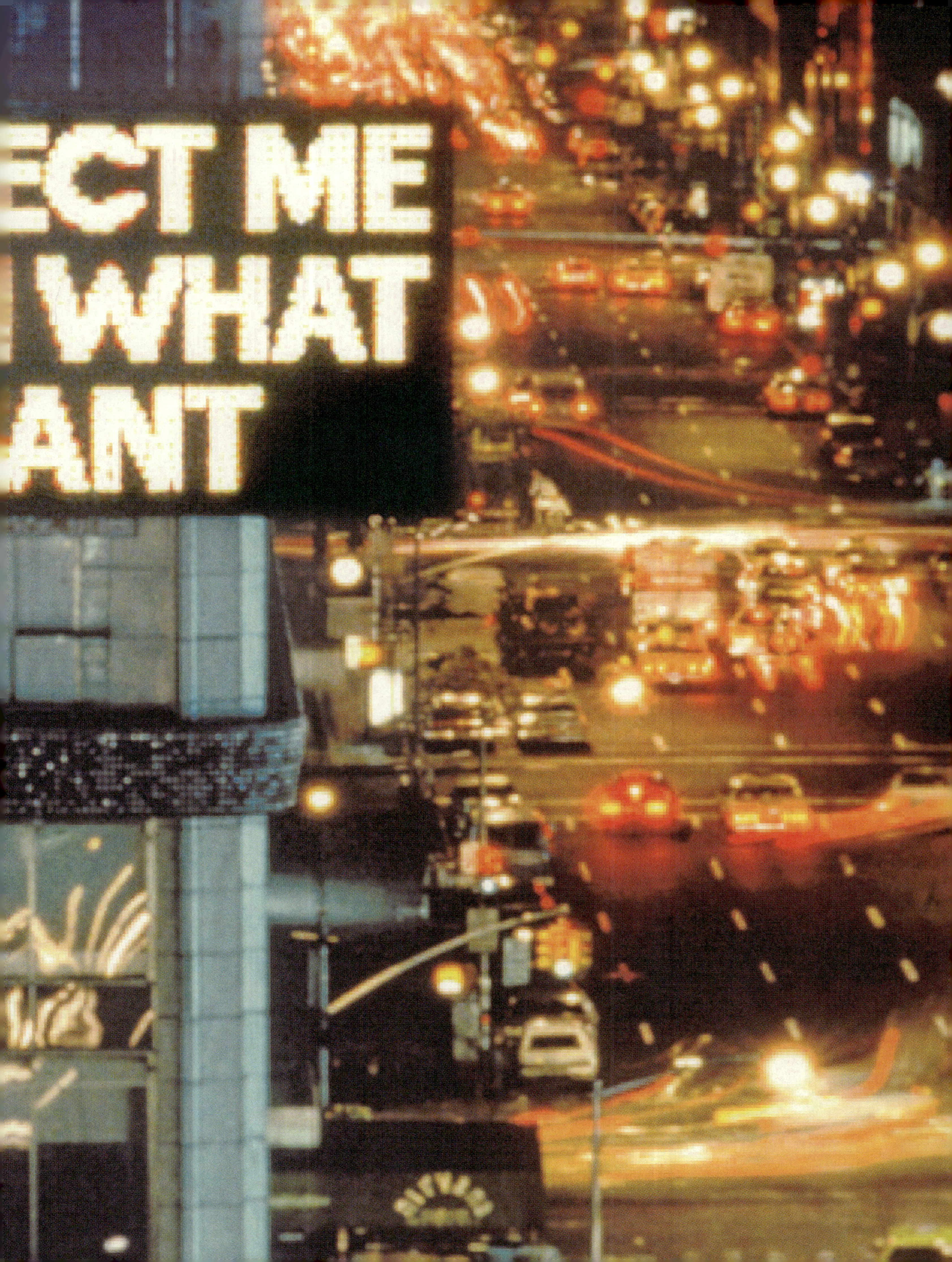
ECT ME
WHAT
ANT

Lenders to the Exhibition

Laurie Anderson
Ara Arslanian
Scott and Yael Braun
The Broad Art Foundation, Santa Monica
Aaron and Leslee Cowen, New York
Dallas Museum of Art
Jeffrey Deitch
The Doris and Donald Fisher Collection
Honor Fraser Gallery, Los Angeles
Barbara and Michael Gamson
Gladstone Gallery, New York and Brussels
Glenstone
Keith Haring Foundation
Marguerite Steed Hoffman
Jenny Holzer
Paul Kasmin Gallery, New York
Robert Longo
Robert Mapplethorpe Foundation
Matthew Marks Gallery
Metro Pictures
Joseph Mizzi
Modern Art Museum of Fort Worth
The Museum of Contemporary Art, Los Angeles
The Museum of Modern Art, New York
Richard Prince
The Rachofsky Collection
Rubell Family Collection, Miami
Julian Schnabel
B.Z. + Michael Schwartz, New York
Gayle and Paul Stoffel
UBS Art Collection
David Zwirner Gallery, New York and London

And those collectors who wish to remain anonymous

Acknowledgments

Group exhibitions always present a challenge, particularly when they address a decade as diverse as the 1980s. Michael Auping, the Modern's chief curator, has worked on this project for the past three years, refining the checklist and the installation. He acknowledges that this show is, to some degree, a personal viewpoint—his recollection of New York in the '80s as a young curator. However, it is also apparent that he has brought together works by some of the greatest artists of that decade, giving the exhibition a deservedly large platform, spreading it over 25,000 square feet of space. What is most impressive is that he has been able to fill this space with some of the most iconic works from New York in the 1980s. Our thanks to Michael for his perseverance in amassing this presentation.

Michael has worked with Leslie Murrell, our editor, and the designer Peter Willberg to produce this beautiful and informative publication. Along with their contributions are insightful essays by curator Andrea Karnes and assistant curator Alison Hearst.

Many of the works in this exhibition have attained very high values and are in considerable demand. Therefore, we are especially appreciative of lenders whose generosity has truly made this presentation possible. Their names are listed on the opposite page.

We are also thankful to the artists and their representatives for their cooperation and assistance in bringing these great works together. To everyone above, and on behalf of the Museum's Board of Trustees, I offer our gratitude.

Marla Price
Director

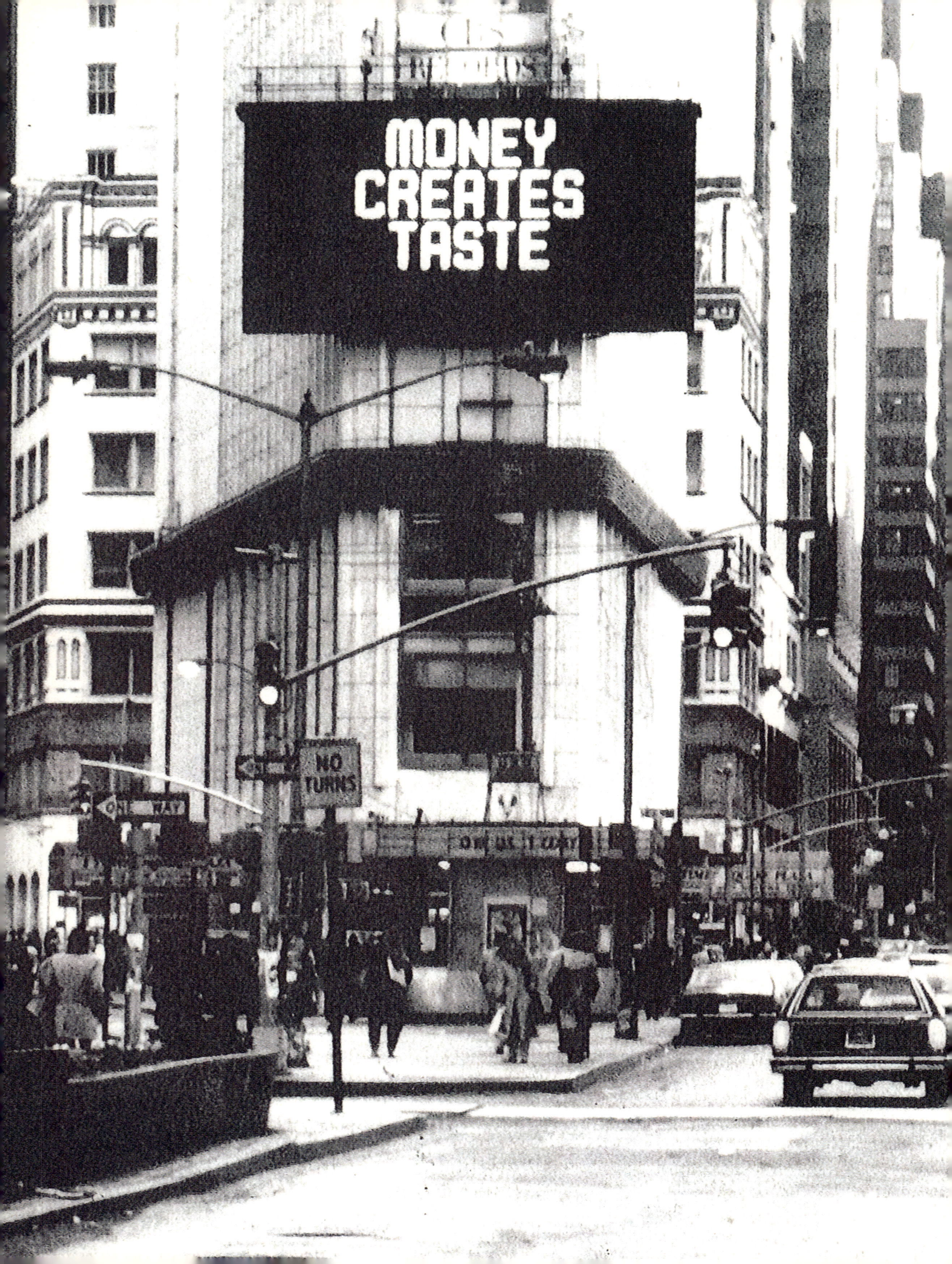
MONEY
CREATES
TASTE
NO
TURNS
ONE WAY

Introduction

In his first column for the *Village Voice* in 1981, Peter Schjeldahl described the American art world of the 1980s as something resembling a feverish onslaught: "More is happening in American art right now than ever before. There is more of everything and of everybody, including critics. There is more public interest and much more money—not necessarily in that order. There is also a lot of confusion, fatigue, hysteria, cynicism, and paranoia. Sometimes I wonder how anyone stays sane. There is something faintly unwholesome—heavily made-up and neon lit—about the scene, but it is very exciting."[1]

The art world entered the '80s in numbers and attitude. A large generation of baby boomers came into the field and expected to be heard. Many of them were art school–educated by some of the best artists of previous generations. Their understanding of postwar art history and its cycles of stylistic overthrows was acute, and their ambitions were grand.

Nowhere was this more the case than in New York City. There is a sense—in part mythic, in part very real—that New York art in the '80s was bigger, brighter, more glamorous, and, in some ways, darker than anything Americans had ever experienced. In an ultra-urban environment thought of as the pinnacle of global economic and cultural cosmopolitanism, the '80s art world in New York represented a neo-Edwardian moment.

The eighties seem out of proportion in respect to the decades that came before and after. Part of this had to do with an expanded art market. Then-president Ronald Reagan's new economy was not just trickling down to the art world, it was transforming art into something that was not only intellectually stimulating, but an investment, a so-called asset class, as well as a means toward upward social mobility. At the time, this gave the '80s a slightly sordid complexion. Critics warned of "a market atmosphere, with its constant demands for something new,"[2] along with "painters that are millionaires at thirty" and "careerist maneuvering and a market quickening to reward it; the ascendancy of

Jenny Holzer
From *Truisms* (1977–79), 1982
Electronic sign
20 × 40 feet
Installation: *Messages to the Public*,
Times Square, New York, 1982

Photograph by Lisa Kahane, NYC

naive and opportunistic collectors."[3] Tom Wolfe, who lambasted the art world in the '60s in *The Painted Word*, 1975, would later discuss a broader New York culture in the '80s, focusing on the theme of greed. The title for that book, *The Bonfire of the Vanities*, 1987, has been used to describe the art world of those years—in some cases, for good reason. One prominent collector of the period supposedly said, "Art collecting is the only socially commendable form of greed."[4] In retrospect, the art market of the '80s was simply a prelude to the art world of today, but without the now-pervasive art fairs and bloated auction results. In some ways, the '80s art world in its optimistic ambitions seems almost romantic by comparison.

The critic Carter Ratcliff titled a series of articles about art and personality in the 1980s *Dramatis Personae*. With a generation raised on Hollywood films and television, and sophisticated in the power and rhetoric of media, the '80s produced large, artistic personalities that helped support the content of their art or became the art itself. Andy

---

New York art in the '80s was bigger, brighter, more glamorous, and, in some ways, darker than anything Americans had ever experienced.

Warhol had predicted that in the future everyone would be famous for fifteen minutes. There is the sense that this generation took that prediction to heart, although many of them have experienced far more than fifteen minutes of fame.

That being said, the '80s was a platform for a generation of artists with complex and layered aesthetic agendas. Ambition was combined with skepticism about the world, and each artist found different ways of exposing their moment in culture either by subverting or magnifying it. Jenny Holzer's electronic Times Square message MONEY CREATES TASTE and Barbara Kruger's declarative text panel "I shop therefore I am" reflect artists who understood the culture in which they play a part. While art criticism had for decades propounded the purity of traditional media as a way of separating art from common culture, these artists explored outside their media and disciplines, often engaging popular culture and the messages it was sending. There is no question that during that period New York artists produced a remarkably diverse range of forms and philosophies: from Julian Schnabel's epic paintings to Cindy Sherman's *Film Stills* and Keith Haring's and Jean-Michel Basquiat's graffiti.

The exhibition that this book accompanies brings together iconic works by many of the artists prominent during the '80s, devoting more than 25,000 square feet to the presentation. Like the decade it represents, the exhibition is outsize. Of course, every decade has many artists that contribute to its effect, even if the focus is narrowed to a specific city, and much more so if that city is New York. However, no group exhibition, regardless of how large, can be comprehensive, and no number of artworks can capture the precise nature of a place and time. We make no claims that this is a definitive presentation of New York art in the 1980s. We have tried to re-create the energy of that moment through very selected works.

Some would argue that the '80s was the last moment when New York held its centrality as a supreme magnet for artists, writers, and collectors. Perhaps it was also the last decade in which New York had an "art community," before the enterprise became dispersed and global—even though that art community was remarkably diverse and competitive. Our hope is to present a visceral and thoughtful outline or cross section of the competing aesthetics that formed the critical themes of that decade and the urban energy of that context.

Michael Auping
Chief Curator

1 Peter Schjeldahl, "First *Voice* Column," *Village Voice*, January 7, 1981, reprinted in *The Hydrogen Jukebox: Selected Writings of Peter Schjeldahl, 1978–1990*, ed. MaLin Wilson (Berkeley: University of California Press, 1991), 62.
2 Suzi Gablik, *Has Modernism Failed?* (New York: Thames and Hudson, 1984), 95–96.
3 Robert Hughes, "On Art and Money," *The New York Review of Books*, December 6, 1984, 20.
4 Eugene Schwartz, quoted in Peter Plagens, "Cents and Sensibility," *Artforum* 41, no. 8 (April 2003): 215.

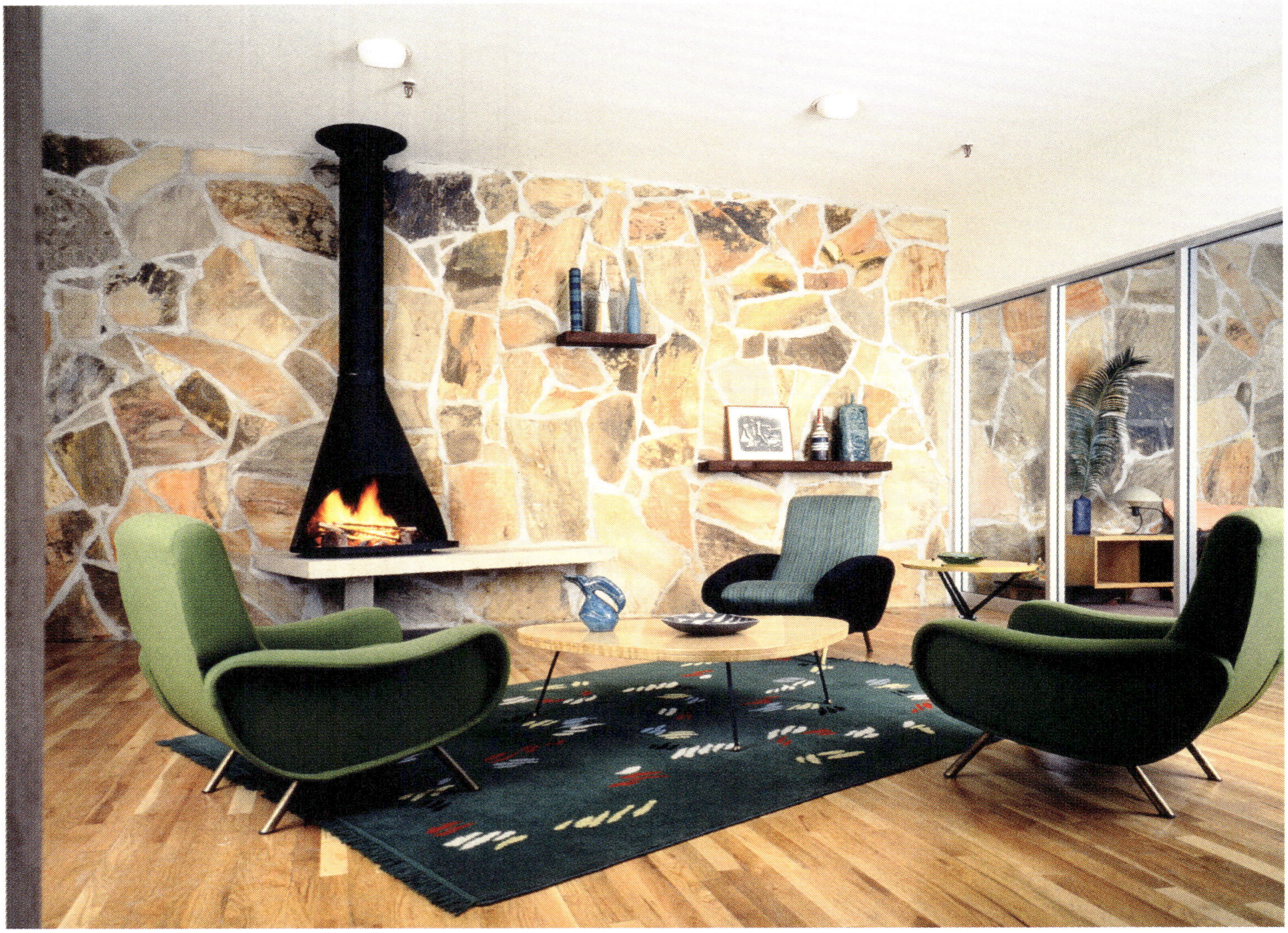

Robert Mapplethorpe
Untitled, David Salle's Loft, 1984

High Performance: Theatricality and the Art of the '80s

Michael Auping

In his controversial 1967 essay "Art and Objecthood," Michael Fried questioned whether Minimalism was art, and if not, under what category should it be placed? The author offered the following: "The answer I want to propose is this: the literalist espousal of objecthood amounts to nothing other than a plea for a new genre of theater; and theater is now the negation of art."[1] By now, most can agree that Fried was wrong in regard to Minimalism being a negation of art. It was, rather, a reformation of the relationship between object and viewer. The viewer became a kind of "performer" moving around the space that was activated by the art. In regard to theatricality, he was quite right, and perhaps unconsciously premonitory in respect to the future of American art. At the time he wrote these words, few in the art world could predict just how theatrical contemporary art would become. They had not seen the 1980s.

While there may not be many things we can agree on about the art of the 1980s, we can certainly say with some confidence that much of it, especially that produced in New York, was theatrical, albeit in different senses of the word. In 1979, the writer and curator Douglas Crimp was early in noting the irony of this creeping theatricality in the works of a number of younger artists, not yet knowing himself just how pervasive the theatrical would become in the art of the next decade.[2]

In Fried's argument, Minimalism was theatrical because the gallery became a stage onto which the viewer walked. During the eighties, this definition of theatricality was compounded, taking cues from television, film, advertising, and performance. If the art of the '70s was raw and often austere, art in the '80s was carefully, sometimes elaborately, staged by comparison.

Theatricality is what gave so much of the art produced in New York in the '80s its flare, as well as its sharp edges. It was a targeted theatricality that could be critical and political, as well as visual. It was also remarkably diverse and inclusive, its theatricality based on an aesthetic of synthesizing content from many different sources. For Fried, theater is "what lies in between the arts," and hence something other than art. The most compelling artists of the '80s understood that there was interesting content and formal invention to be found in that "in between" area. The result was a decade of hybrid media: painting being informed by photography and film; photography blurring into advertising; painting and sculpture literally becoming theater events.

Paintings and Pictures

Painting, generally considered the purest medium, was under the greatest pressure to adapt to a decade that embraced this new hybridity. Given the dominance of minimalist sculpture, conceptualism, and installation art during the 1970s, painting as a medium came under attack. It had found itself in a formalist cul-de-sac, hemmed in by a small list of formalist imperatives. Both abstract and representational painting were deemed by many in the art establishment to be theoretically irrelevant. So much so that *Artforum*, perhaps the most authoritative voice of contemporary art at the time, sent out to painters what now seems like a humorous parody of a questionnaire designed by a conceptual artist, challenging them with the assertion that paintings "abstract and representational, have outlived their usefulness to the current scene."[3]

A new generation coming of age in the '80s set out to "re-stage" painting, making it not just theatrical, but often audacious and flamboyant. In response to the clean and spare aesthetics of Minimalism, Julian Schnabel crammed his paintings with broken crockery overlaid with grand, painterly gestures, creating dramaturgic surfaces. Robert Rauschenberg's combine paintings of the late 1950s and early 1960s, which incorporated objects and found images, offered a precedent for painting as large-scale collage, but Schnabel magnified both the scale and the materiality to a point where painting approached the condition of a theatrical backdrop or tableau. His is a sincere and hyperventilated romanticism. His studios are not just work spaces, but stage sets embellished with tall drapes and antique furniture.

The scale of Schnabel's paintings and his infamously outsize personality beg a reinvention of epic painting for postmodern cathedrals rather than art galleries. They are more Neo-Baroque than Neo-Expressionist, the latter being the '80s movement for which he would become one of the most prominent figures. His professed interest in the Spanish "baroque" architecture of Antoni Gaudí is clearly evident in his shifting and tilting grandiloquent picture planes. The broken plates, long billowing gestures, and undefinable stains that animate his surfaces

Ignatius of Loyola
Julian Schnabel's studio
360 West 11th Street
New York, NY, 1988
Photograph by Jean Kallina

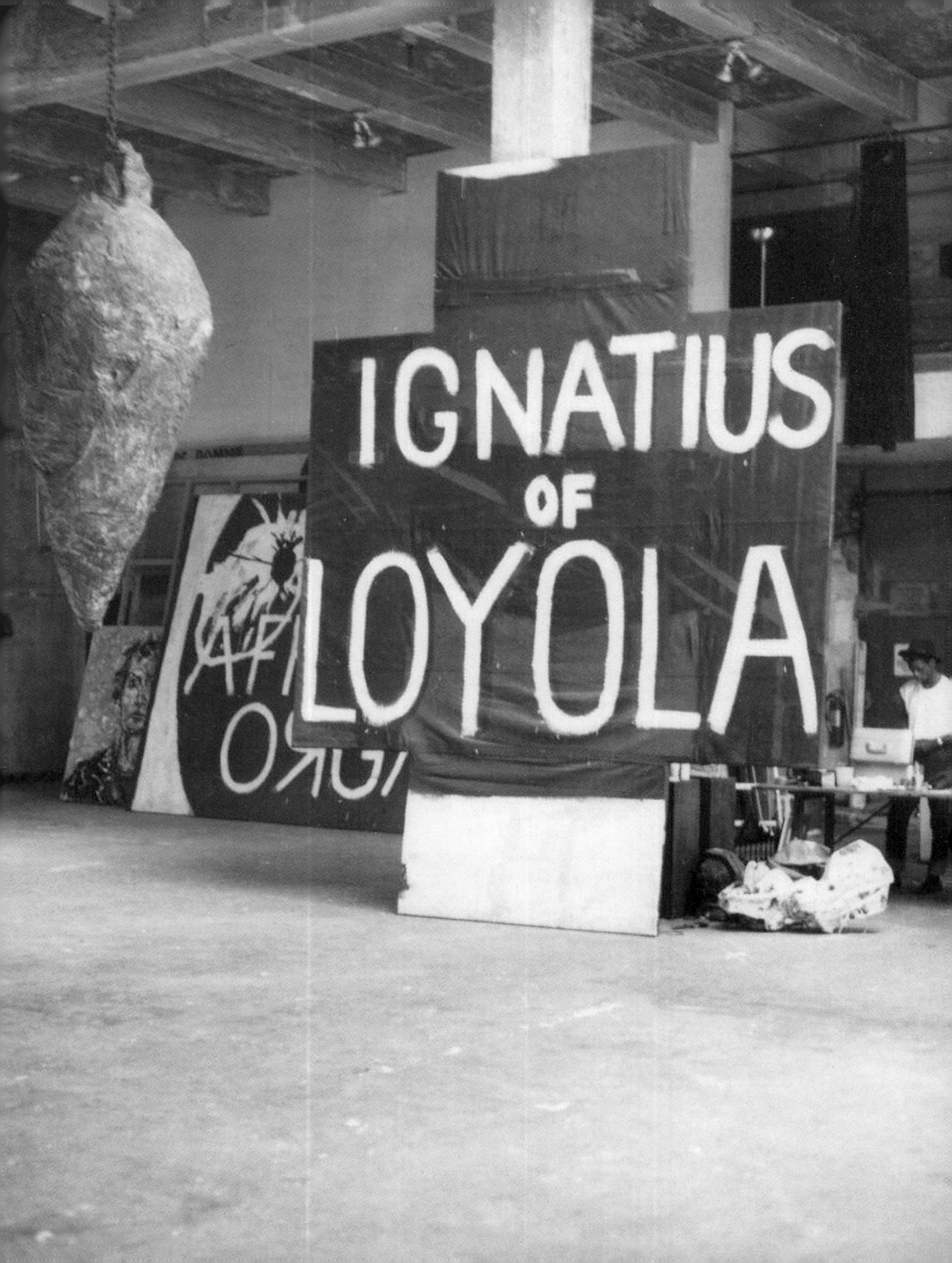
IGNATIUS
OF
LOYOLA

essentially re-create what scholars have referred to as the "phantasmagoric" theatricality of the baroque, in which the viewer is presented what appears to be "an unfolding, geologic process rather than a fixed and finished composition."[4]

In the late 1970s, Schnabel spoke of another source for his interest in the theatrical: the cinema. In hindsight, his later development as a filmmaker puts his interest in creating a "motion picture" in another light. The large tarps and sheets of velvet he has employed as painting surfaces have a wavy and shimmering quality that suggests movement on a Panavision scale. In a poignant early interview, the artist remarked on some of the relationships between painting and film: "Film doesn't want to stop. It's always moving. And painting doesn't want to move, physically I mean. A painting has weight and mass so it's hard to get it moving. It fights against that. I think every image has some kind of momentum. . . . I think all good painting moves in some way. It's just a matter of how fast. Great painting never just sits there. That's part of the drama. . . . Sometimes I think a blank movie screen is better than Minimalism."[5]

His early interest in using plates for his paintings came about with the idea of covering the dark interior of the closet in his hotel room in Barcelona, an idea that conflates both Gaudí and cinema. The plates would not only impart the rugged materiality of Gaudí's architecture, but a panoramic "flicker" effect as well.[6] He made notes for titles, such as *Painting for the Italian Cinema*, *Painting for the French Cinema*, and *Painting for the American Cinema*.[7]

One of the ways Schnabel supported himself in the seventies (along with driving a cab) was as head chef at Mickey Ruskin's Lower Manhattan Ocean Club on Chambers Street (a source for broken plates). An assistant chef was David Salle, whose work would also be placed in that vague category Neo-Expressionism. Salle had attended the California Institute of the Arts, founded in 1961 by Walt Disney as an interdisciplinary program for the visual and performing arts. The performing arts aspect of its mission would have an effect on the artists that attended the school. John Baldessari, an early and distinguished teacher at CalArts, remarked, "Quite a few of the art students who were attending [CalArts] were affected by the performing arts and theater aspect of the school. It was new information for them. They were surrounded by actors and filmmakers, not just artists. And, of course, there was Hollywood right down the Freeway."[8]

By the mid-1970s, distinctions between media were blurring, particularly at CalArts, where Salle worked among painting, drawing, video, and performances that involved props, music, theatrical lighting, and scenery. His early chronology is riddled more with references to the performing arts than to painting.[9] He took a class in theater direction, saw Merce

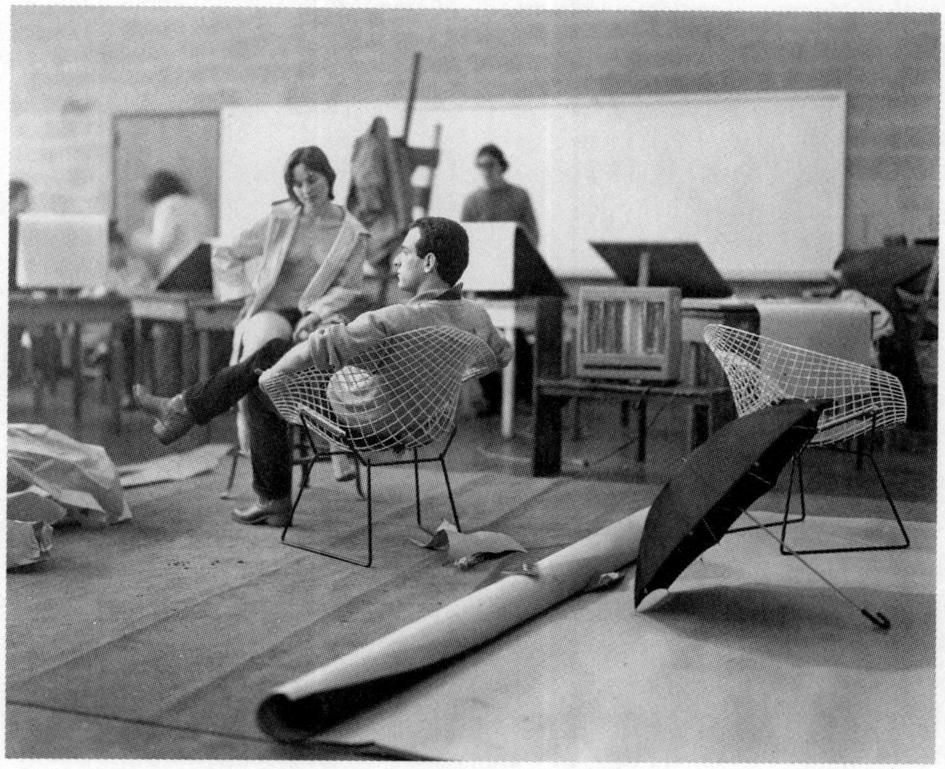

Cunningham's Dance Company, and attended concerts by Terry Riley and Steve Reich. He saw the plays and read the writings of Richard Foreman about his Ontological-Hysteric Theater and was familiar with the films of Rainer Werner Fassbinder, Samuel Fuller, Douglas Sirk, and Preston Sturges. As Salle later put it, "The most interesting things were happening in performance, installation, and theater."[10]

Salle described one of his early installations as "a large photograph of a race car on one wall, a photograph of an African tribal dancer on the opposite wall, and a row of light bulbs on the floor that flashed in a random sequence after a piece of music was played. I've forgotten what the music was; very atmospheric, theatrical, and obscure. I was after a kind of temporal sequence that was supposed to produce a hypnotic rhythm. I still have a very kinesthetic way of reading pictures."[11] These installation pieces employ what Salle referred to as "theatrical time and space."[12]

Salle would eventually form a practice in which the language of painting would be infused with that of the cinematic and the performative. Salle's oddly juxtaposed figures, objects, and scenes suggest cinematic techniques as much as they do the fragmentation of cubist collage. The disorienting close-ups, deep spaces, abrupt changes of subject and background, and atmospheric lighting in his paintings have been

Robert Cumming
David Salle and Model,
Life Drawing Class Coffee Break,
Hartford Art School, W. Hartford, Conn.
March 1979
Vintage gelatin silver print
8 × 10 inches
Copyright Robert Cumming
Courtesy Janet Borden, Inc.

compared to "the splice, jump-cut, dissolve, wipe, zoom, split frame and soft focus" used in filmmaking.[13]

Salle's moody fields of female nudes, still lifes, and pieces of furniture positioned laterally across a canvas or through painted overlays are also reminiscent of the late Dada-Surrealist paintings of Francis Picabia, a source Salle has often acknowledged. However, he sees Picabia's paintings through his interest in film, "being the closest thing to a Douglas Sirk movie I could imagine."[14]

Like Sirk's noir films, Salle's paintings have the quality of being melodramatic and deadpan at the same time. The lurid and melancholic lighting of film noir is found in many of his paintings. Salle's interest in film and theatrical settings seems to even have seeped into his living space. The "living room" of his studio, as photographed by Robert Mapplethorpe, looks like a stage set based on a 1950s living room. Salle would eventually extend his art into set design, collaborating on ballets with his partner, choreographer Karole Armitage, who was the model for a number of his paintings, and film directing (*Search and Destroy*, 1995, starring Griffin Dunne and Christopher Walken).

Many have been critical of Salle's presentation of women. Indeed, his females, often nude, appear to represent the classic "male gaze," in which women are presented as just another piece of furniture set on a pictorial stage. Salle pushes the theatrical envelope on this gaze by using female poses that are often salacious, reflecting the in-your-face drama of pornography. In the '70s, Salle worked for the semipornographic magazine *Stag*. Yet, Salle's women seem quietly and strangely ice cold, like foreign objects to be analyzed. Their revenge is that they not only do not seduce him, they ignore him.

In the '80s, it was common to play the "macho" theatrics of the so-called Neo-Expressionists against the cooler approach of the "Pictures Generation" of photo-based artists, such as Cindy Sherman.[15] Sherrie Levine, however, noticed an odd symbiosis between Salle's cinematic viewpoint and that presented through the various female types played by Sherman in her *Untitled Film Stills*, 1977–80. Speaking of her early encounter with Salle's paintings, she said, "I had the idea that they were pictures of a man looking at a woman looking at a man. And I thought that was pretty interesting, because I've always seen the self-portraits of Cindy Sherman as pictures of a woman looking at a man looking at a woman. His are pictures that posit a man's consciousness in relation to a woman's consciousness."[16]

Salle's and Sherman's work are oddly related, with 1950s and 1960s film culture as a common denominator, particularly film noir, in which gender polarizations were key elements of a plot. One could say Salle was playing the hard-boiled, typically misogynist, noir detective to Sherman's femme fatales. Levine's observation reflects the complexities of gender viewpoint being explored by '80s artists, and how those viewpoints had been exploited in film and media.

Sherman's *Untitled Film Stills* consist of black-and-white photographs that present a female character, played by Sherman, in various guises, each representing movie characterizations of women. Sherman followed a generation of conceptual artists who documented common, ubiquitous aspects of postwar life. Ed Ruscha's gas stations, Dan Graham's apartment buildings, and Bernd and Hilla Becher's water towers pushed Pop art into the realm of typology. Sherman brings a feminist perspective to this typological aesthetic, documenting how Hollywood, and mass media in general, typecasts women. The success of Sherman's images is based not only on her ability to deconstruct Hollywood's portrayal of

---

Salle's women seem quietly and strangely ice cold, like foreign objects to be analyzed. Their revenge is that they not only do not seduce him, they ignore him.

---

female identity, but on her talent for delivering those identities by creating poignant situational dramas through both acting and minimal, but carefully constructed, theatrical sets.

Sherman began her career experimenting with performance, film, and installation. Living in Buffalo in the 1970s, she tried acting out different identities in public, attending art openings "where I was dressed in character. I decided I just wanted to go in character, some kind of character."[17] She also made a film, *Doll Clothes*, 1975, featuring a paper doll self-portrait wearing different outfits, and an installation titled *A Play of Selves*, 1976, which consisted of a four-act visual play with 245 cutout photographic figures embodying characters such as Agony, Desire, Frivolous Young Woman, and the Narrator (all played by Sherman) pasted on the walls in a continuous flow of scenes. Eventually these performative and theatrical forms came together in her later studio work.

In making her *Film Stills*, Sherman essentially became a synthesis of director, actress, set designer, wardrobe adviser, makeup artist, and prop person. The reverse of Schnabel and Salle, who brought film ideas into painting, Sherman employs a device initially developed by painters—the theatrical tableau—and later used in photography and film. Sherman exploits the melodramatic possibilities of the tableau, while creating a quality of realism through an attention to specific details. Using a minimum of props and backdrops—a period chair or lamp, a drink in the hand, a cigarette, a ruffled sheet, an empty alley with a single, dim light—she creates narrative suspense, and sometimes humor. Her portrayals can be so spot-on, we laugh at ourselves for believing them in movies. What is most remarkable about Sherman's images, however, is they use theatricality to compress a narrative, as if a single Sherman photograph can distill a sixty-minute film. Through this one image, it is as if we know the entire plot.

Sherman's generation understood instinctively that Hollywood and Madison Avenue advertisers had created an artifice of reality, and their response was to expose the reality of the artifice. As Thomas Lawson wrote about this so-called Pictures Generation, "Our daily encounters with one another, and with nature, our gestures, our speech are so thoroughly impregnated with a rhetoric absorbed through the airwaves

---

Sherman employs a device initially developed by painters—the theatrical tableau—and later used in photography and film.

---

that we can have no certain claim to the originality of any one of these actions. Every cigarette, every drink, every love affair echoes down a never-ending passageway of references—to advertisements, to television shows, to movies—to the point where we no longer know if we mimic or are mimicked."[18]

There is some irony and message in the fact that the president of the United States who crystallized much of the politics (conservative and liberal) of the '80s was an ex-actor and a cowboy. The cowboys played by Ronald Reagan, John Wayne, and others were icons of American cinema. "Cowboy movies" were a standard genre and a symbol of American independence and self-reliance. Richard Prince takes us back to those movies, filtered, as it were, through Marlboro cigarette ads. By the eighties, the cinematic image of a cowboy riding across vast American plains was appropriated by the Philip Morris Company for one of the most successful advertising campaigns of all time. The famous Marlboro Man reinvigorated cigarette sales using the American western as its theatrical backdrop. The photographer employed by Philip Morris was shrewd to replicate the grand western landscapes captured by the CinemaScope technologies developed for movies in the early 1950s.

Prince's photographs are, like Sherman's movie stills, a theatrical compression or trigger for a familiar movie. Stripping away the Marlboro logo and text from the image and re-photographing it, Prince takes us back to that moment of innocence when we imagined that a complex American culture could be simply defined as a rugged cowboy riding across an unspoiled landscape. In the 1950s and 1960s, the loner male cowboy was a symbol of national pride. Yet Prince's photographs have a vague quality of despair or ennui. Perhaps especially for men, they suggest a melancholic parody of a lost and once-dominant male identity.

While female identity was a critical theme that helped define an '80s aesthetic (with women finally playing a central, if not dominant, role in the art world), the issue of male identity was also one that lurked in the shadows of many male artists of the period. Eric Fischl, another CalArts graduate, and also one that fit uneasily into the Neo-Expressionist label, explored the myth of suburban wholesomeness as it was reflected in the American TV family. Choosing the psychological viewpoint of an adolescent boy growing up in the suburbs, he debunks the idea of the cute and comforting baby boomer environment depicted in such network hits as *Leave It to Beaver*, *The Adventures of Ozzie and Harriet*, and *The Donna Reed Show*.

In one of the artist's most iconic paintings of the '80s, *Bad Boy*, 1981, a young boy is seen staring at an older woman, perhaps his mother or sister, who lies in bed nude with her legs spread as she picks her toenails, evoking the impression that she is not concerned about her naked state and the boy's presence in her room. Although we cannot see his face—our viewpoint is from behind the boy—he appears to be talking to her while he steals money from her purse, which sits on a dresser behind him and out of her sight. Our viewpoint is positioned like a camera on a Hollywood set—in this case, not unlike the famous seduction scene in Mike Nichols's 1967 movie, *The Graduate*.

Bad Boy is a daring subversion of the American TV family. It could also be an oblique reference to the complex gender relations that were taking place in the '80s. Fischl has said, "It [*Bad Boy*] was an important painting for me in the sense of my being aware of how the content of a painting can come about almost secretly. It started as a still-life and then morphed into something very psychological. I thought about it in terms of various meanings. . . . I think part of it had to do with feminism. Feminism had a big effect on all the male painters, though it wasn't talked about. Male painters felt we were under a microscope, being confronted and at the same time watched. We had been in control and now all of a sudden we weren't."[19] In *Bad Boy*, it is indeed difficult to determine who is in control of the situation—the woman, in all her gender display, or the boy, stealing her money.

Promotion and Display

As the art market boomed through the mid-1980s, the nature of art dealing was transformed. The changes not only involved how art was sold—waiting lists of collectors, for example, and selling works prior to openings to special clients—but also how the art was shown. The intimacy of the back room at Wildenstein's uptown gallery or even the elegance of Leo Castelli's shows of the '70s was replaced with the one-person megashow. Gallery exhibitions became increasingly staged, with larger and larger works spread over more and more square feet of space.

Today we are used to galleries allotting massive amounts of real estate to the presentation of an artist's work, but it was the art dealers of the eighties that started this inflation of exhibition space.[20] Moreover, the artist as "bohemian" or cool conceptualist was replaced by the "art star," and a number of the stars of the '80s received special promotion. The "triple show," in which an artist exhibits work at three galleries simultaneously, was an '80s invention. Schnabel, Salle, and Francesco Clemente all had such multi-venue shows devoted to their work, and Schnabel and Clemente both covered huge walls with paintings that looked like theater backdrops. Indeed, some of the artists acknowledged they were aspiring not to contemplation, but theatrical effect. "Art has always been a form of theater," Clemente said. "We are only expanding that role to our time."[21]

Some artists played off of the negative criticism that commercial galleries were becoming oversize fine art boutiques. As early as 1939, the critic Clement Greenberg warned that capitalism was becoming decadent and mired in "kitsch" and the banal aesthetics of popular culture.[22] Greenberg's prophecy seemed to ring true in the 1980s, when the avant-garde increasingly imitated features of consumer and entertainment culture, from the art of display to the cult of personality. These phenomena would be examined and finely polished by Jeff Koons, who was of a slightly younger generation than the Neo-Expressionists and Pictures artists, and who had a keen sense of the '80s art market and its commodity aesthetic. By parodying it in a grand and ambitious fashion, he became one of the emblematic figures of the decade. Bluntly put, Koons spliced Marcel Duchamp's readymades of 1913–17—common, functional objects placed in the context of art—to Greenberg's kitsch. However, while Duchamp's readymades set themselves apart by their sheer ordinariness, Koons's objects glow with the newness of shiny surfaces and the seductive drama of display advertising.

Koons's approach has not been to simply choose common objects and place them in a space, but to carefully stage them. His early series of works—titled *Pre-New, The New, Equilibrium, Statuary, Luxury and*

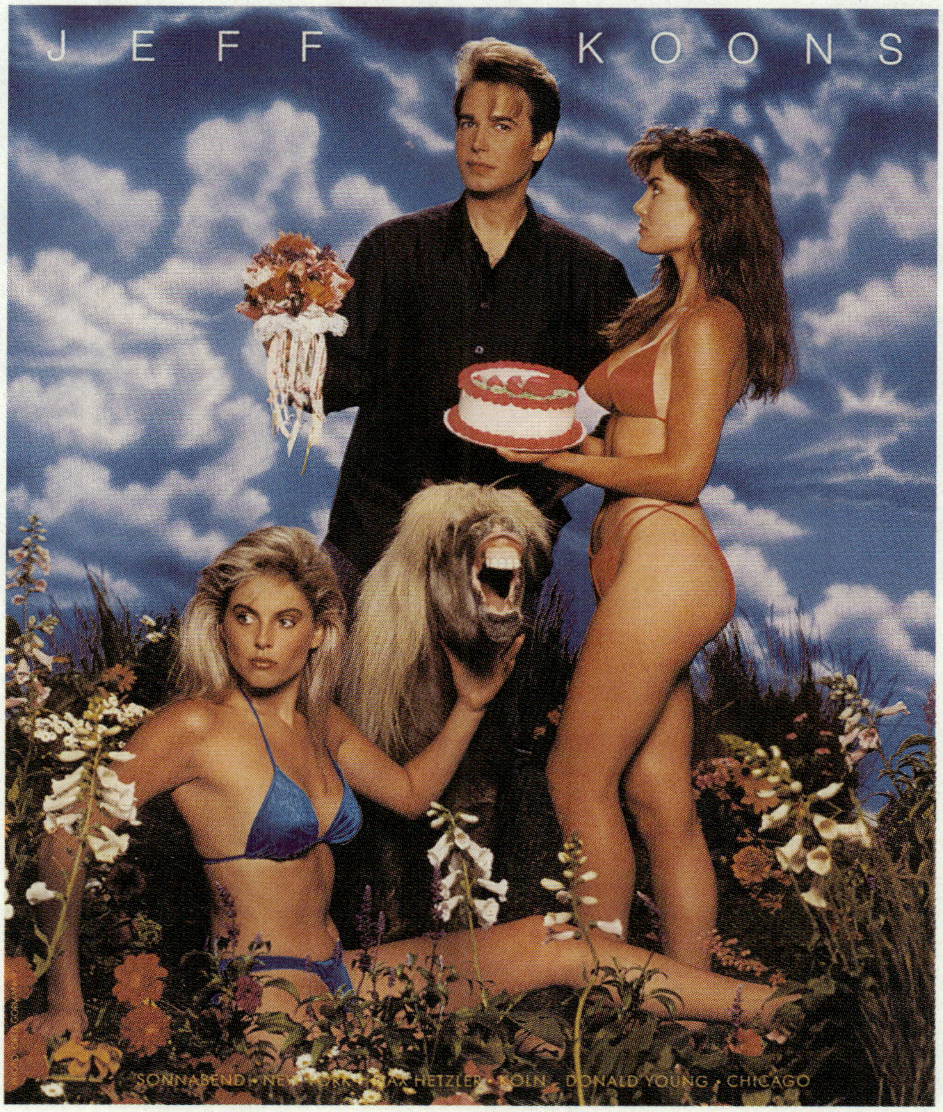

Degradation, and *Banality*—take commodity aesthetics to a new level, high or low, depending on your viewpoint. The son of an interior designer, which the artist often cites as an inspiration, Koons has cultivated a talent for presentation and showmanship. In their early careers, Jasper Johns and Robert Rauschenberg supported themselves making department store displays. However, their goal was to leave that commercial world behind in order to pursue full-time studio careers in fine art. In an ironic reversal, Koons's early work led to what often appeared as commercial display cases.

In his 1980 exhibition at the New Museum of Contemporary Art in New York, simply titled *The New*, Koons placed spotless vacuum cleaners in Plexiglas vitrines as if they were in a retail showroom. With dramatic

Jeff Koons
Art Magazine Ads (Art in America), 1988–89
Lithograph, edition of 50 plus 10 artist proofs
45 × 37 ¼ inches
Collection of the Modern Art Museum of Fort Worth, Anonymous Gift
© Jeff Koons

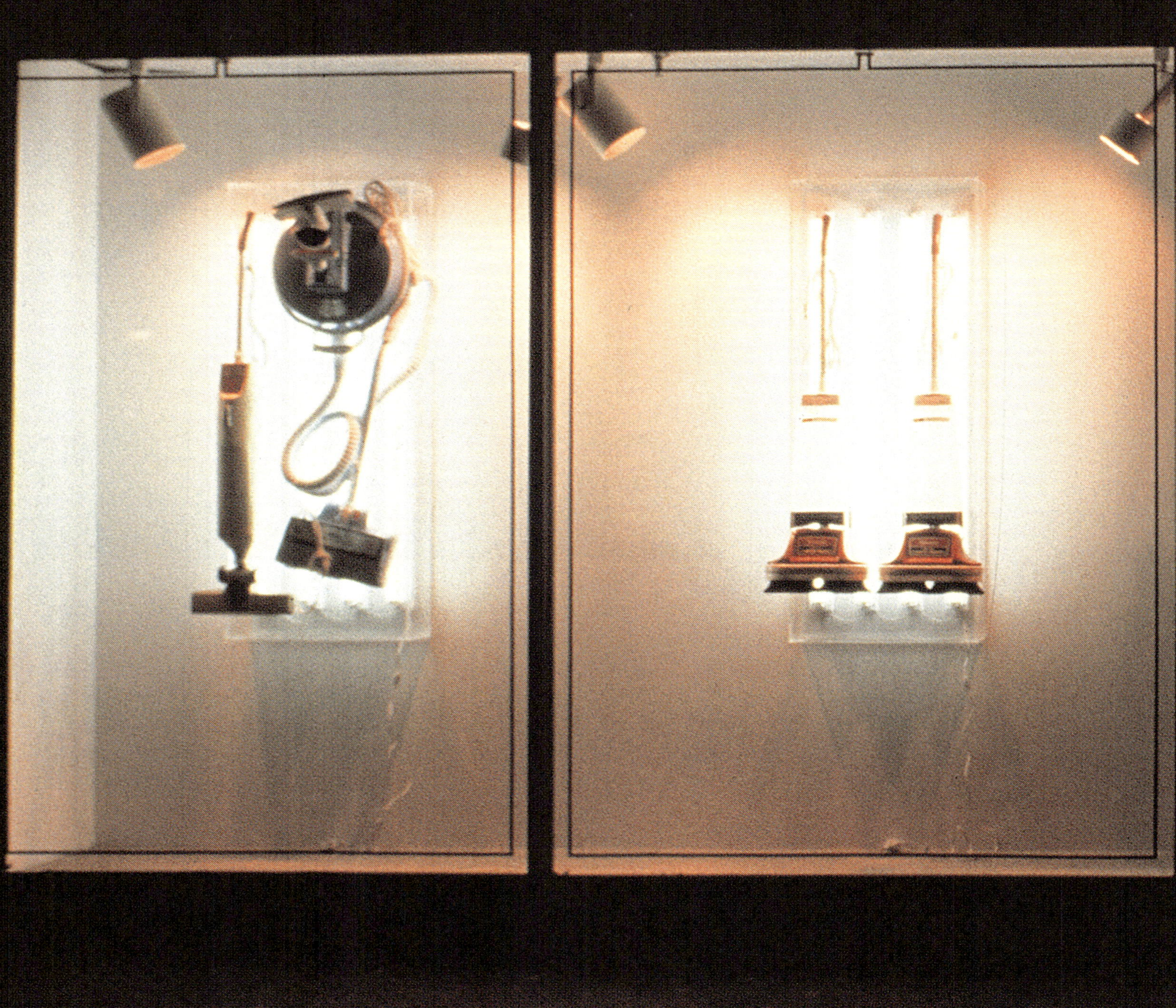

Jeff Koons
The New (Installation view),
New Museum of Contemporary Art,
New York, 1980
Courtesy of the Artist and New Museum Archive

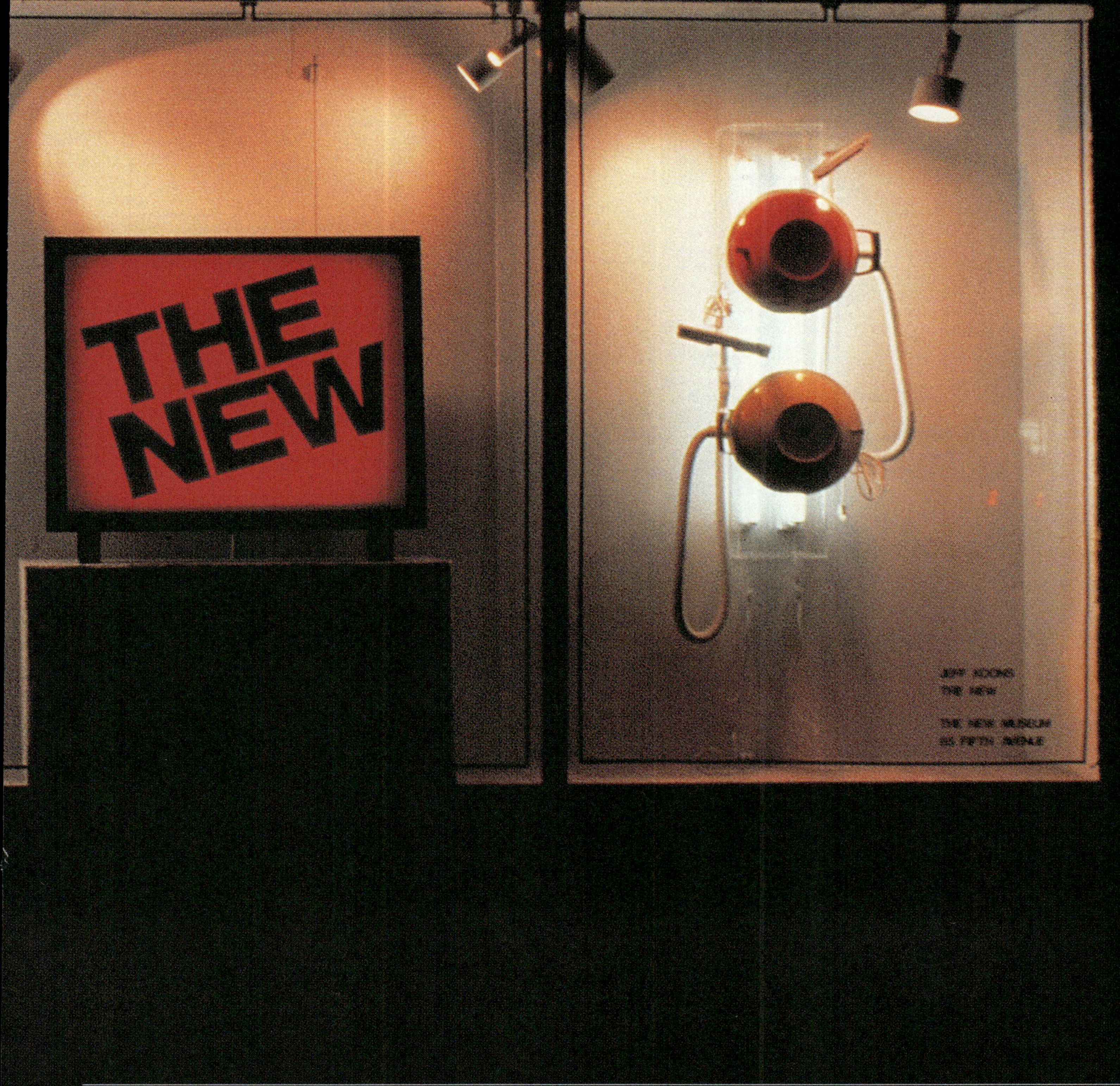
THE
NEW

lighting, they became Minimalism-as-consumer-icon, their cleaning function a wry comment on the pristine nature of Minimalist sculpture. In his *Equilibrium* series of 1985, new basketballs were surreally suspended in tanks of distilled water with a small amount of salt to assist the hollow balls in remaining in the center of the liquid, creating a sculptural parallel for how players magically suspend themselves in space when dunking a basket. Searching for the magic trick that keeps the ball suspended, we peer into these tanks as if they were liquid dioramas.

Koons also pointed out the simple beauty of a new basketball, its circular perfection and geometric lines floating in clear water. These basketball tank pieces were accompanied by a series of posters originally produced by Nike, and now appropriated by Koons, picturing uniformed star NBA players to promote the company's tennis shoes. The artist saw a parallel with the art world. In his *Art Magazine Ads*, 1988–89, Koons implied that art was also a product that required star promotion, placing advertisements in international art magazines of himself in various guises. In elaborately staged scenes, the artist is photographed variously with bikini-clad models and exotic animals or at a blackboard, magnanimously teaching children, portraying himself as a leader of a new generation of art consumers.

Koons has gone so far as to equate the beauty of banality to the "spiritual." Such histrionics beg the question of a transcendent commodity

---

Clemente has compared New York of the '80s to the late Roman Empire in terms of its grittiness, decadence, and diverse cast of characters.

---

culture. Koons is often described as a latter-day Duchamp, but in many respects his art is closer in its effect to that of the French artist Yves Klein. Both have portrayed themselves as Pop shamans, coupling art production with theatrical public personae that create a metaphysical context for their art. Koons's Hoover vacuum cleaners encased in glass containers suggest the quality of shrines, their choice as an object of devotion an ironic reference to the modernist "purity" espoused by Greenberg. Benjamin Buchloh's skeptical analysis of Klein's reception could be equally applied to Koons. "What makes Klein's work so attractive is its construction of a paradox in public: the suggestion that the attempt to redeem spirituality through art at the moment of consumer culture's rise to power would inevitably fashion the spiritual in (involuntary?) travesty."[23] In dramatizing this paradox, both artists highlight the cynical times that we live in.

White Cubes versus Dark Streets: "When you talk about the '80s, it depended on which neighborhood you were talking about."

In many ways, New York art in the '80s was a study in contradictions. Speaking of the artistic content of art from this decade, Jenny Holzer said that "it depended on which neighborhood you were talking about."[24] Midtown and downtown New York were not all white cubes and market boom. There were still low-rent streets, and many of the younger artists coming into the city found their community in those fringe areas, where the aesthetics and politics were more radical.

Clemente moved to New York in 1980, via Rome and Madras, India. What attracted him to all three urban cities was the "squalor and the energy."[25] In his painting *Perseverance*, 1981, he depicts himself carrying the Pantheon through the streets of downtown New York, as excrement flies around him. He has compared New York of the '80s to the late Roman Empire in terms of its grittiness, decadence, and diverse cast of characters. In his 1981 exhibition at Sperone Westwater, he created a room of frescoes of various artists and personalities from the '80s, thinking of it as a form of cinema. "I imagined that frescoes were the equivalent of movies, in terms of having an extremely wide screen, a cast of characters, and strong communal value. So I had [curator] Diego Cortez cast my room."[26]

One could argue that the '80s was the last decade when the New York art world had an art community in a neighborhood sense of the term. For many, the clubs and performance spaces were the heart of that community. Until recently, every generation in New York had its art bar. The '50s and '60s had the Cedar Tavern, where the Abstract Expressionists congregated. The '70s had Mickey Ruskin's Max's Kansas City, where Warhol and his entourage could be found almost nightly. The generation of the '80s required multiple social venues: the Mudd Club, CBGB, Club 57, Hurrah, Tier 3, and the Palladium.

These clubs were a melting pot of all types of artists—musicians, painters, poets, performers, and filmmakers. The associations that developed through performance, painting, drawing, and discussions long into the mornings reinforced the idea that traditional distinctions among media—painting, sculpture, performance, film, etc.—were becoming less relevant. Everyone was working out of a hybrid, experimental context that did not necessarily lend itself to the art market. If you could not find a gallery to show your art or your performance,

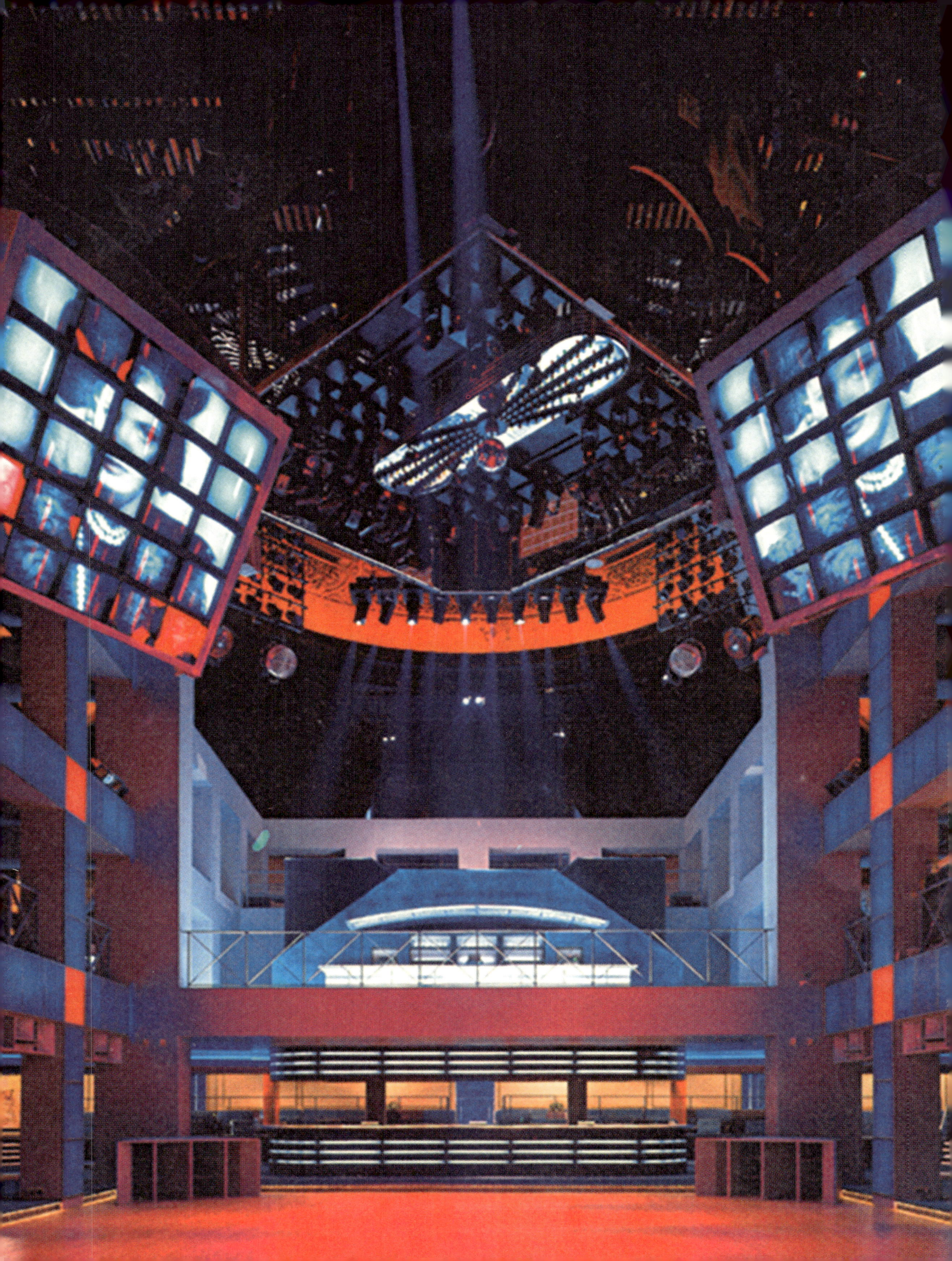

the clubs were a possibility. Some of these clubs grew to mammoth proportions, rivaling the expansion of commercial galleries. The old Palladium on East 14th Street at Third Avenue was converted by Steve Rubell (an investment guru who overextended himself and went afoul of the IRS) and the high-end designer Ian Schrager to a nightclub on steroids. Artists were commissioned to create site-specific works for the club, which then attracted more and more artists who wanted to be seen there. It was an all-night art gallery with a major sound system. Anyone who attended the Palladium in its heyday of the '80s remembers it as a form of social theater.

In stark contrast to the Palladium, however, there were also unoccupied buildings in Lower Manhattan. Regardless of the economic prosperity that had developed, the downtown and midtown areas were only in the

Anyone who attended the Palladium in its heyday of the '80s remembers it as a form of social theater.

beginning stages of renovation. When there are too many artists and not enough galleries, artists find other platforms for their work. Vacant or very low-rent buildings were an alternative for artists who were not yet noticed and whose work tended to be more political in nature or street- and community-based.

The Times Square Show in 1980 was one of the first events of the decade to define a new street sensibility, distinguishing itself by its democratic curatorial approach. It included more than one hundred artists, some of whom would later receive individual renown, among them Keith Haring, Jean-Michel Basquiat, and Jenny Holzer. A youthful and optimistic feeling, and what Holzer has called "the best kind of naïveté," pervaded the show. A few collectors came, but it was mostly people in the neighborhood and off the streets. "We didn't have collectors following us around, so we were happy to make our art for whoever was on the street."[27]

In the end, graffiti—an art literally of the streets—was the most direct route to taking art and ideas to a larger urban audience. Throughout the decade, graffiti became a ubiquitous part of downtown New York. Temporary by nature, it is not a commodity, but an event. At its most dynamic, graffiti is street theater, a late-night performance, leaving spray-painted images as its residue. Ironically, Basquiat, Haring, and Holzer began their careers as anonymous messengers, but later became even more well-known than many of their gallery counterparts.

Palladium nightclub, New York, 1976–97

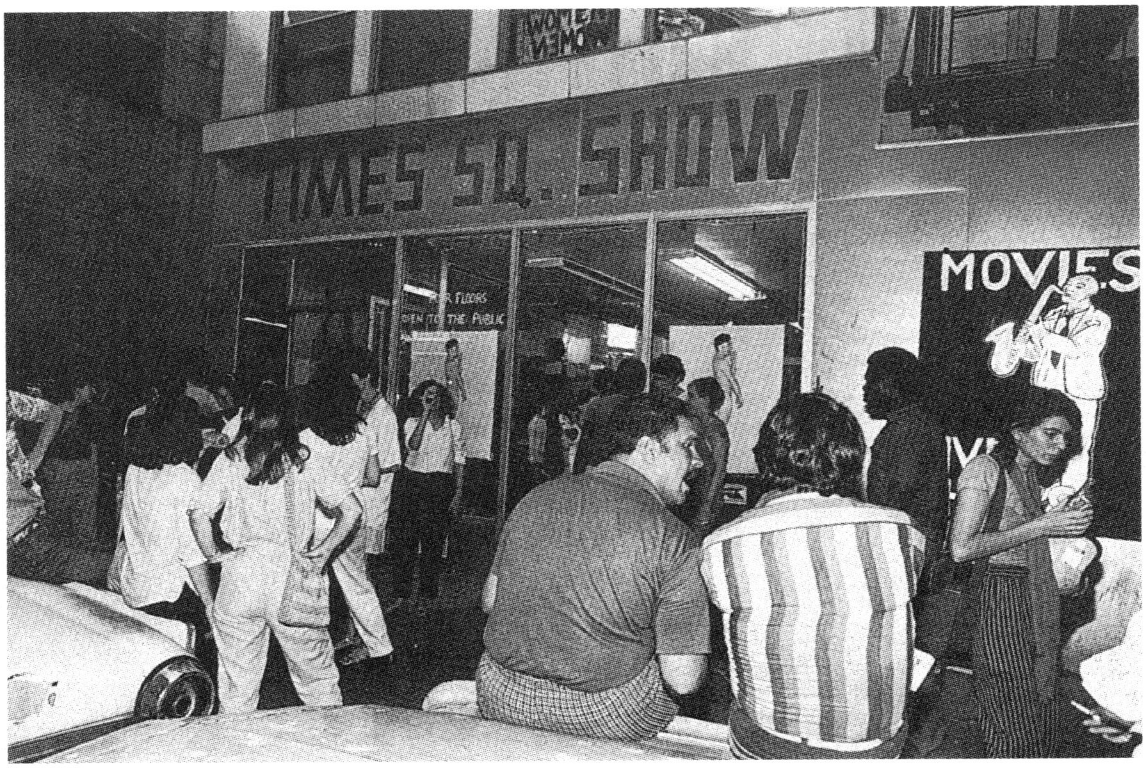

In the later part of the 1970s, spray-painted, exclamatory messages began appearing on downtown walls: SAMO AS AN END TO MINDWASH RELIGION, NOWHERE POLITICS AND BOGUS PHILOSOPHY; SAMO SAVES IDIOTS. Basquiat and his high school friend Albert Diaz invented an imaginary religion (SAMO for "same old shit"), and Basquiat appeared on Lower Manhattan streets late at night to deliver their message like a street preacher with a spray can. Part of the drama of these stealth actions was the fact that no one could identify the sender, despite the efforts of the downtown newspapers, the *Village Voice* and the *Soho News*, and residents. Finding new messages on a given morning was like reading a new act, which would later be described as "language performed," and a cryptic, visual art precursor to hip-hop music.[28] He was also a member of the band Gray, playing clarinet and synthesizer. Gray's music has been characterized as "composed noise music . . . not so much the sounds of a dance bar, but the sound of traffic. It was a theater of the streets."[29]

Basquiat was the son of a successful Haitian immigrant, but his penchant for outrageous, self-destructive behavior meant that he barely graduated from high school. Living on and off the streets from as early as fifteen years of age, he was self-taught, but street-smart. By design, much of his graffiti was in SoHo near the gallery scene, and Basquiat secured an introduction to Andy Warhol, who inspired the young artist's energy and

Times Square Show,
Entrance to the exhibition,
New York, 1980
On right: Tom Otterness,
Untitled Times Square Sign (Sax Player), 1980
Photograph by Teri Slotkin

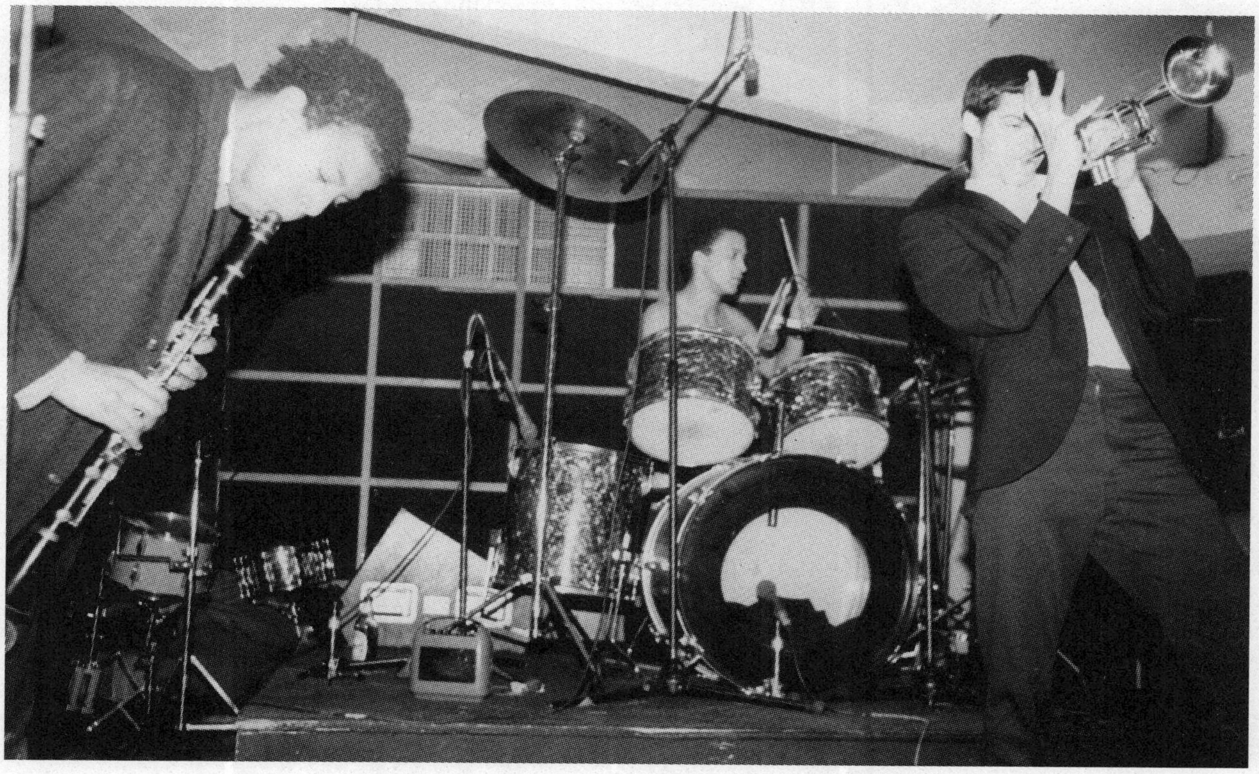

bravura and became a champion of his art. In turn, Basquiat and other painters of the '80s generation inspired Warhol to return to painting after years working in movies, television, and publishing.[30] Ironically, many of these artists saw Warhol's film and television work as more radical than painters of Warhol's generation.

Basquiat was one of only a few graffiti artists to make the successful transition from street painting to the galleries. He shifted his late-night

At its most dynamic, graffiti is street theater, a late-night performance, leaving spray-painted images as its residue.

energies and nervous obsession with drawing into all-night bouts of painting on horizontal canvases that now stood in for walls, creating stream-of-consciousness meditations on pop culture, particularly as it related to black Americans. A central theme in his subject matter was the issue of "performance" and the special talents of black athletes and musicians. He famously had himself photographed as a professional boxer, wearing Champion boxing gloves. Basquiat's paintings were

Gray at Hurrah nightclub in New York.
Left to right: Jean-Michel Basquiat,
Michael Holman, and Shannon Dawson
Autumn 1979
Photograph by Nick Taylor

diaristic, riffing between African and Mexican symbolism, modernist art brut (he has often been compared to Jean Dubuffet), jazz, and contemporary advertising.

When Basquiat was invited to join the Annina Nosei Gallery in the early 1980s, he was cast by the art world as a performer of a different sort. Still maintaining his itinerant ways, partly as a result of an addiction to drugs, the artist lived and worked for a time in the gallerist's basement, leading to speculation that he was a primitive genius being held hostage

> Basquiat's paintings were diaristic, riffing between African and Mexican symbolism, modernist art brut (he has often been compared to Jean Dubuffet), jazz, and contemporary advertising.

to produce paintings. He played to the part with humor and wit, allowing himself to be photographed in his studio with dreadlocks, barefoot, but in an expensive suit.

Basquiat played a high-profile role in the theater of downtown art. He was a new kind of celebrity for the art world, one that could negotiate a segregated world between fine art, pop culture, and the politics of the outsider. He regularly appeared on Glenn O'Brien's New York cable television show *TV Party* and was cast by O'Brien to play the lead role in the film *Downtown 81*. He was a symbol of the aspired hybridity of the downtown scene. Sadly, his celebrity often overshadowed the inclusive character of his paintings.

Keith Haring would not only make the leap from the street to the galleries, but also into the much larger world of commercial advertising. His signature image of a "radiated" baby eventually became one of the most dynamic logos for Ford Motor Company. Spreading over stairways, the walls of buildings, and sidewalks, Haring's simple but energetic figures reflected the vigorous drive of their maker. Haring's high-strung character was a perfect fit for the action-oriented nature of graffiti. Those who witnessed the artist executing his graffiti work in public described it as a pop-up graphic performance. Kenny Scharf has said, "It was all about drawing and performance. I used spray paint, but Keith performed drawings. Consciously or unconsciously, graffiti artists think of art as theater. We were doing our art in public with a time limit. Even if it's at night with no one around, you felt like people were watching. In effect, it was a performance people had to re-imagine when they saw the work the next morning."[31]

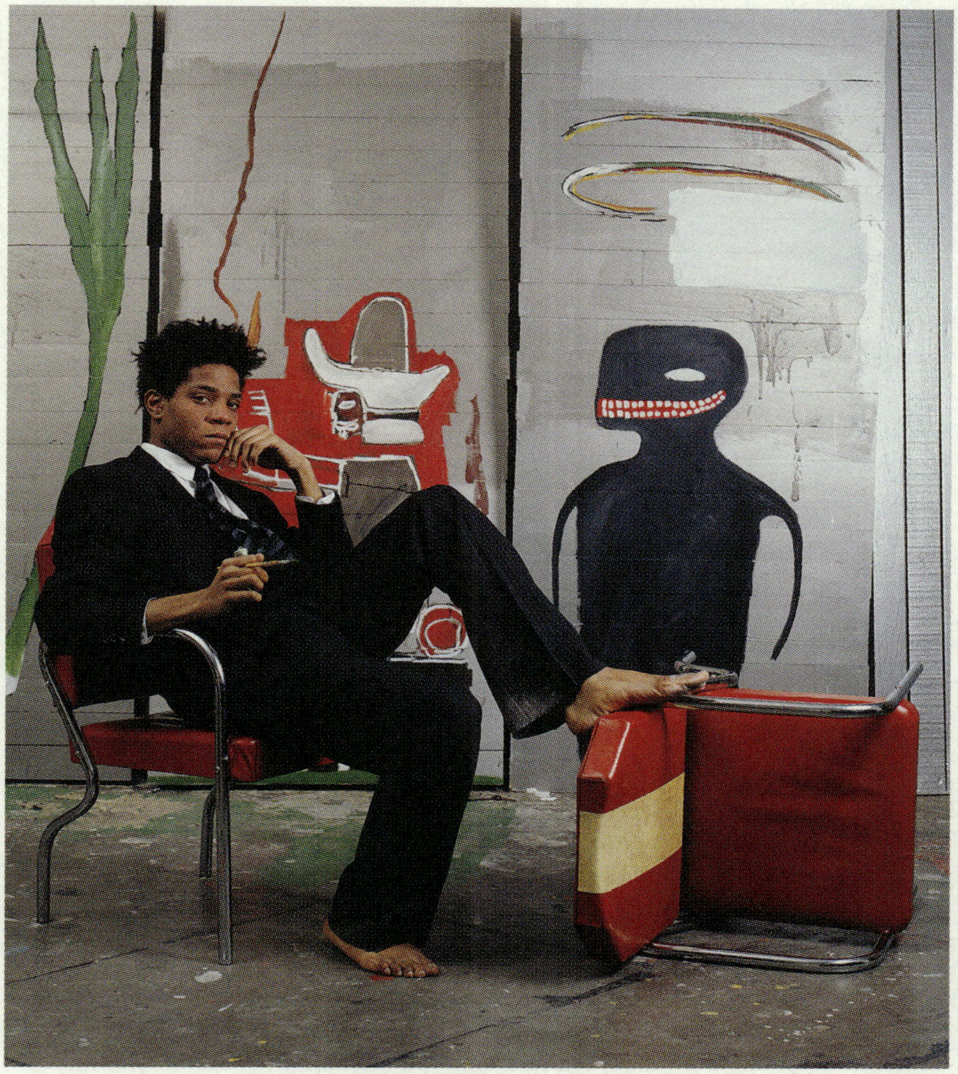

Roommates Haring and Scharf were inspired by cartoon animation they had seen in their youth, and both took up the challenge of transforming those kinetic comedies and dramas into a public, graphic form. Scharf invented hybrid characters based on cartoon families like the Jetsons. His deft use of a spray brush gave his graffiti and his later paintings the look of liquid figuration and the landscapes that distinguished early color cartoons. "The idea of giving painting that kind of performative elasticity was what we were after," Scharf said.[32] With Haring, Scharf also created a black light disco installation in the closet of their Times Square apartment. Titled *Cosmic Closet*, circa 1981, it was a surreal, three-dimensional landscape that could also be thought of as a theater-in-the-round with various hanging and moving elements. For Scharf, Surrealism—with its melting forms and oddly tilted landscape

Basquiat in his studio, 1985
Photograph © Lizzie Himmel

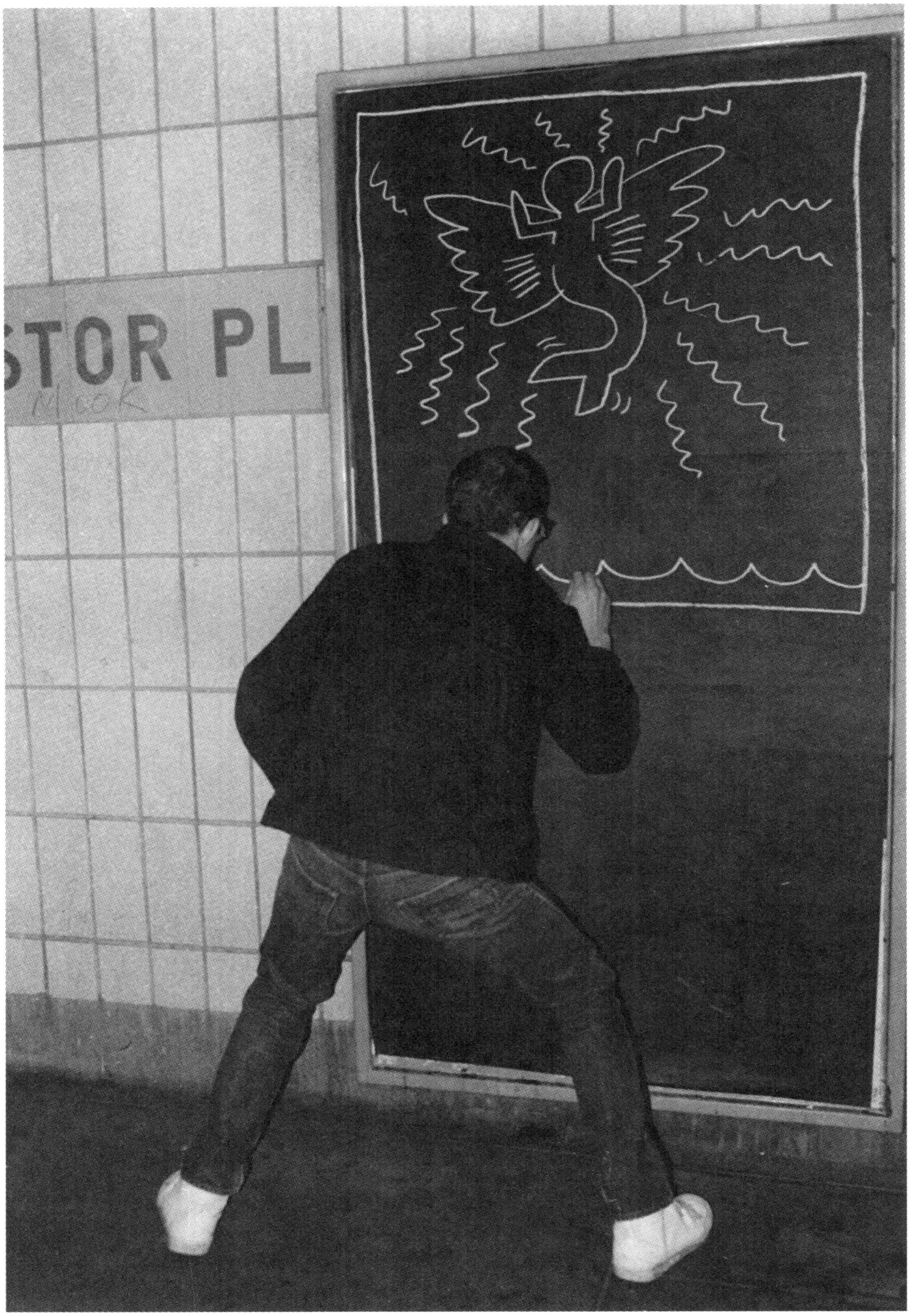

Keith Haring in the New York subway
Keith Haring artwork © Keith Haring Foundation
Photograph © Elinor Vernhes

planes that suggest moving images—was a precursor to animation. His later paintings combine the slow, "psychedelic," implied movement of Surrealism with the more hyped-up cartoon animation of the 1950s.

Haring's later paintings take animation back to a more ancient source. His imagery is made up of long, linear paint strokes, accented by short, linear blips that give his images a vibrating presence, as if exerting electricity or radiation. They are, in essence, speedy pictograms. His works on large sheets of vinyl or paper have the same immediacy as his graffiti. With the works on paper in particular, the animation effect seems less related to cartoons than to Japanese ink painting, where an artist executes a scene with both speed and accuracy.

Graffiti gave a decade often mired in philosophy and theory a sense that art could be very direct—dare we say fun?—and relatable to a large audience. The burst of imagistic vigor brought to the '80s art world by Basquiat and Haring seems even more amazing considering their short-lived careers. Both died in their early thirties, Basquiat of a drug overdose and Haring of AIDS.

Basquiat and Haring posited public art as an art of the hand and body. Jenny Holzer shaped the concept of public intervention for a new type of "graffiti," transforming her art into the delivery systems of contemporary advertising. After graduating from the Rhode Island School of Design in 1977, Holzer entered the Whitney Museum of American Art's Independent Study Program. Her now well-known *Truisms* developed when an instructor gave her an intimidating study list of philosophical texts as required reading, which Holzer pared down to a series of simple—often questionable, depending on your viewpoint—one-line aphorisms: AN ELITE IS INEVITABLE; ABUSE OF POWER COMES AS NO SURPRISE; CLASS STRUCTURE IS AS ARTIFICIAL AS PLASTIC; FAITHFULNESS IS A SOCIAL NOT A BIOLOGICAL LAW; PEOPLE WHO GO CRAZY ARE TOO SENSITIVE. The *Truisms* were placed on commercially printed broadsides that the artist pasted onto walls and fences in Lower Manhattan, sharing space with advertising posters for music and performance events.

None of Holzer's *Truisms*—there are now a total of 253—can be proved, and they take their inspiration from different viewpoints, from liberal to conservative and male or female. The posters were not signed or attributed to anyone. The neutral, bold typeface of her messages suggests a voice of authority, but in fact the statements are more accurately described as a lexical portrait of society. In this sense, they suggest an interesting parallel to Sherman's photographic, female personae; but in this case, the cast of characters is broadened, taking us through a range of identities and stereotypes.

following spread:
Jenny Holzer
Exhibition view: *Jenny Holzer*,
Solomon R. Guggenheim Museum, New York, 1989

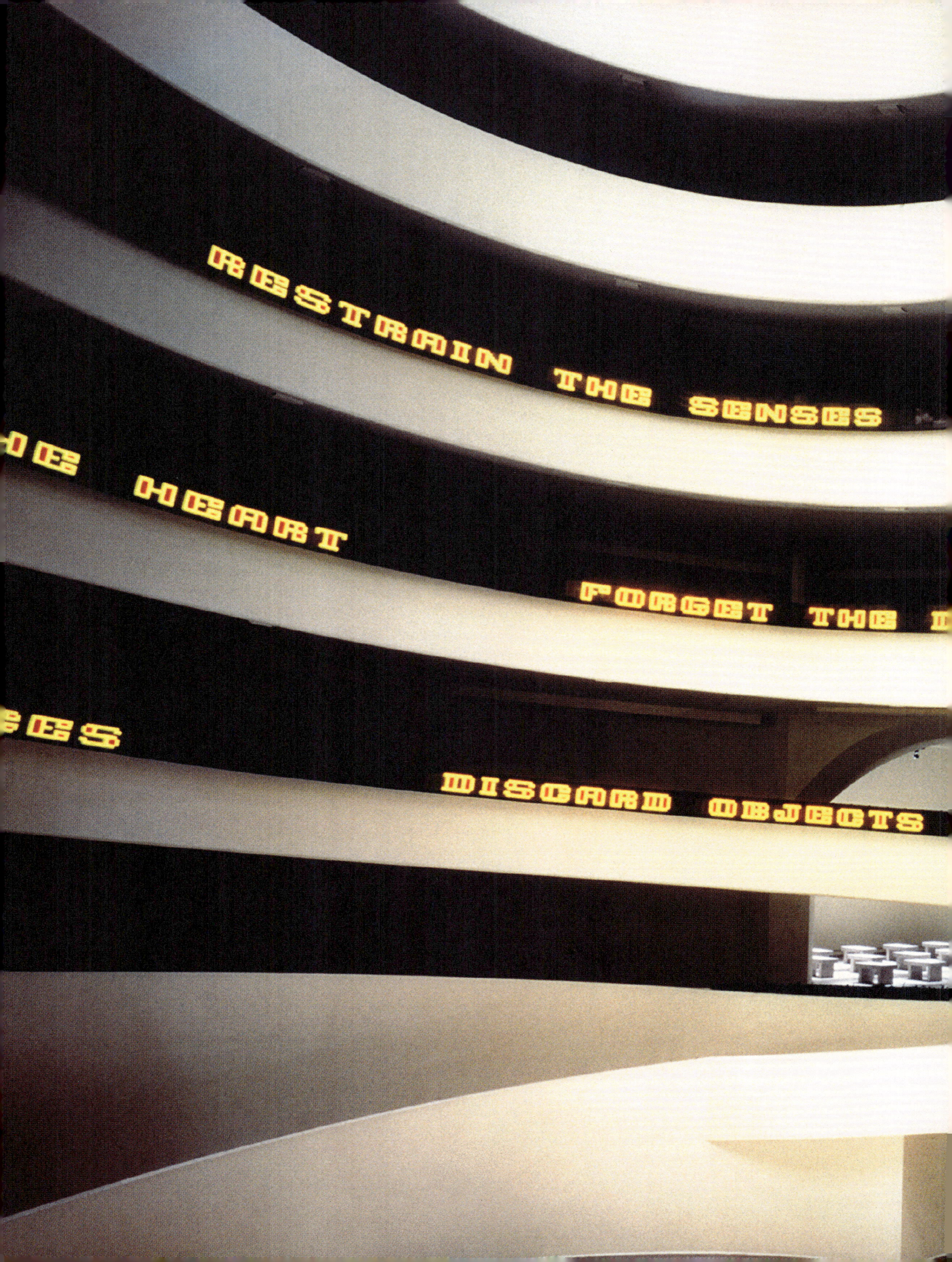
RESTRAIN THE SENSES
HEART
FORGET THE
ES
DISCARD OBJECTS

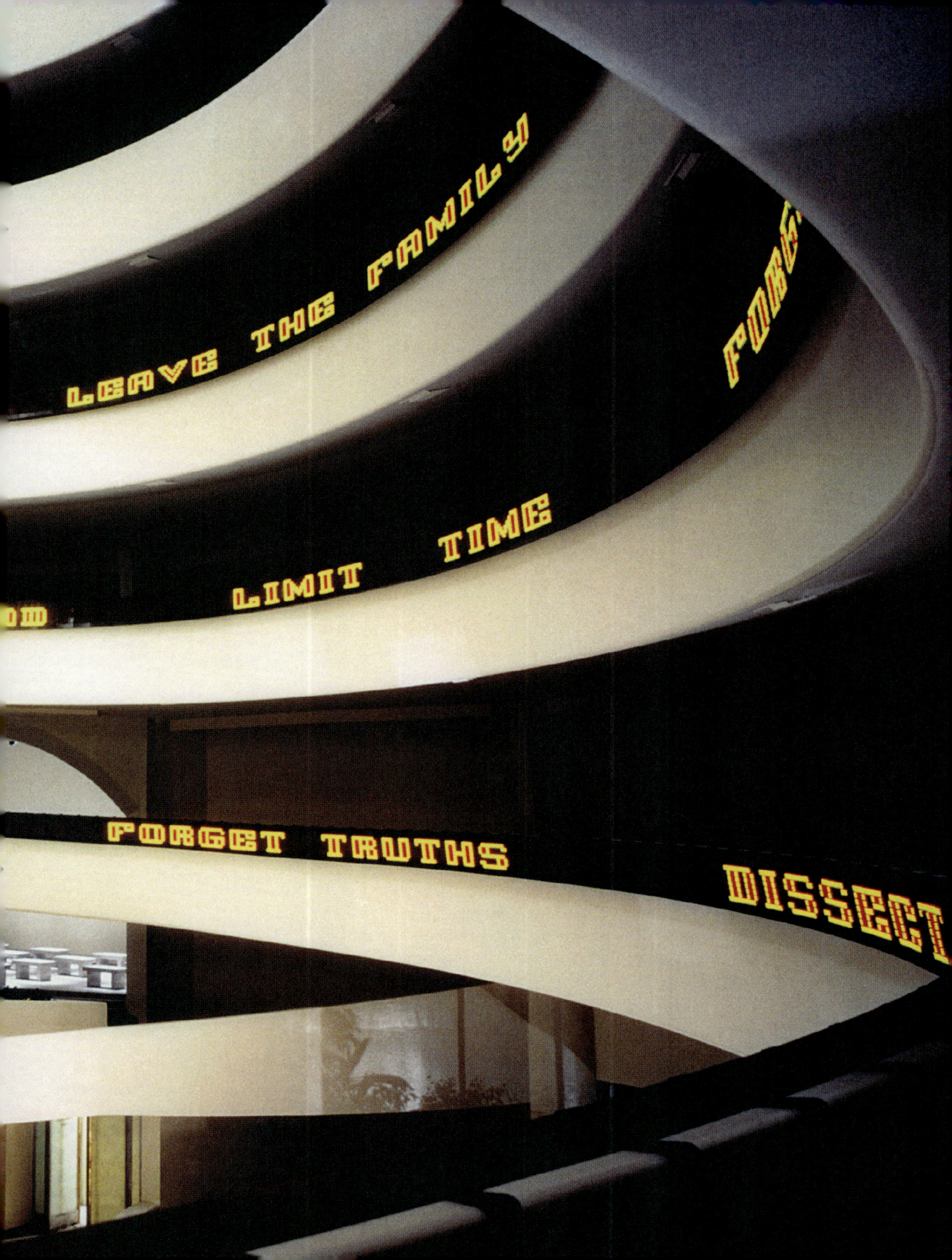
LEAVE THE FAMILY
LIMIT TIME
FORGET TRUTHS
DISSECT

Because her art is text-based, it is logical to assess Holzer's impact solely in terms of the content of her language. However, her ability to stage her messages has been equally important to its presence. The artist's early use of billboards and electronic signage brought public art to a new scale, competing with the bold images of corporate advertising.

While Holzer has used a variety of delivery systems for what have become increasingly personal texts, her signature medium has been the electronic LED (light-emitting diode) signs that flicker out texts and images that move across walls, creating dramatic installations that put the viewer in an almost stagelike environment. Installing these in dark rooms with somber stone benches (also carved with her texts), Holzer creates surreal scenes that parallel the futuristic, technological, noir classic film *Blade Runner*, 1982. Throughout the '80s, the artist's stage became grander and more ambitious. Snaking her signs along the entire ramp of the Guggenheim Museum in 1989 created a remarkably dramatic vortex of language and abstract light swirling around the spiraled architecture of Frank Lloyd Wright's building. The theatricality Fried attributed to Minimalists like Dan Flavin, Donald Judd, and later Bruce Nauman was reinvented and magnified a hundred-fold by Holzer. She has referred to her environments as striving for a "stadium-like" atmosphere,[33] and her ability to program hundreds of signs with both image and text reflects all the theatricality the term *stadium* implies.

The Literal Stage

Robert Longo has said, "At a certain point in the '80s, it seemed like all roads led to performance, whether you were a painter, sculptor, or a video artist. Everything had a performance element, and if you were ambitious, you wanted to find a real stage, not just a performance space."[34] Given this continually developing theatrical aesthetic, the literal stage was the logical destination for a number of artists in the decade. The model, however, was not one of abandoning the gallery for the stage, but of combining the two avenues in a give-and-take relationship.

Longo's early work brought the traditional medium of drawing together with the new interest in performance. His *Men in the Cities* drawings of 1979–82 have become an iconic symbol of the performative drama that heralded in the '80s. These large, almost life-size drawings depict his friends twisting into acute poses, which seem especially exaggerated in light of the conservative, black-and-white business attire they wear. Longo photographed his subjects as essentially one-person performances. As "director," the artist provided stimulation for his performers, at times playing music or throwing things in their direction to get them moving quickly and unself-consciously. “I thought of the drawings as if I were scoring a dance piece or a movie, like large storyboards, but just using images.”[35] He photographed his subjects from low angles so the viewer would be looking up, as if we were seeing the performers on a stage or movie screen from a front row seat. He also used dramatic lighting to set the performers off. “When you see them together, they are like action stills. In that sense, Cindy [Sherman] and I are flip sides of the same coin.”[36]

Longo and Sherman were a couple in Buffalo in the late ’70s and moved to Manhattan together. They both found inspiration in performance and film. Not surprisingly, they chose to deconstruct movies from different gender viewpoints. While Sherman zeroed in on scenes that stereotyped femininity, Longo deliberately explored the theater of the masculine—what he calls “the hard-hitting parts, the action clips.”[37] Sherman’s scenes draw us in, while Longo’s drawings project outward.

“Projection” has a double meaning for Longo in that his drawings come from projected images, but also in the fact that he sees imagery as a physical projection. His drawings have a sculpturelike presence, achieved by the sharp graphic line of his dark pencil. The drawings led to larger tableaux and sculpture. Like the drawings, he read his sculptures as being a form of three-dimensional cinema, portraying qualities of motion and the rhetoric of pose, often influenced by Sergei Eisenstein’s films.

The 1970s had also seen a proliferation of what came to be known as

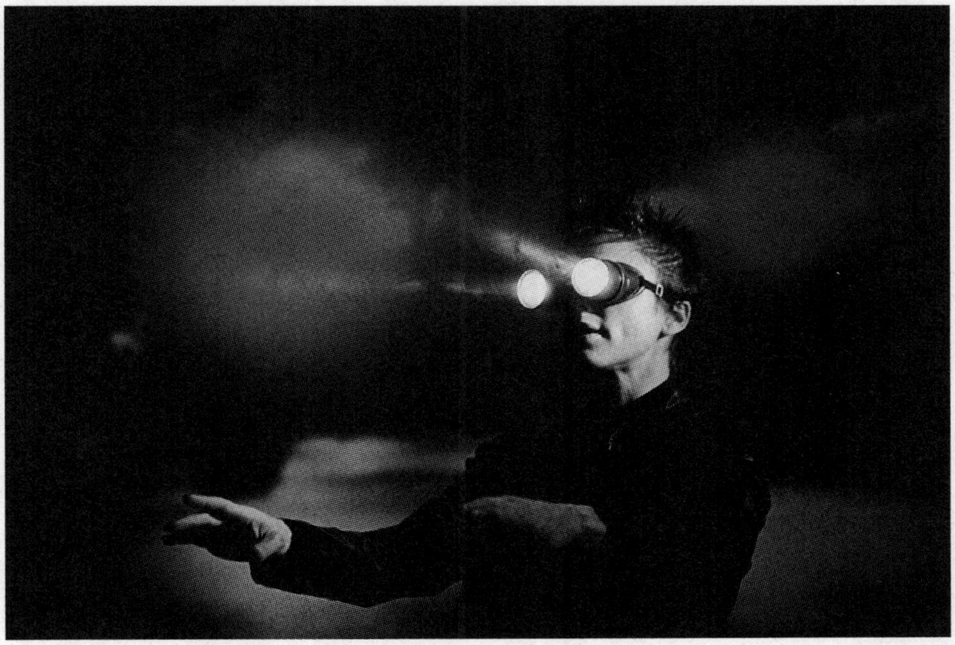

Laurie Anderson
United States I–IV,
Brooklyn Academy of Music, 1983
Courtesy of the Artist

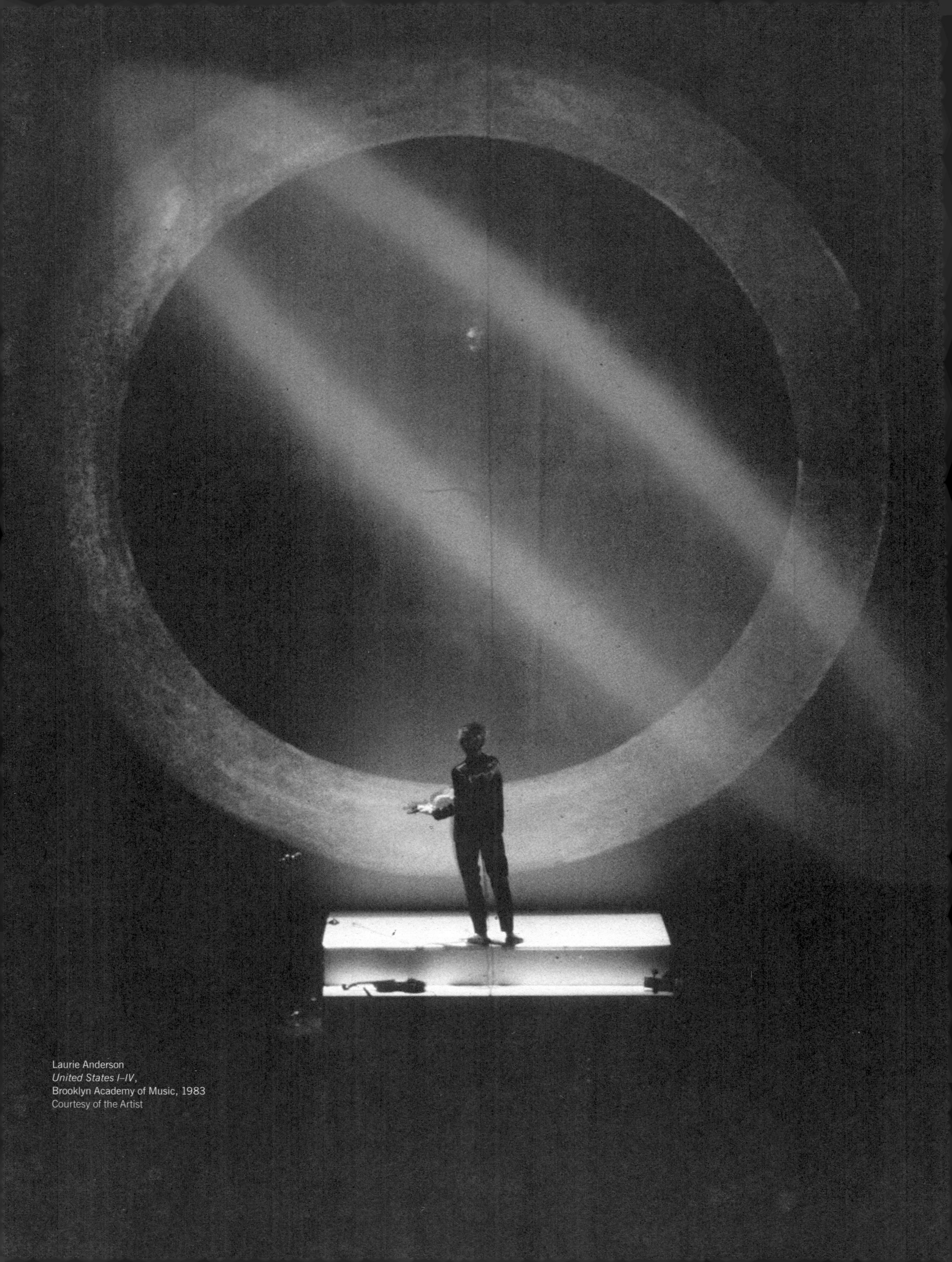

Laurie Anderson
United States I–IV,
Brooklyn Academy of Music, 1983
Courtesy of the Artist

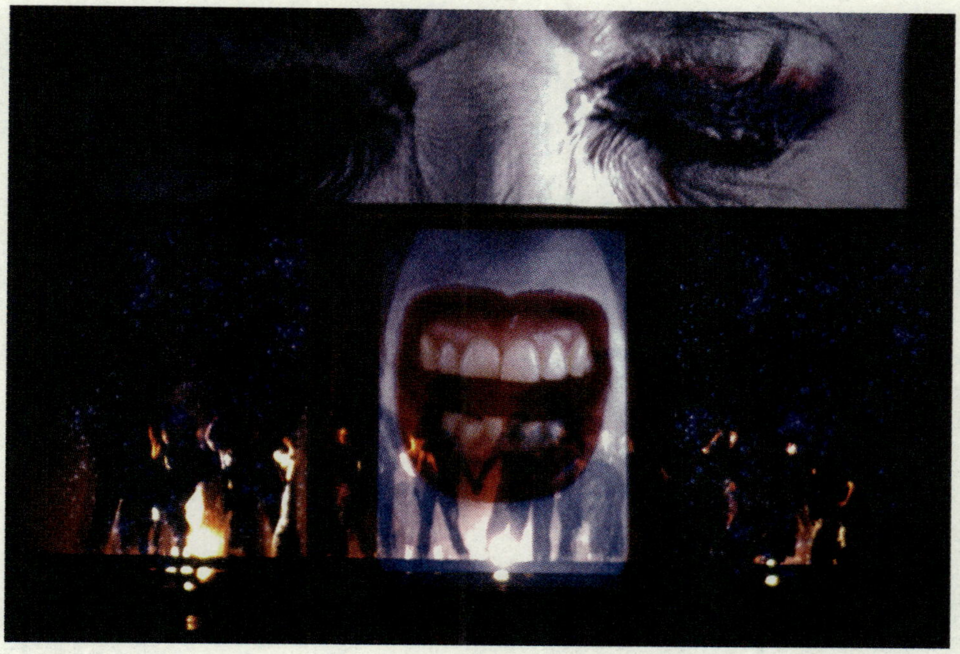

"performance art," which influenced Longo and other artists of his generation. However, much of it was presented in a casual and experimental vein. Recorded on video cameras (which were becoming more widely available) or presented live to audiences, it often had a rough, made-in-the-studio quality, as well as an intimacy due to the fact that the works were performed in studio lofts or small venues. By the '80s, this type of performance had evolved into much grander and more technically sophisticated presentations such as Robert Wilson's ambitious operas, which were eye-opening for Longo. Inspired by Wilson, Longo combined his graphic and sculptural sensibilities, as well as his rock guitar experience, into theatrical stage productions. *Killing Angels*, first performed in 1985, for example, contained drawing, tableaux, dance, rock music, and film. When the gestural drama of Longo's drawings and sculpture are transformed to the stage with rock music and deep lighting, the result is a '70s performance on steroids.

One of the most dynamic artists to emerge from the '70s performance and gallery scene to forge a grand synthesis of art, music, and theater was Laurie Anderson, who became the consummate multimedia artist. Anderson studied violin and took art classes as a child, later studying art history at Barnard College and graduating magna cum laude and Phi Beta Kappa. In 1972, she earned an MFA in sculpture from Columbia University. A captivating documentary photograph from 1974 looks like a scene from an urban fairy tale. In a long white dress, Anderson is wearing ice skates frozen in blocks of ice while she plays the violin.

Robert Longo
Marble Fog, 1985
Performance still
Brooklyn Museum, New York
Courtesy of the Artist and Metro Pictures, New York

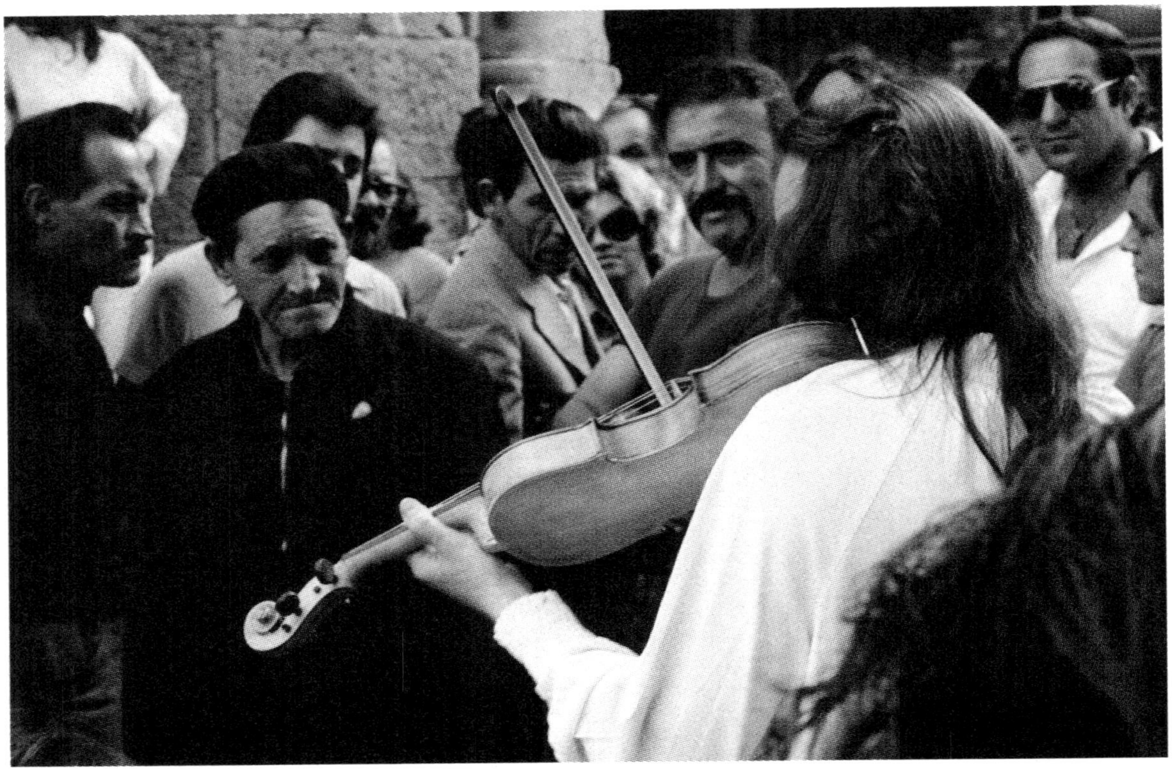

Duets on Ice was titled for the fact that while a song played from a hidden tape inside her violin, she played the same song on the instrument. This dialogue between human and electronic sound and image was a thread that would run through much of her future work, tying together a wide range of subjects and media.

At the core of Anderson's art is her interest in telling stories, and in the ways in which communication is in a constant state of transformation. During the '70s, Anderson became a catalyst in introducing narrative content into contemporary art, following years in which formalist abstraction was paramount. Anderson's essentially autobiographical narratives are fragmentary and layered, not only in terms of their content, which is often nonlinear, but also in their delivery. A fundamental question embedded in Anderson's art is, how many ways can you tell a story? Her narratives have taken the form of children's books and comics, drawings, gallery installations, poems, records, films, and performances.

Over the past four decades, Anderson's evolution as an artist has continually moved her onto the stage, but she uses the stage almost like an artist's studio, where things seem invented and unexpected transformations occur. Watching the artist standing alone on the stage surrounded by hidden wires that feed various visual and sound effects activated by her sly touch, the audience can never predict where one

Laurie Anderson
Duets on Ice, 1975
Genoa, Italy
Courtesy the Artist

of Anderson's performances is going. She does not just put different media together, she mixes our perception of them; when we might expect a song, we are presented an image, then the image is transformed into the text of a song.

Anderson's stage pieces are as much changing art installations as they are performances. She is also a master of special effects in which voice, body, imagery, and electronic equipment continually dissolve into one another. In 1981, Anderson made the unusual crossover from poet-performer-artist to the pop record charts with her hit song "O Superman." Like her performances, her songs have a sculptural edge. Chantlike and haunting, they project intimately and powerfully into the space of a record or auditorium. Using audio filters, she switches her voice into different personae, sometimes human, sometimes ghostly and electronic.

Anderson does not just put different media together, she mixes our perception of them; when we might expect a song, we are presented an image, then the image is transformed into the text of a song.

Anderson is often a conductor, both metaphorically and sometimes physically. In *Drum Dance*, 1986, the artist is a performer and musical instrument. Tapping sound sensors hidden under her clothing, she dances to a loud drumbeat that she creates as she plays her body—a techno-shaman, performing a trancelike ritual.

Her more elaborate performances have been described as "Electronic Cabarets" for good reason. They contain music, recitation, backdrops, comedy, and drama. But they are, in fact, quite a bit more than that. Scored for voice, violin, electronic sound, horns, keyboards, percussion, and multiple visual backdrops, Anderson's performances create a polyphonic field that extends beyond the aural, the performative, or the visual to something much grander than a cabaret. The '80s art world would experience Anderson's multimedia practice in what is a reinvention of operatic form.

If anything reflects the ambitions of art in New York in the 1980s, it is Anderson's *United States I–IV*, which premiered at the Brooklyn Academy of Music in February 1983. Seven hours in length, the piece was presented over two successive evenings in a theater with a distinguished history of classical symphony and performance. Different aspects of Anderson's early books, films, writings, drawings, sculptures, performances, and music became a story with a very wide lens under the subtitles of "Transportation," "Politics," "Money," and "Love." With dozens of performers and unseen technicians operating electronic equipment, *United States* presented a theatrical landscape of bold and experimental proportions—a grand aural, visual, and textual landscape of opera and of America.

This could be the French playwright and director Antonin Artaud's vision of his 1938 collection of essays *The Theater and Its Double*, which argued for something more complex than theater as a contrived literary event, but rather "a kind of unique language half-way between gesture and thought."[38] Indeed, the complexity and ambition of *United States* begs some lofty comparisons, from Gertrude Stein's *The Making of Americans* of 1925 to James Joyce's and William S. Burroughs's disjunctive novels. Imagine Burroughs's "cut-up" novels as addressing the state of America and presented in multimedia. Anderson's art does not have a category. She has become a new kind of artist, whose work is a quintessential symbol of Fried's theatricality, which operates "in between the arts."

In 1977, the writer Michel Benamou asked, "Has everything from politics to poetics become theatrical?"[39] Certainly by the next decade it seemed so. No doubt the term may still retain some of the negative connotations that Fried attributed to it, and some will wrongly equate the theatrical with hype or overreaching. In fact, during the '80s it came to be defined as a quality that was complex and deeply embedded in the art of the era. It allowed artists to reach outside their comfort zones and engage something more than private expressions and formalist revisions. Art at the turn of the twenty-first century has certainly been fueled by eighties ambitions. Indeed, one wonders what art would look like today without the theatrical '80s.

1 Michael Fried, "Art and Objecthood," *Artforum* 5, no. 10 (June 1967): 21.
2 Douglas Crimp, "Pictures," *October*, no. 8 (Spring 1979): 75–88.
3 The *Artforum* questionnaire was written by Robert Pincus-Witten. Responses from painters were published in "Painter's Reply . . . ," *Artforum* 14, no. 1 (September 1975): 26–36.
4 Robert Harbison, *Reflections on Baroque* (Chicago: University of Chicago Press, 2000), viii.
5 Julian Schnabel, in an unpublished interview with Michael Auping, New York, 1979.
6 Ibid.
7 David Moos, *Julian Schnabel: Art and Film* (Toronto: Art Gallery of Ontario, 2010), 9.
8 John Baldessari, in a telephone conversation with Michael Auping, May 2011.
9 Fiona Irving, "Chronology," in Janet Kardon, *David Salle* (Philadelphia: Institute of Contemporary Art, University of Pennsylvania, 1986), 82–87.
10 David Salle, quoted in Robert Rosenblum, "'80s Then: David Salle talks with Robert Rosenblum," *Artforum* 41, no. 7 (March 2003): 74.
11 Ibid.
12 Ibid.
13 Lisa Phillips, "The Equivocal Touch in the Vicinity of History," in Janet Kardon, *David Salle*, 31.
14 David Salle, quoted in "David Salle talks with Robert Rosenblum," 75.
15 See Douglas Crimp, "Pictures."
16 Sherrie Levine, quoted in Paul Taylor, "How David Salle Mixes High Art and Trash," *The New York Times Magazine*, January 11, 1987.
17 Cindy Sherman, quoted in "Interview with Cindy Sherman," in Heather Pisanti, *Wish You Were Here: The Buffalo Avant-Garde in the 1970s* (Buffalo: Albright-Knox Art Gallery, 2012), 96.
18 Thomas Lawson, *A Fatal Attraction: Art and Media* (Chicago: The Renaissance Society at the University of Chicago, 1982), 3.
19 Eric Fischl, in a telephone conversation with Michael Auping, January 24, 2014.
20 Ann Fensterstock, "Decade of Decadence: SoHo 1980 to 1990," in *Art on the Block* (New York: Palgrave Macmillan, 2013), 75–97.
21 Francesco Clemente, in an unpublished interview with Michael Auping, in his New York studio, May 1984.
22 Clement Greenberg, "Avant-Garde and Kitsch," in *Clement Greenberg: The Collected Essays and Criticism*, ed. John O'Brian, vol. 1 (Chicago: The University of Chicago Press, 1986), 5–22.
23 Benjamin H. D. Buchloh, "Into the Blue: Klein and Poses," *Artforum* 33, no. 10 (Summer 1995): 95.
24 Jenny Holzer, in a telephone conversation with Michael Auping, November 10, 2013.
25 Clemente, interview with Auping, May 1984.
26 Francesco Clemente, quoted in Brooks Adams, "Francesco Clemente talks with Brooks Adams," *Artforum* 41, no. 7 (March 2003): 58.
27 Holzer, conversation with Michael Auping, November 10, 2013.
28 Franklin Sirmans, "In the Cipher: Basquiat and Hip-Hop Culture," in *Basquiat*, ed. Marc Mayer (Brooklyn: Brooklyn Museum, 2005), 91–105.
29 Clemente, in conversation with Michael Auping, May 1984.
30 Joseph D. Ketner II, "Warhol's Last Decade: Reinventing Painting," in *Andy Warhol: The Last Decade*, ed. Joseph D. Ketner II (Milwaukee: Milwaukee Art Museum in association with Prestel Verlag, 2009), 14–47.
31 Kenny Scharf, in a telephone conversation with Michael Auping, March 16, 2014.
32 Ibid.
33 Jenny Holzer, in conversation with Michael Auping in New York, Buffalo, and Venice between 1988 and 1991.
34 Robert Longo, in a telephone conversation with Michael Auping, February 17, 2014.
35 Ibid.
36 Ibid.
37 Ibid.
38 Antonin Artaud, "The Theater of Cruelty (First Manifesto)," *The Theater and Its Double* (New York: Grove Press, 1958), 89.
39 Michel Benamou, "Peresene and Play," in *Performance in Postmodern Culture: Theories of Contemporary Culture*, vol. 1, ed. Michel Benamou and Charles Carmello (Madison, WI: Coda Press and the Center for 20th Century Studies, University of Wisconsin, Milwaukee, 1977), 3.

Laurie Anderson • Jean-Michel Basquiat • Ross Bleckner Troy Brauntuch • Francesco Clemente • Eric Fischl Nan Goldin • Jack Goldstein Peter Halley • Keith Haring Jenny Holzer • Jeff Koons Barbara Kruger Sherrie Levine • Robert Longo Robert Mapplethorpe Allan McCollum • Richard Prince • David Salle • Kenny Scharf • Julian Schnabel Cindy Sherman • Donald Sultan Philip Taaffe • Andy Warhol Christopher Wool

Laurie Anderson

O Superman (For Massenet)

O Superman. O judge.
O Mom and Dad. Mom and Dad.
O Superman. O judge.
O Mom and Dad. Mom and Dad.
Hi. I'm not home right now. But if you want to leave a
message, just start talking at the sound of the tone.
Hello? This is your Mother. Are you there? Are you coming home?
Hello? Is anybody home?
Well, you don't know me, but I know you.
And I've got a message to give to you.
Here come the planes.
So you better get ready. Ready to go.
You can come as you are, but pay as you go. Pay as you go.

And I said: OK. Who is this really?
And the voice said:
This is the hand, the hand that takes.
This is the hand, the hand that takes.
This is the hand, the hand that takes.
Here come the planes.
They're American planes. Made in America.
Smoking or non-smoking?
And the voice said: Neither snow nor rain nor gloom
of night shall stay these couriers from the swift completion
of their appointed rounds.

'Cause when love is gone, there's always justice.
And when justice is gone, there's always force.
And when force is gone, there's always Mom. Hi Mom!

So hold me, Mom, in your long arms.
So hold me, Mom, in your long arms.
In your automatic arms. Your electronic arms. In your arms.
So hold me, Mom, in your long arms.
Your petrochemical arms.
Your military arms.
In your electronic arms.

Laurie Anderson
Drum Dance, Home of the Brave, 1986
Courtesy of the Artist

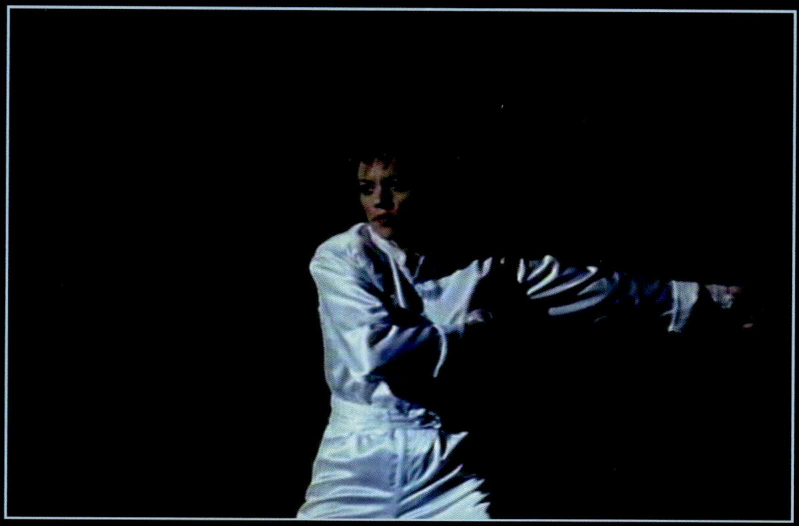

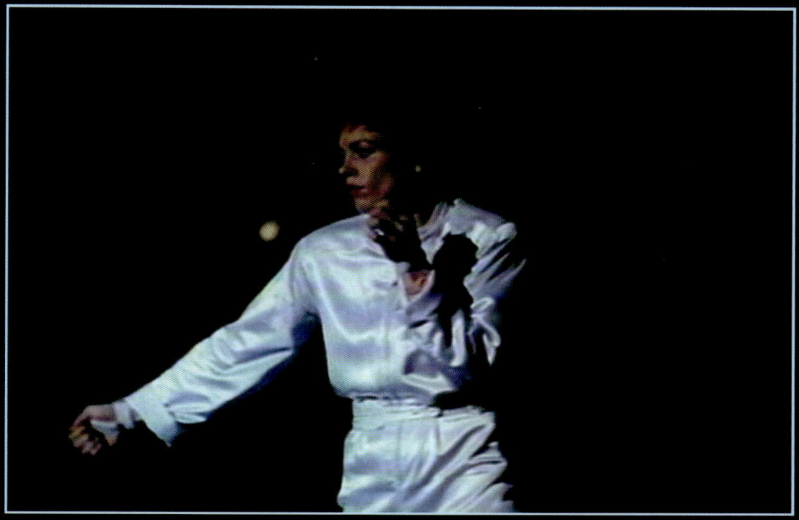

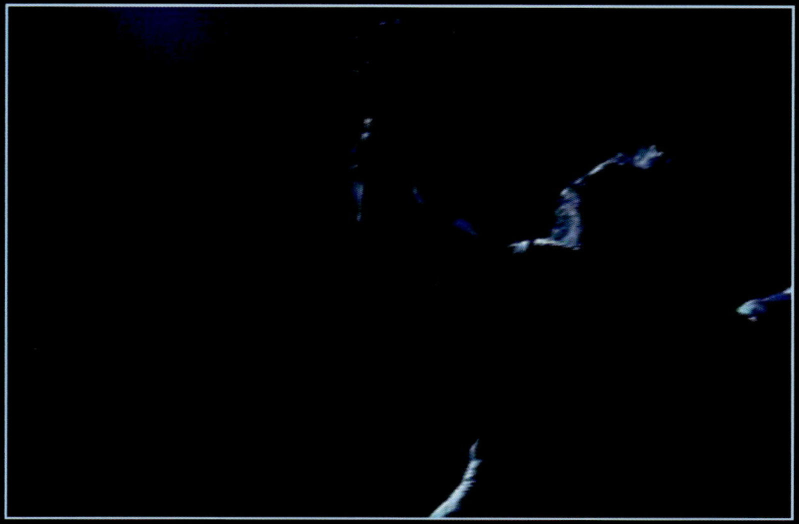

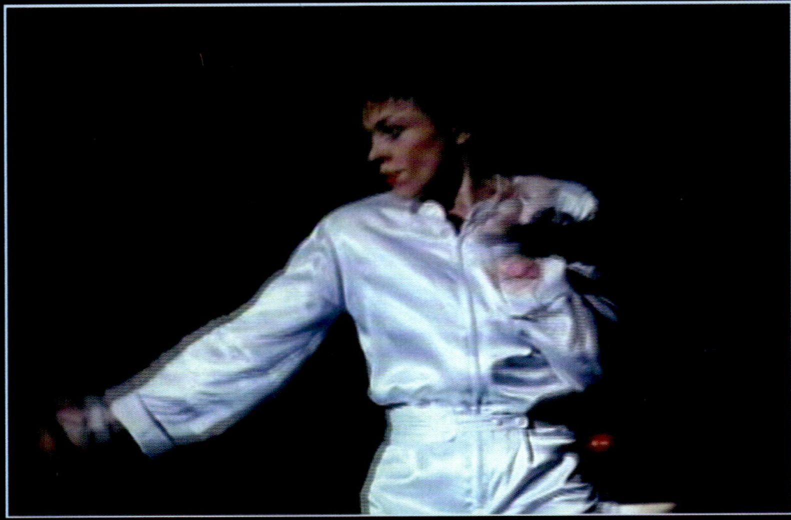

At heart, I'm an anthropologist. I try to jump out of my skin. I normally see the world as an artist first, second as a New Yorker and third as a woman. That's a perspective that I sometimes would like to escape. It's why in my performances I use audio filters to change my voice. That's a way to escape as well.

Quoted in Kenneth R. Fletcher, "Laurie Anderson," *Smithsonian Magazine*, August 2008

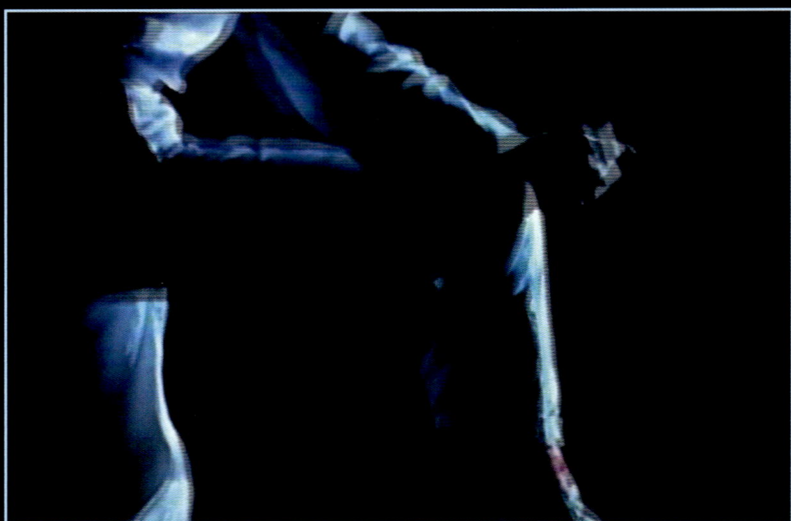

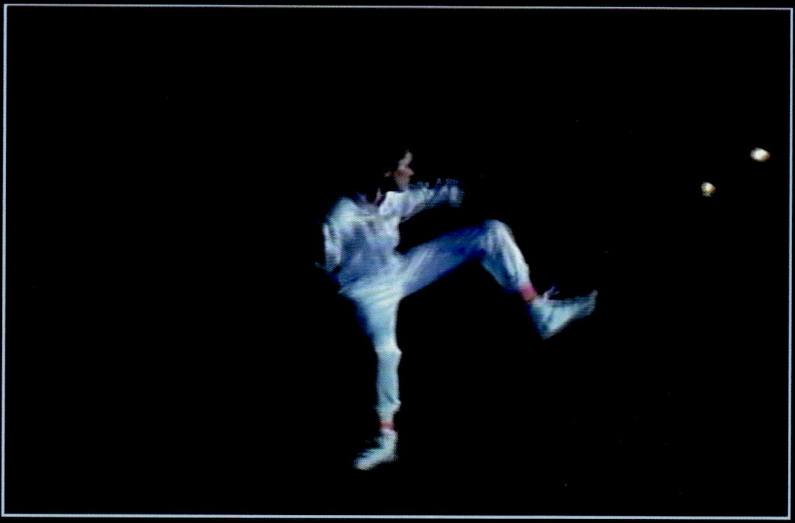

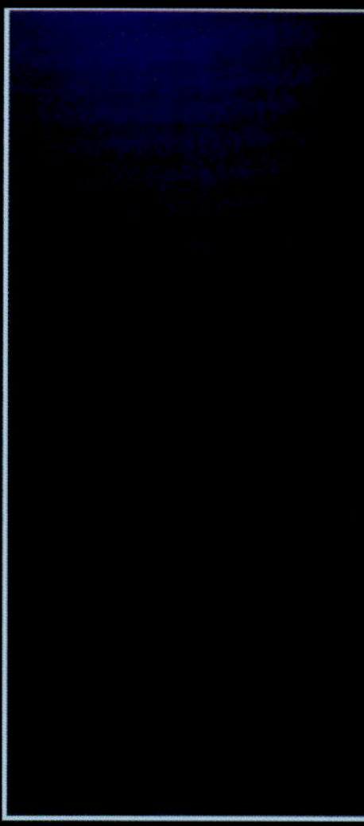

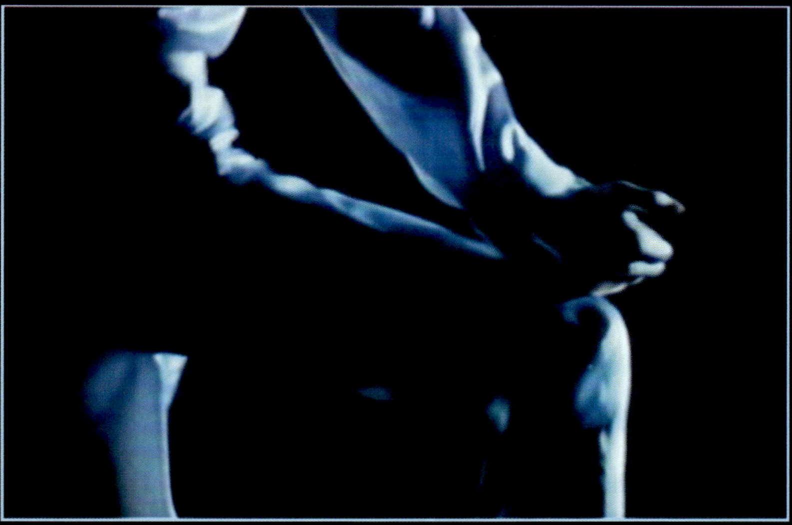

Jean-Michel Basquiat

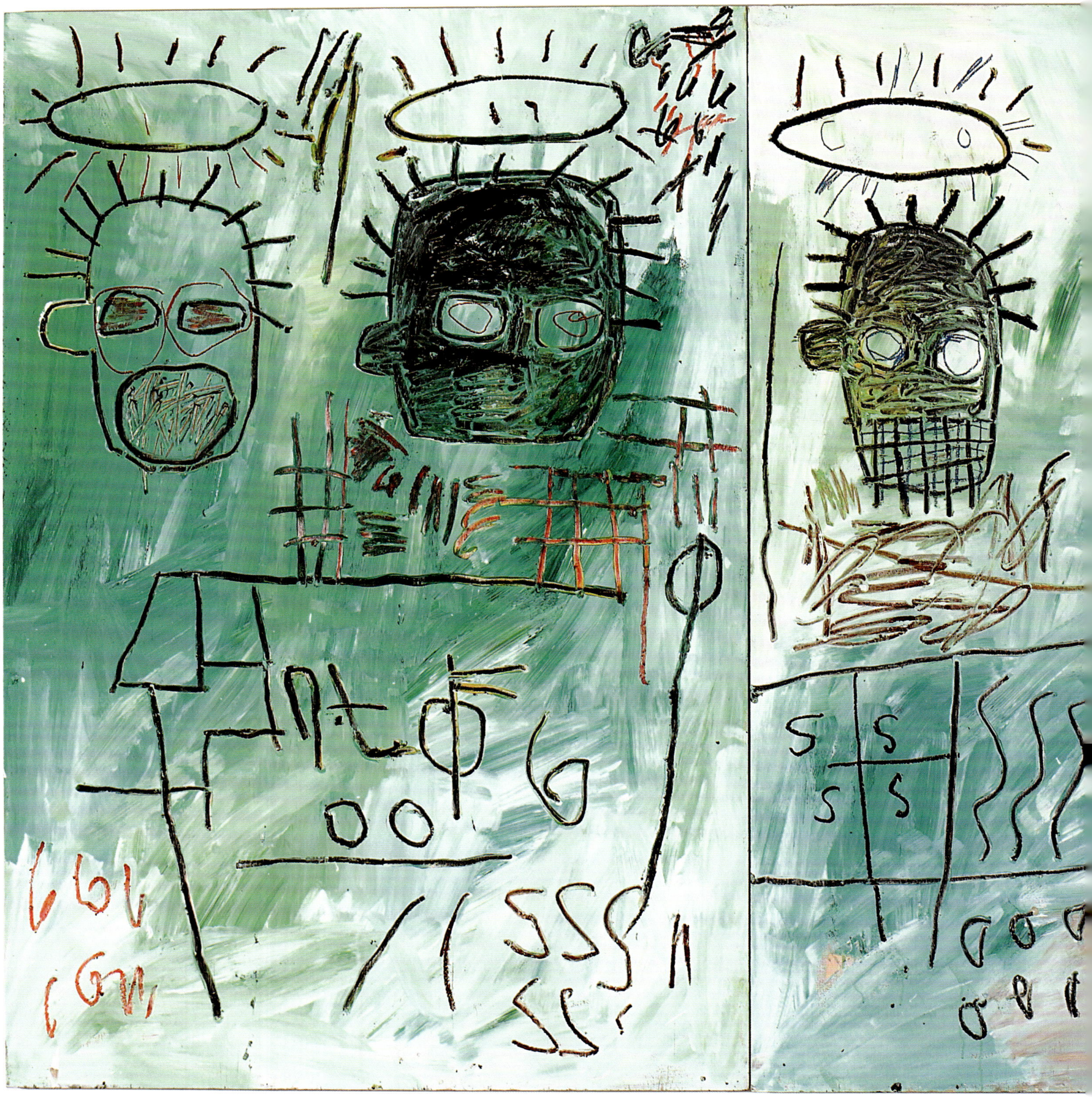

Jean-Michel Basquiat
Six Crimee, 1982
Acrylic and oil paintstick on Masonite
Overall, 72 × 144 × 1 inches
Each panel, 72 × 48 × 1 inches
The Museum of Contemporary Art, Los Angeles,
The Scott D. F. Spiegel Collection

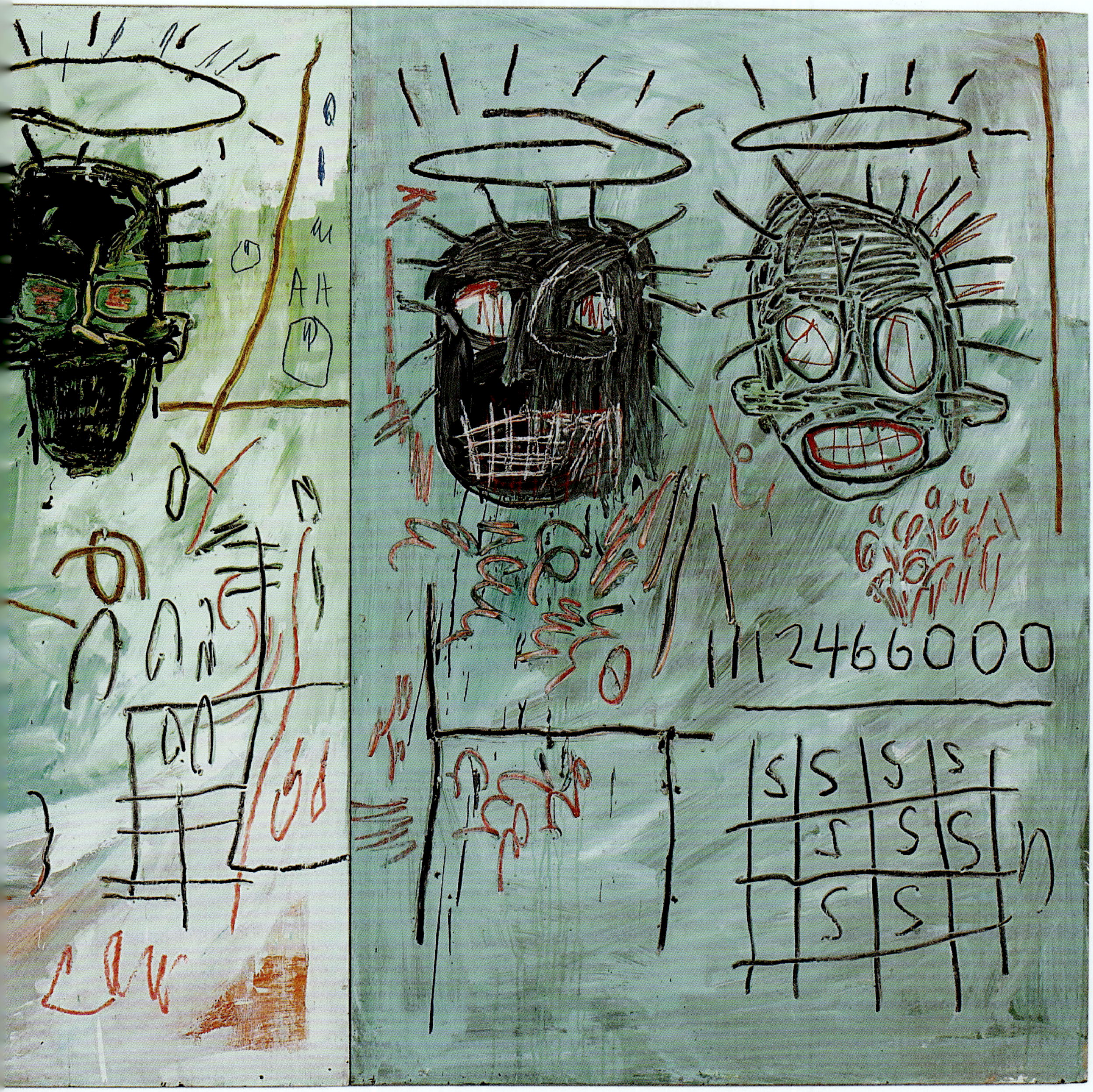

The more I paint the more I like everything.

Yesterday was the first time I'd drawn in a long time. I'd been sort of living off this pile of drawings from last year, sticking them onto paintings.

For a while I was drawing on good paper, but now I've gone back to the bad stuff. I put matte medium on it. If you put matte medium on it, it seals up, so it doesn't really matter.

I like the ones where I don't paint as much as others, where it's just a direct idea.

Most of the pictures have one or two paintings under them. I'm worried that in the future, parts might fall off and some of the heads underneath might show through.

[The list of pre-Socratic philosophers in the recent paintings] was from going to Italy, and copying names out of tour books, and condensed histories.

Originally I wanted to copy the whole history down, but it was too tedious so I just stuck to the cast of characters.

[My subject matter is] royalty, heroism, and the streets.

Jean-Michel Basquiat: I was a really lousy artist as a kid. Too abstract expressionist; or I'd draw a big ram's head, really messy. I'd never win painting contests. I remember losing to a guy who did a perfect Spiderman.

Henry Geldzahler: But were you satisfied with your own work?

B: No, not at all. I really wanted to be the best artist in the class, but my work had a really ugly edge to it.

G: Was it anger?

B: There was a lot of ugly stuff going on at the time in my family.

G: Is there anger in your work now?

B: It's about 80% anger.

G: But it's also humor.

B: People laugh when you fall on your ass. What's humor?

Quoted in Emma Brown and Henry Geldzahler, "New Again: Jean-Michel Basquiat," *Interview*, January 1983.
Excerpt of article originally published in *Interview* magazine, January 1983. Courtesy BMP Media Holdings, LLC

Jean-Michel Basquiat
Untitled, 1982
Oilstick on paper
42 3/4 × 30 3/8 inches
Collection of the Modern Art Museum of Fort Worth, Museum purchase

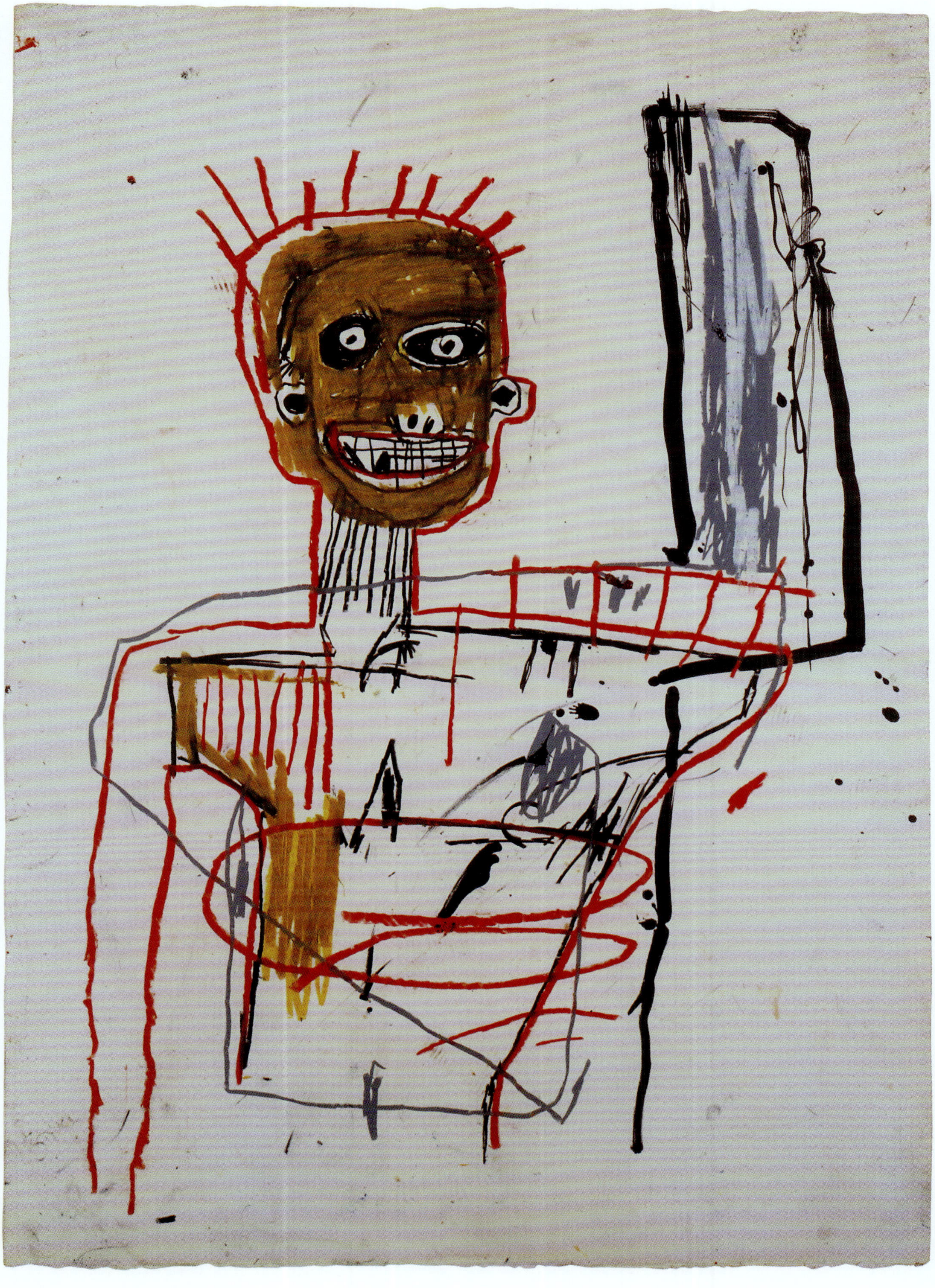

Ross Bleckner

There were these lights inside the painting and as a viewer I would be this person who was perpetually locked out of the painting. I think a lot of the theme of death was also implied in the sense that you have ideas, you put them in a painting, and they are locked in there forever. They die in there. Then you move on. My work is very much about a kind of degraded sublime.

Quoted in Jeanne Siegel, "Geometric Desurfacing: Ross Bleckner, Alan Belcher, Ellen Carey, Peter Halley, Sherrie Levine, Philip Taaffe, James Welling," *Arts Magazine* 60 (March 1986): 28

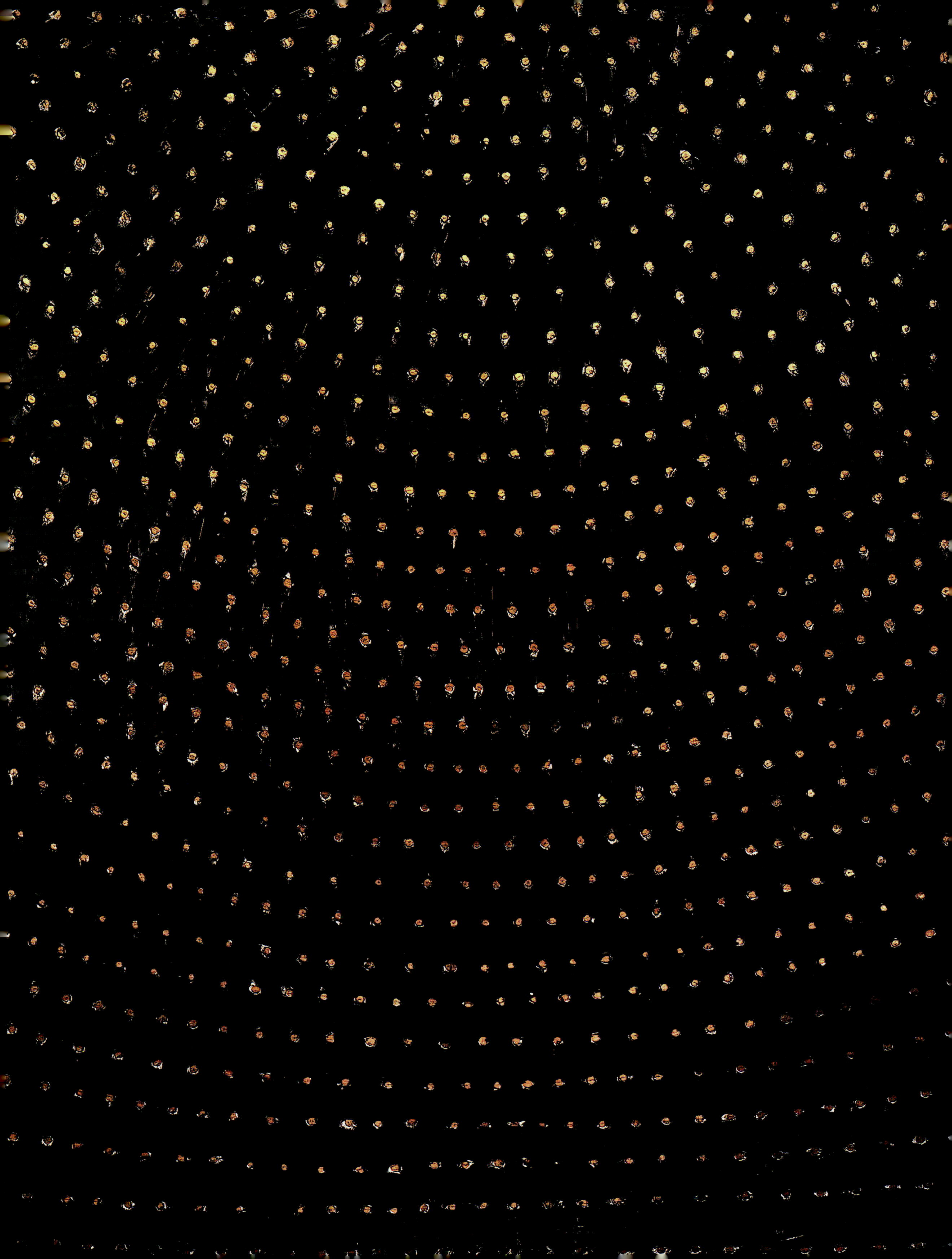

A lot of my work deals metaphorically and literally with the idea of death. I've read the obituaries since I was a child. I used to want to be the obituary writer for the *New York Times*. Only because I thought that's the ultimate criticism.

A lot of our beliefs have to do with hope, an infantile idealism that things get better and life gets more equitable. I had an aunt who was dying of pancreatic cancer, the worst kind of cancer, very painful, very slow. I remember her always saying as she was withering away, "Well, if I could last a few more weeks there'll be a cure." Well, here we are twenty years later and God knows how many billions of dollars and I know now she could have dragged on for all these years and there'd still not be a cure. There's not a cure. These diseases are cultural problems. It's not about technology or progress. I think that's the kind of death that the Twentieth Century is going to be seeing now in its reposing years. We're ending it with a plague that's totally, totally unstoppable. Totally out of control and completely environmental.

My paintings memorialize a lot of different things simultaneously: the culture, immediate ends, relationships and the people who have just passed. The people who've died from, in this case, AIDS. They memorialize the death of our own idea about that so that as an artist you can continue to grow and go on. In a way they memorialize the tragedy of being subsumed in the marketplace, too. Because in order to keep your art going, you also have to keep upping the stakes formally.

Quoted in Aimee Rankin, "Ross Bleckner," *Bomb Magazine*, no. 19 (Spring 1987): 22–27.

Ross Bleckner
Sanctuary, 1989
Oil on canvas
84 × 60 inches
The Doris and Donald Fisher Collection

There is that tragedy, that beauty, that fear and fascination. It's a scary beauty.

Quoted in Dan Cameron, "'80s Then: Ross Bleckner Talks to Dan Cameron," *Artforum* 14, no. 7 (March 2003): 230–31. © Artforum

Troy BraUntuch

I love films, yeah. I think actually, going back to the Pictures Generation, it was so much film-based, coming up out of the early '70s, '60s—cinema was just really amazing. So I think myself and others were sort of quite entrenched in film and image. Certainly more than art.

Because art at that moment wasn't anything like that in that sense. It was post-Pop, and minimalism and conceptual art. Anything but an image. Anything but a picture of something, or something real.

[My work] seems to need a personal history, investigation, because everything seems sort of arbitrary. There's such an abundance of imagery in media. It sort of finds that seam, that moment that's really not identifiable as being a critique of that. I think I'm more interested in how I choose an image, what that image is, what that narrative is, how it reads when someone looks at something, thinks about something. So at the moment, I guess I wouldn't think about that. I think because it's already in the work. It's sort of like, whether there's a camera, or a racing horse, or a criminal, or a state trooper—in the end, they're not replaceable. I couldn't take something out of this and put something else in that would make sense. So, it's sort of how you make meaning with it, in the end.

Quoted in Hannah Mandel, "Troy Brauntuch's Dark Matter," *Interview*, May 10, 2013.

Troy Brauntuch
Untitled, 1984
Inks and pigment on linen
60 × 60 inches
The Rachofsky Collection

Francesco Clemente

I like squalor and energy—places where you have to use your wits as well as your inner spirit. When I first came here [to New York in the 1980s], I had amazing dreams. I had dreams that it was raining shit. In the painting *Perseverance*, I carry my Italian heritage through the streets, and it's raining shit. ... Great cities are spiritual and depraved. It's where artists have to live today to make art.

Francesco Clemente, in an unpublished interview with Michael Auping, in his New York studio, May 1984

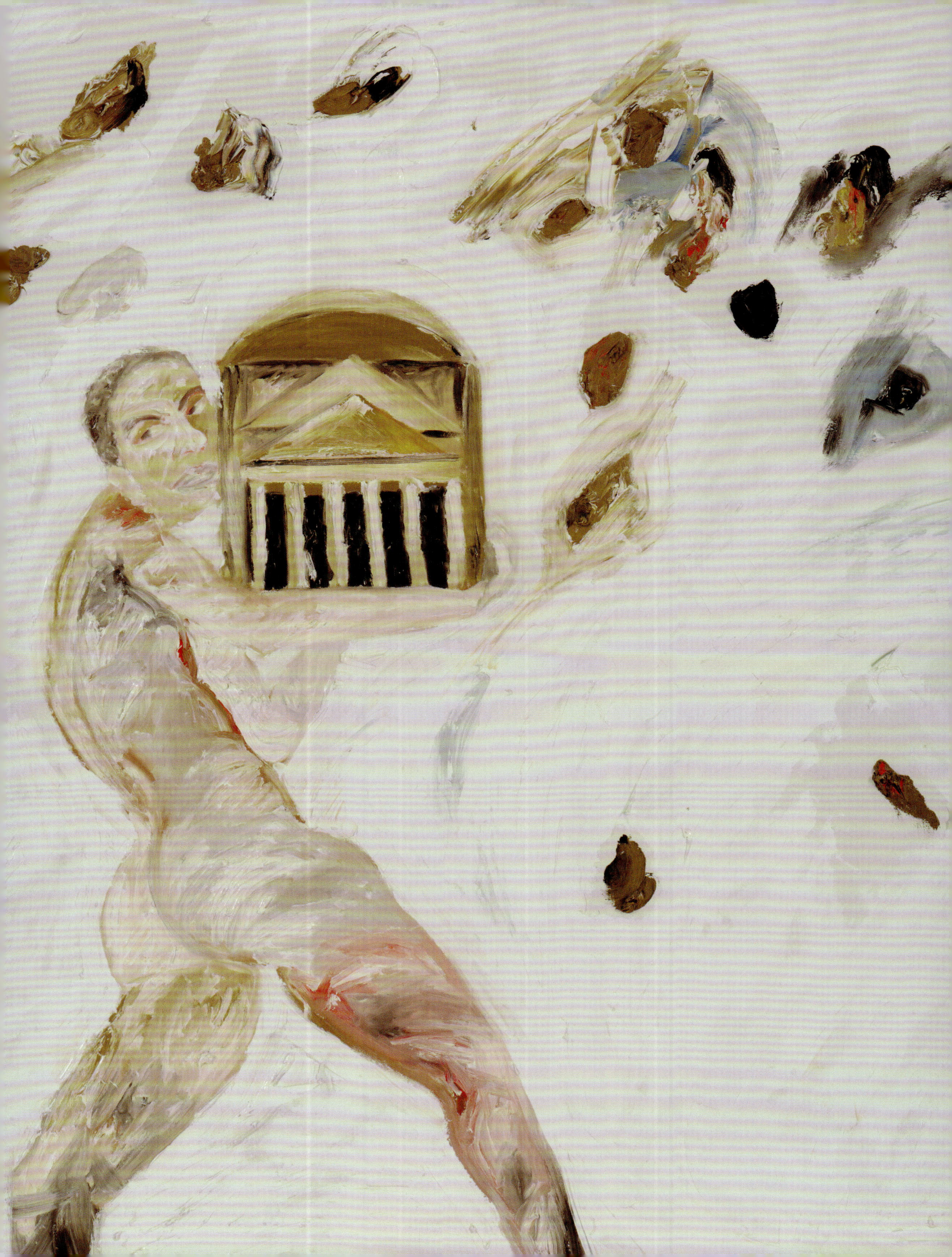

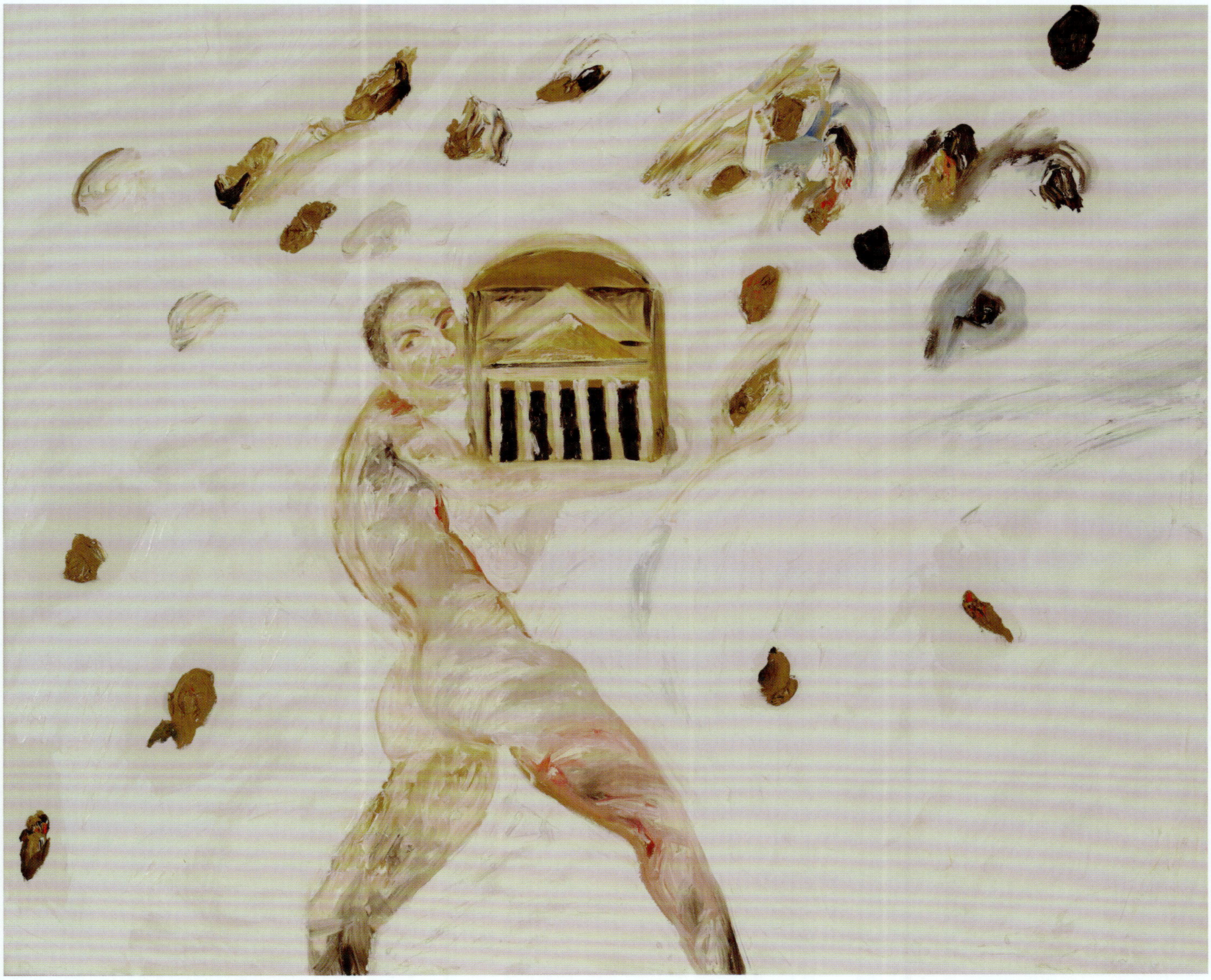

Francesco Clemente
Perseverance, 1981
Oil on canvas
78 × 93 inches
The Museum of Modern Art, New York, NY, USA;
Partial and promised gift of UBS

Eric Fischl

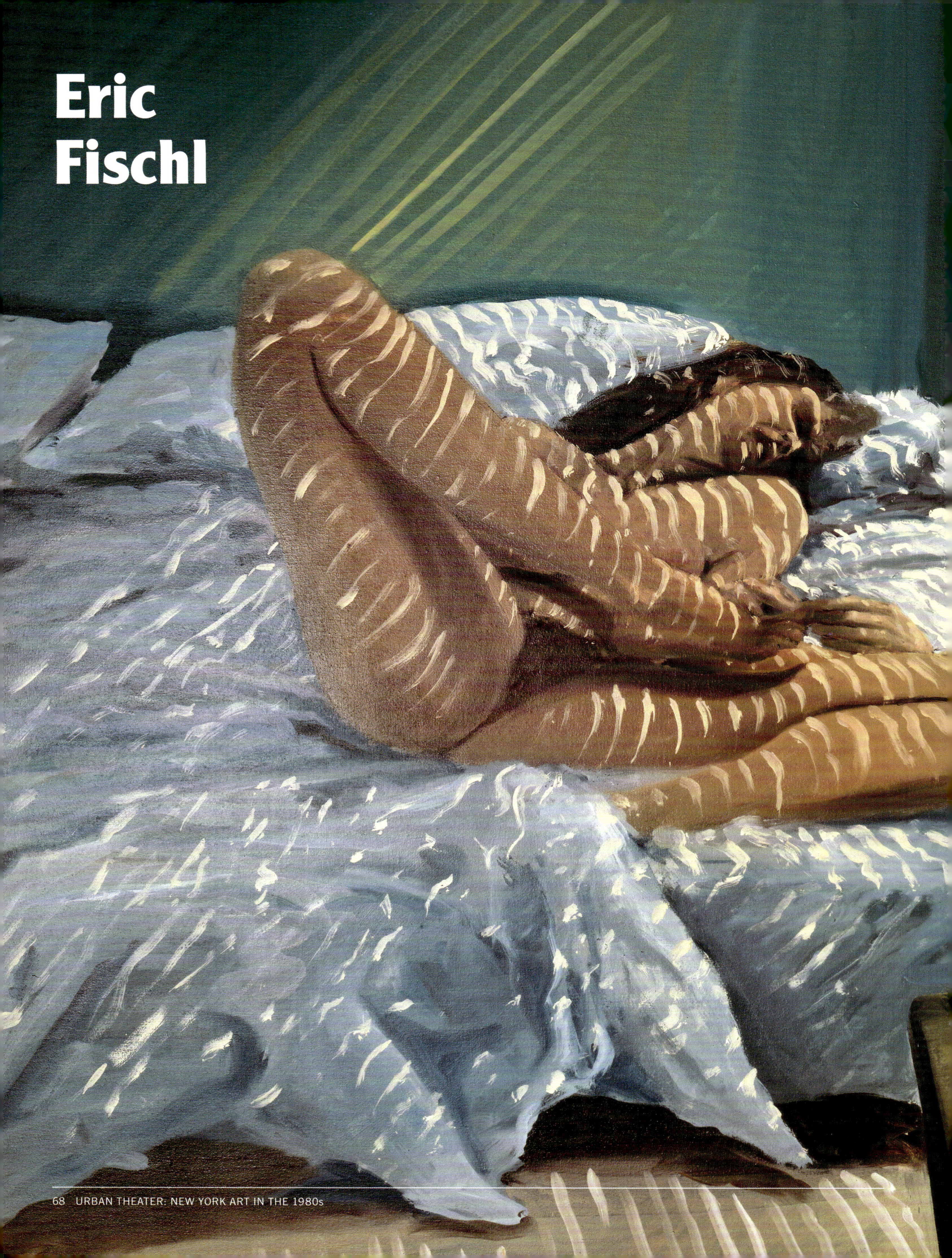

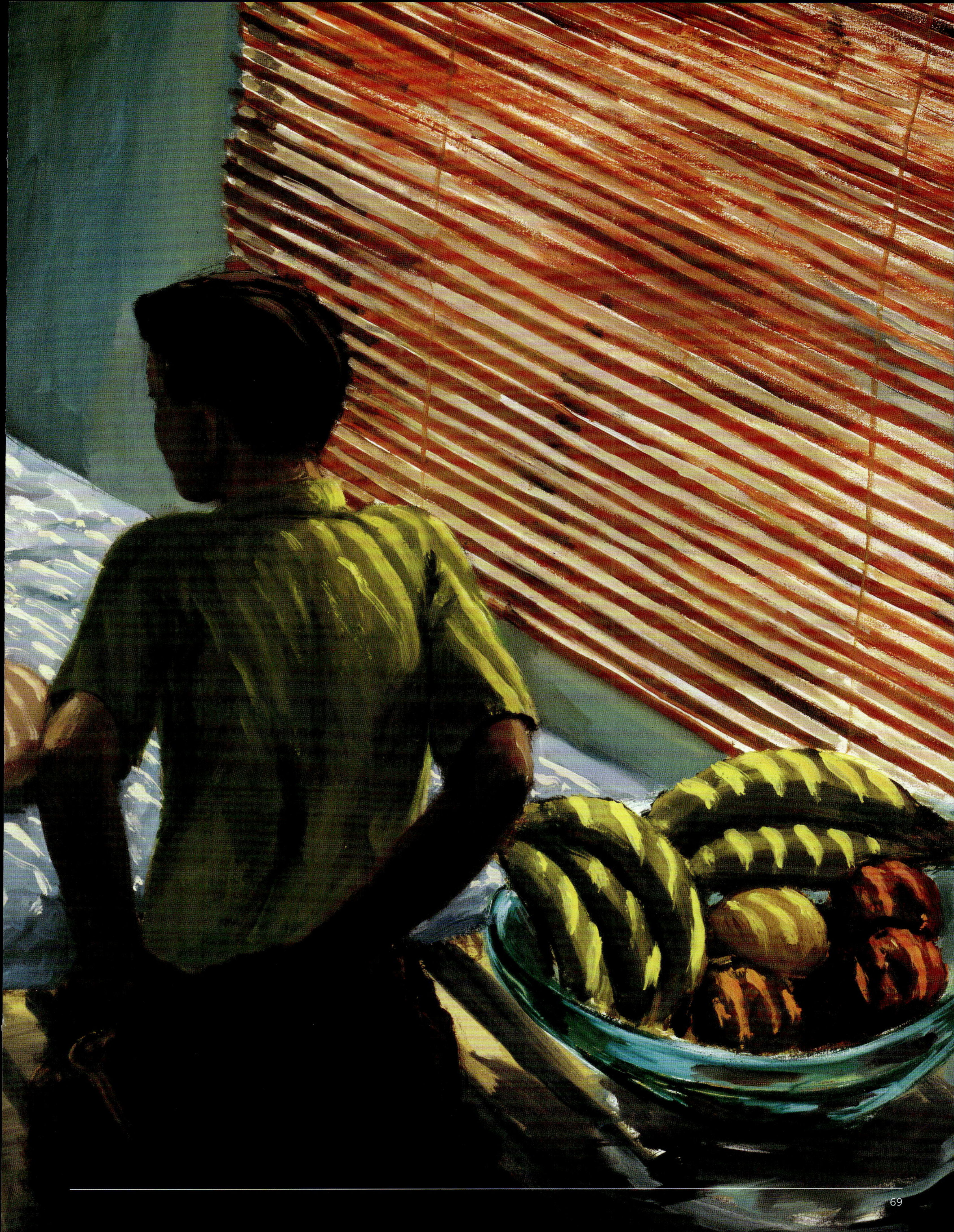

Take, for example, *Bad Boy*, a picture I made in 1981 that touched on themes of incest and voyeurism and is to date my most famous and notorious painting. Before its exhibition, I was viewed as just another up-and-coming artist with one New York solo show on my résumé and a day job crating art. Afterward I became known as that sex painter from the suburbs.

The truth is my choice of themes was not entirely innocent. After *Sleepwalker*, I deliberately painted psychosexual subjects—the taboos of middle-class suburban life—and I wasn't altogether unhappy with the reputation it earned me. I didn't fully trust my painting skills then and felt that painting—especially old-fashioned realist painting—needed a little shock therapy to rescue it from the throes of modernist ennui. But I was also trying to explore those taboos, to express what they actually felt like and how they came to be, to expose their presence behind the prim, unexamined surfaces of suburban life, and to reveal their natural—or at least commonplace—role in adolescence.

The picture is about desire, voyeurism, appropriateness, and boundaries. It draws attention to the disjunction between the private and public spheres, between the woman's intimate movements, her indolence and sexuality, and the boy's—and by extension the viewer's—taut, penetrating gaze. The boy's age, of course, introduces Oedipal themes that are underscored by his actions. Though painted in shadow, they show the boy holding the woman's purse behind his back, apparently stealing something from it, most likely money or a credit card.

Bad Boy equates the boy's moment of sexual discovery to a theft, with its attendant feelings of trespass, guilt, and an intense, vagrant excitement that the boy, it seems clear, will memorialize in all his future encounters. But if the boy is breaking taboos, so too is the woman. At the very least, her negligence makes her complicit in the boy's transgression. And viewed from another angle, she seems to be luxuriating in her sexuality, exhibiting herself seductively, indiscriminately, as a way of taunting or projecting power over the boy and, it seems clear, all men.

Bad Boy re-created the troubling feelings I experienced during puberty when I saw my mother naked on a fairly regular basis. No doubt she felt it was natural, but I already didn't know how to deal with my emerging sexuality, much less the illicit impulses her naked body triggered in me. In this context, the boy is stealing from the woman's purse because he does not know what else to do, because he can't do anything else.

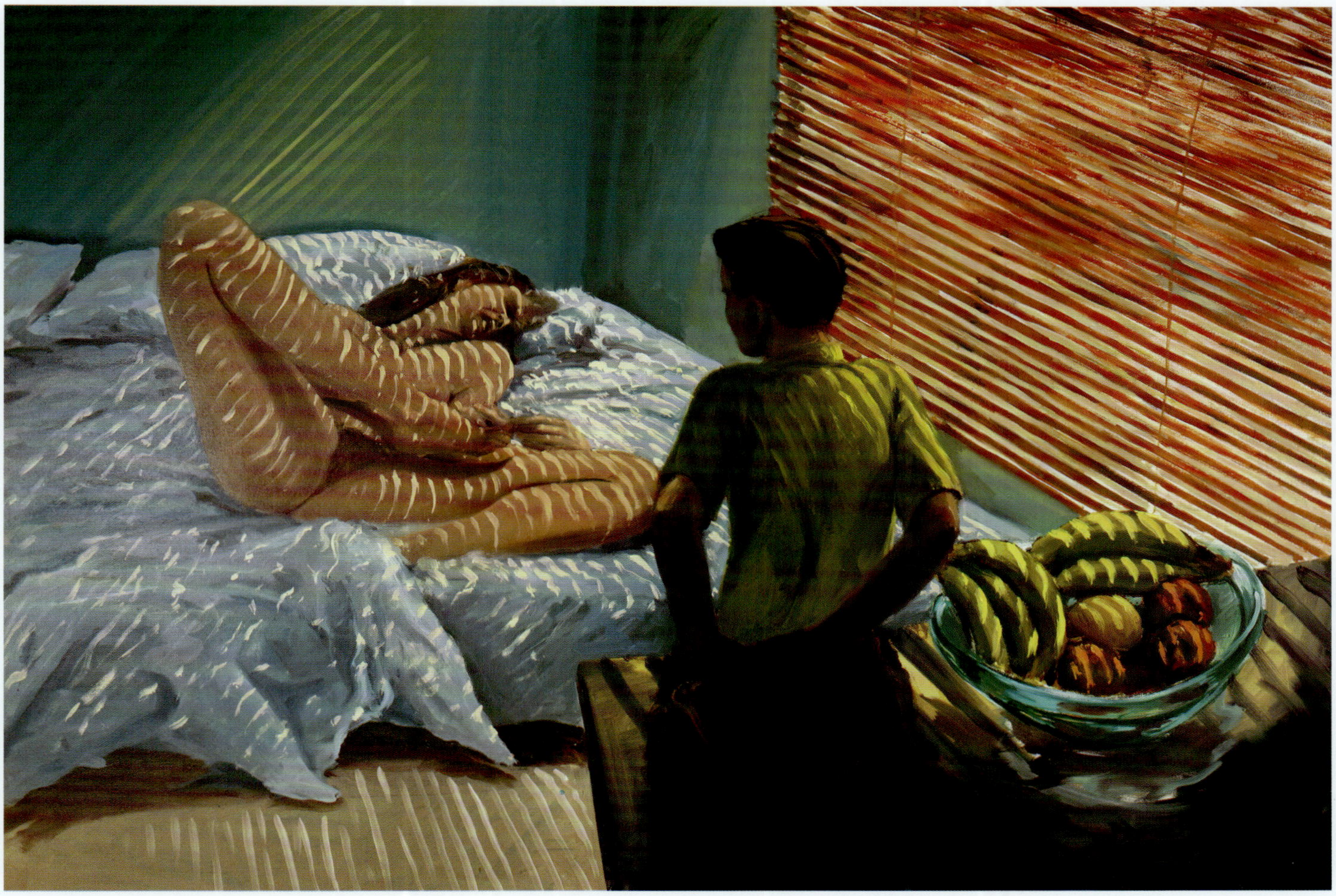

Eric Fischl
Bad Boy, 1981
Oil on canvas
66 × 96 inches
Private Collection,
Courtesy Thomas Ammann
Fine Art AG, Zurich

Nan Goldin

It's still my family. Ten years have passed since the *Ballad* was published and I don't really look at the book anymore. That was then; this is now. I continue to keep my diaries, both written and photographic. They take care of the past for me, and allow me to live totally in the present. I took the pictures in this book so that nostalgia couldn't ever color my past. I realize I took the picture of myself battered so I wouldn't go back to the man who beat me up. I wanted to make the record of my life that nobody could revise: not a safe, clean version, but instead, a record of what things really looked like and felt like.

Nan Goldin, "Afterword," *The Ballad of Sexual Dependency* (New York: Aperture Foundation, Inc., 1986), 145.
Afterword published in 1996 reprint

Nan Goldin
The Hug, New York City
(from *The Ballad of Sexual Dependency*), 1980
Cibachrome
Image 13½ × 9⅞ inches; Sheet 14 × 11 inches

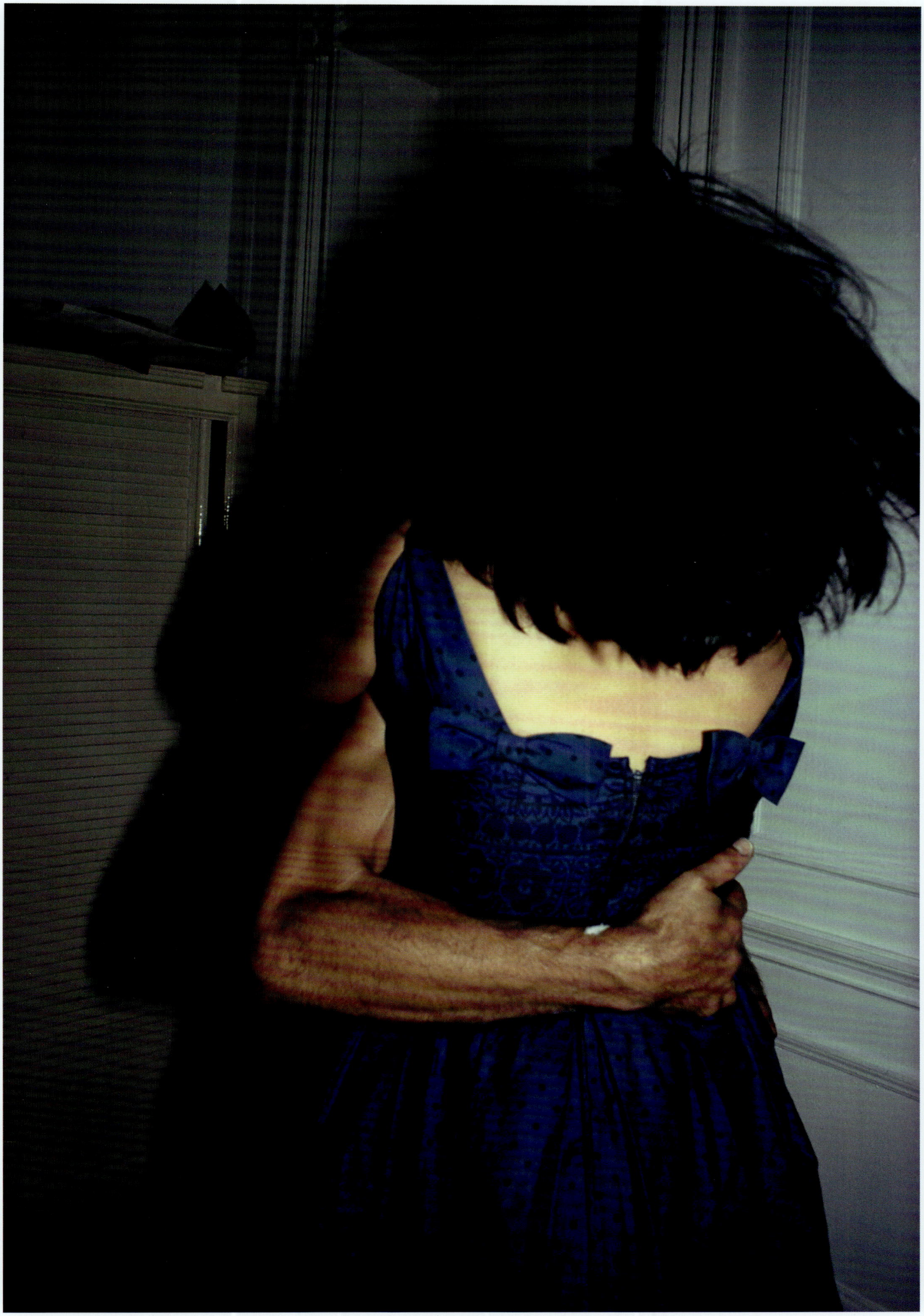

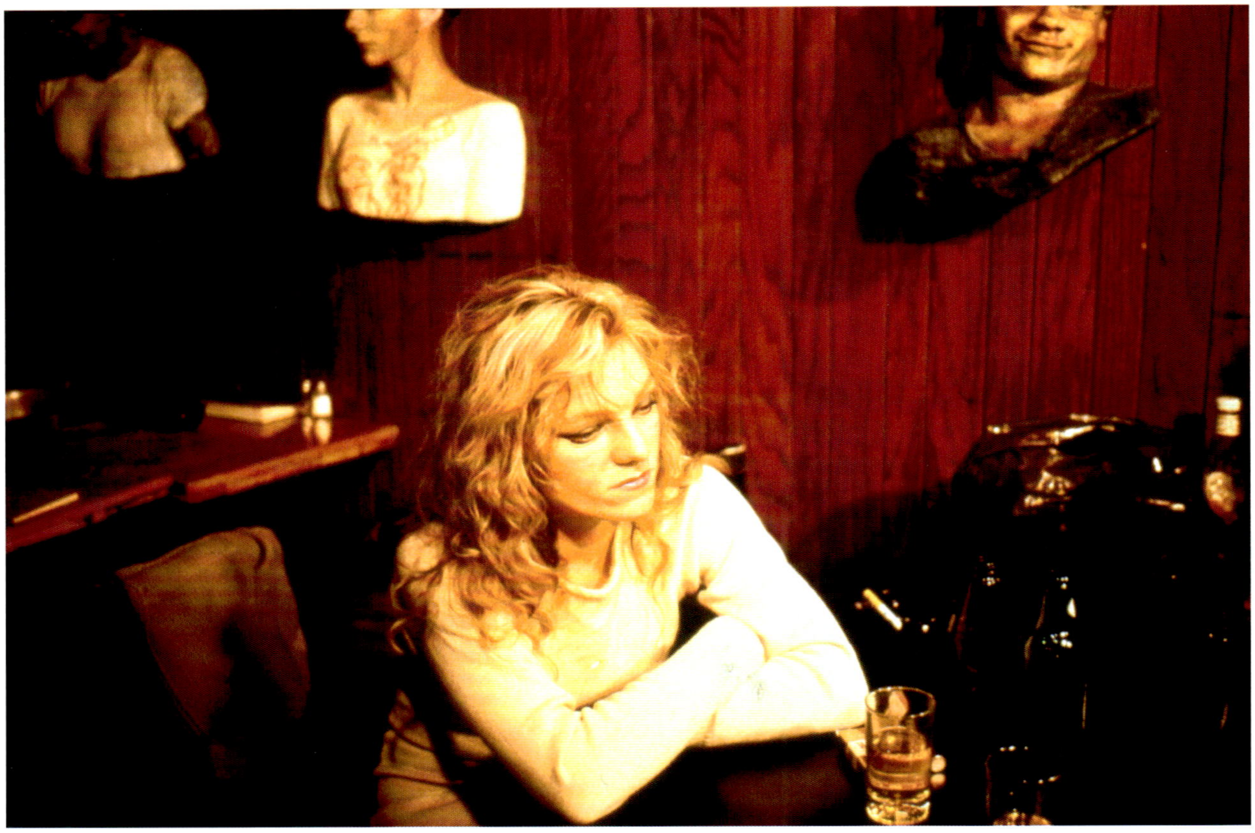

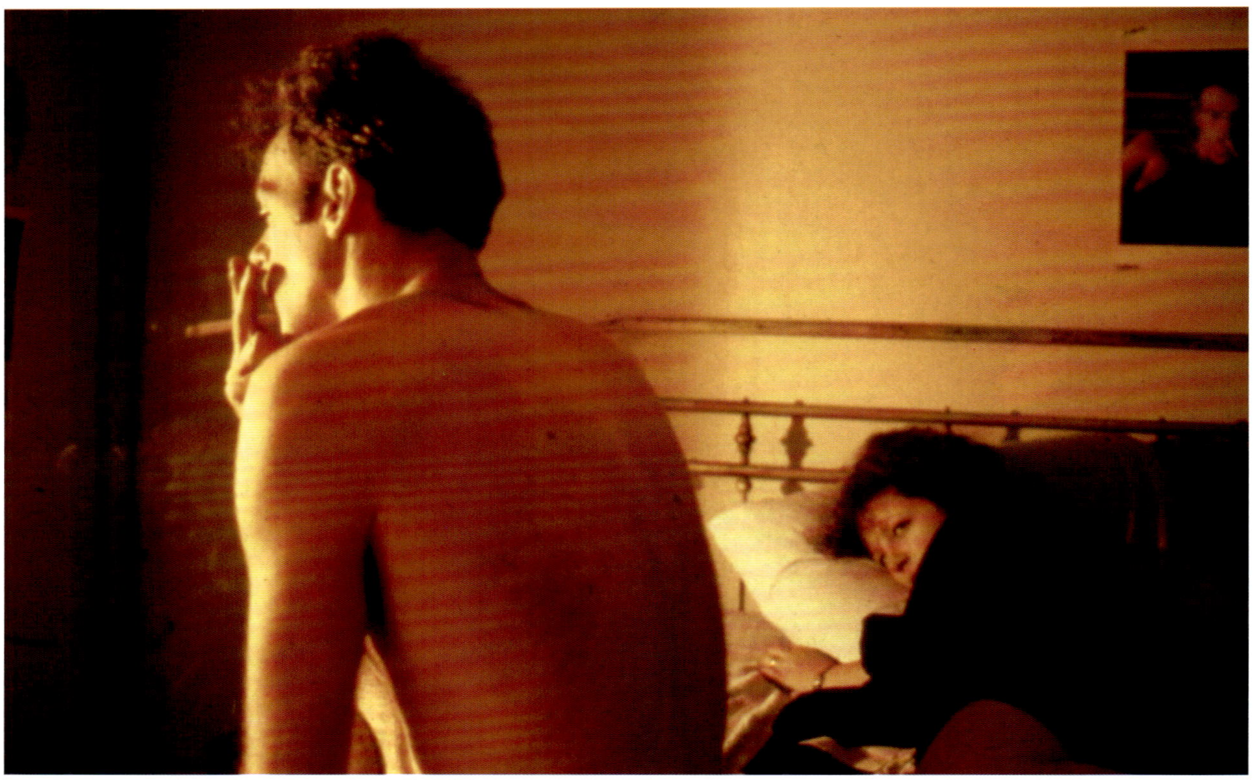

above:
Nan Goldin
Cookie at Tin Pan Alley, New York City
(from *The Ballad of Sexual Dependency*), 1983
Cibachrome
Image 9⅞ × 13½ inches; Sheet 11 × 14 inches

below:
Nan Goldin
Nan and Brian in Bed, New York City
(from *The Ballad of Sexual Dependency*), 1983
Cibachrome
Image 9⅞ × 13½ inches; Sheet 11 × 14 inches

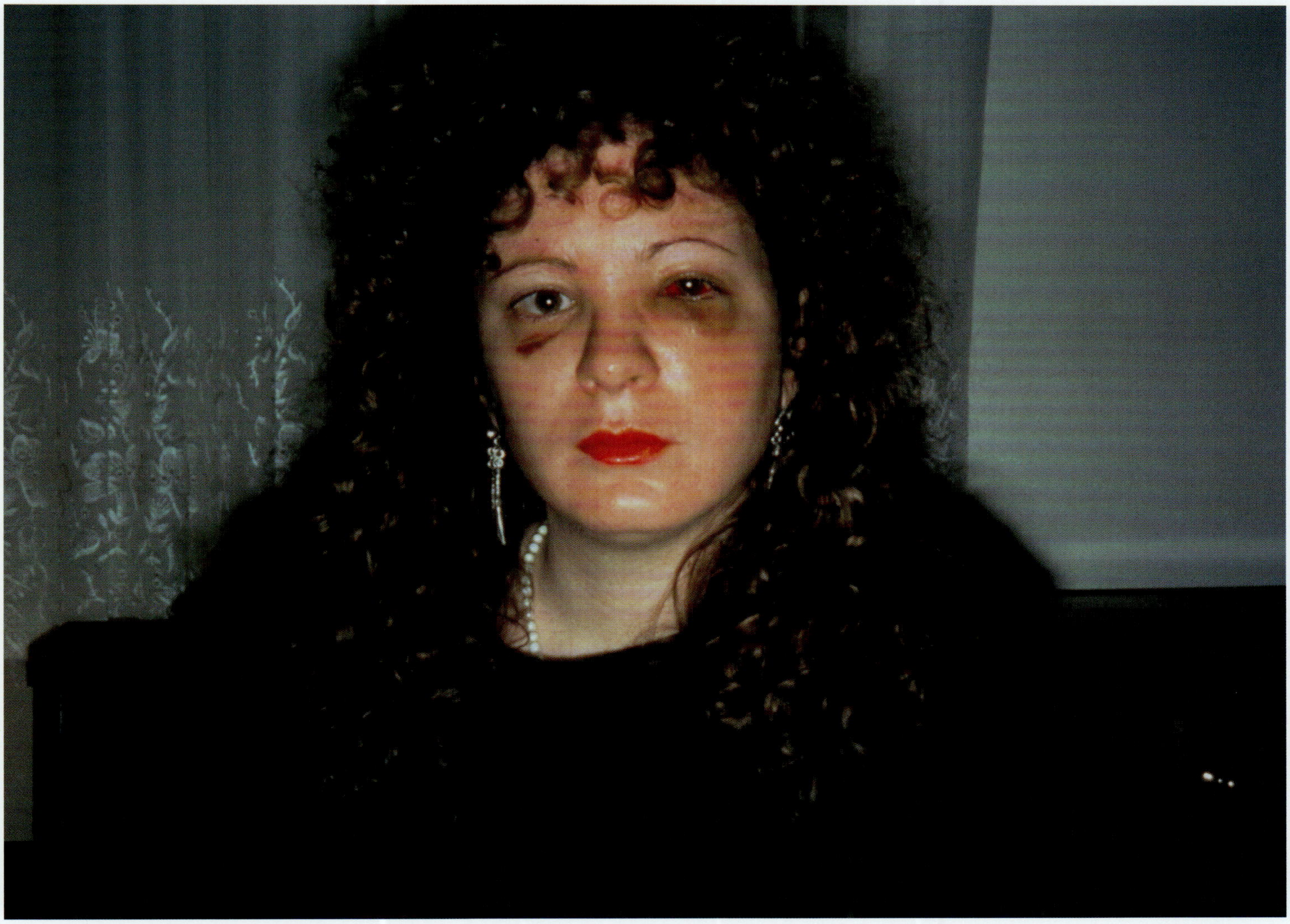

Nan Goldin
Nan after being battered
(from *The Ballad of Sexual Dependency)*, 1984
Cibachrome
Image 9⅞ × 13½ inches; Sheet 11 × 14 inches

Jack Goldstein

It began with performance, performances that had to do with my disappearance, and the evolution of those performances led to making films, because the work could be edited. Then the making of films moved into the making of records, in which both, the soundtrack and the image, are separated. And the making of records led to doing stage performances with actors and that turned into the making of paintings.

I use media for its mediation. And so I rely on what media can do, that certain things would not work as a film, but would work as a performance. So my use of media has a lot to do with playing with those kinds of things, it's being very conscious of that mediation.

Quoted in Chris Dercon, "An Interview with Jack Goldstein," 1985. Reprinted in *Jack Goldstein* (Frankfurt am Main: MMK Museum für Moderne Kunst and Verlag der Buchhandlung Walther König, 2010), 165

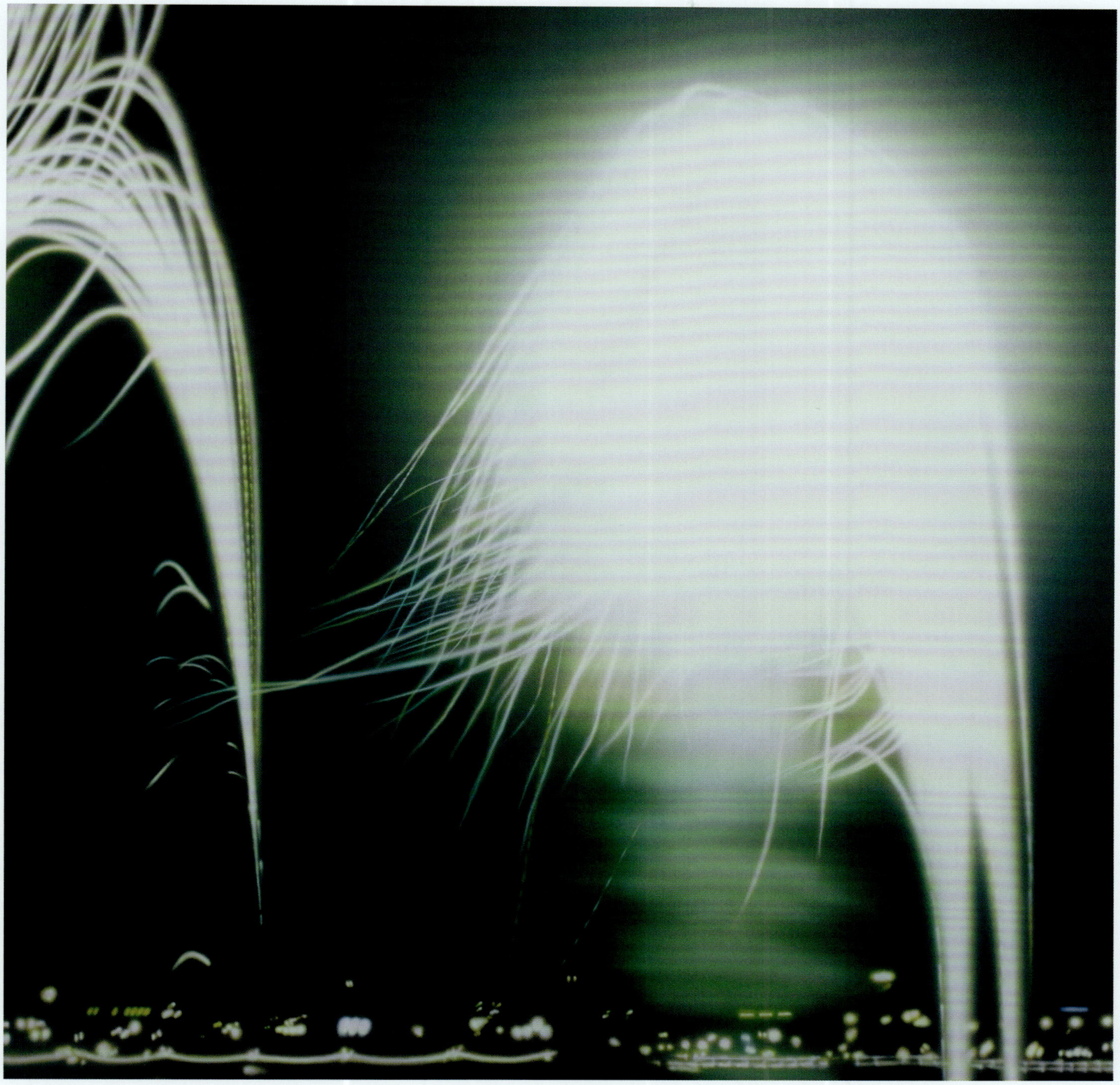

Jack Goldstein
Untitled (Fireworks Exploding), 1984
Acrylic on canvas
96 × 96 inches
Collection of B.Z.+ Michael Schwartz, New York

Peter Halley

Surprisingly, most of the current discussion of abstraction continues to focus on the idea of abstraction as a stylistic device or invention, borne out of artists' formal concerns; it treats abstraction as a phenomenon whose history can still be traced as a series of stylistic changes within the language of Modernist art itself. Further, abstraction continues to be seen as a superior language of emotional expression, in which the "free" play of "pure" color, form, and gesture enable artist and viewer to commune on an emotive or spiritual "plane" beyond the narrative and representational.

In thinking about this most rarefied of visual languages, it seems we intellectually retreat into the cloister of high culture; we deny that abstraction is a reflection of larger historical and cultural forces. We deny that the phenomenon of abstraction only gains meaning to the extent to which it does reflect larger forces and is embedded with their history.

In addition, the rapid changes made in travel and communications in this century have pushed us exponentially into a world that no longer depends on "real" or "natural" time or space. We take it for granted that we can speak with someone halfway around the world or that it takes just a few hours to travel thousands of miles. Such disjunctions in space and time have also created a world that is both highly malleable and free from natural referents.

If we examine the daily life of a middle class person in the United States or Europe, we get a picture of an existence of extraordinary hermeticism. People live in sealed houses or condos in highly controlled landscapes. They travel in the sealed environment of the automobile along the abstract pathway of the highway to equally artificial office parks and shopping malls. When one speaks of abstract art, it is essential to remember that it is only a reflection of a physical environment that has also become essentially abstract.

Whenever Andy Warhol spoke about death, or sex, or any other troubling emotional situation, he would say, "it's so abstract." While the history of postwar abstraction reflects these intellectual and technological changes, abstract art has by no means constituted simply their chronicling or representation. Rather, postwar abstraction is characterized by a certain emotional refusal brought out by alienation. If postwar abstraction chronicles anything, it is the emotional blankness, emptiness, and numbness of an abstract world where social relations have become as untethered as technology has.

Peter Halley, "Abstraction and Culture," *Peter Halley: Selected Essays 1981–2001* (New York: Edgewise Press, 2013), 163–71

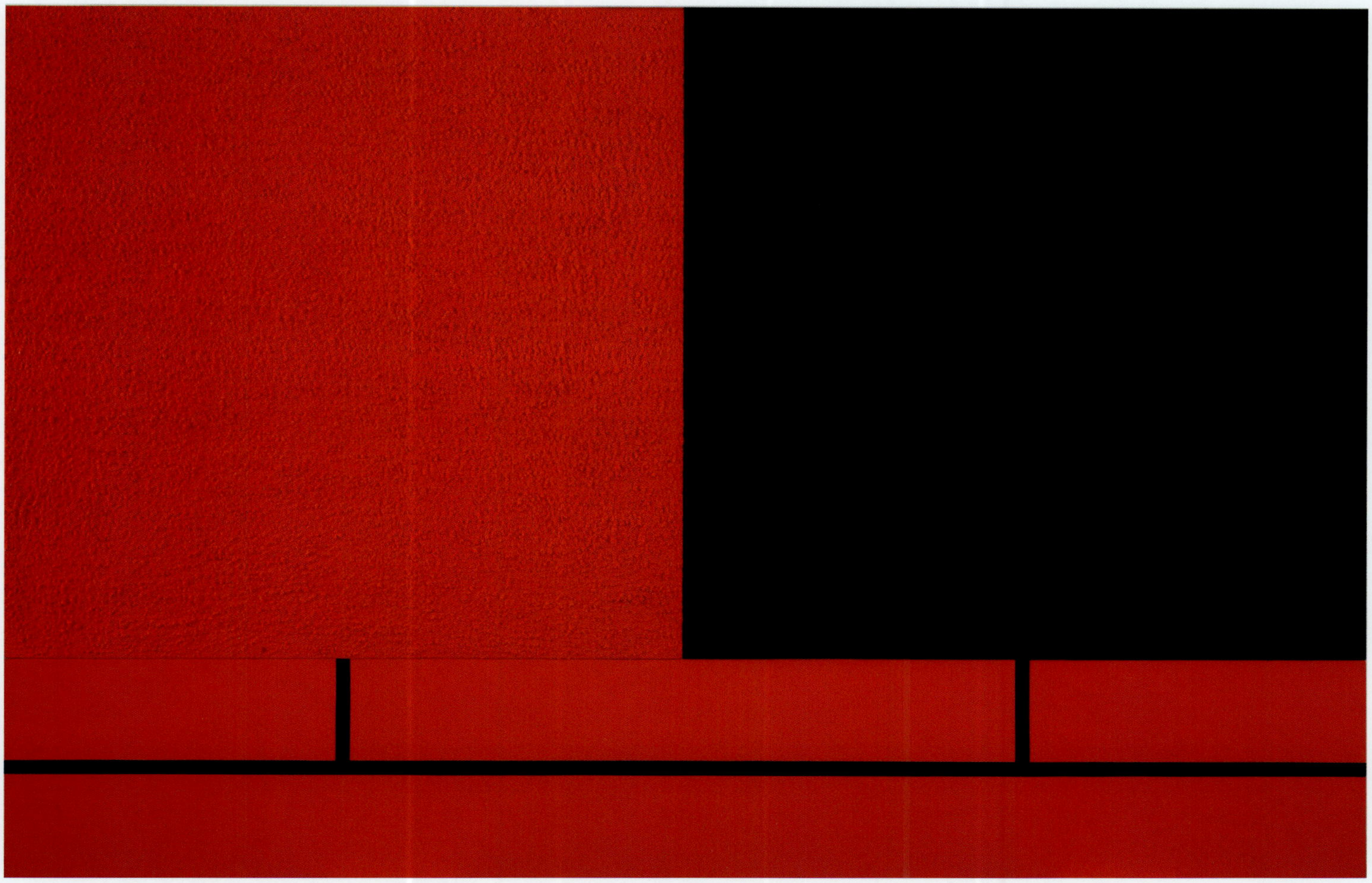

Peter Halley
Glowing and Burnt-Out Cells with Conduit, 1982
Acrylic, Day-Glo acrylic, and Roll-a-Tex on canvas
64 × 96 inches
Collection of B.Z. + Michael Schwartz, New York

Keith Haring

Keith Haring
Red, 1982–84
Gouache and ink on paper
106 ¾ × 274 inches
Courtesy Gladstone Gallery, New York and Brussels
Keith Haring artwork © Keith Haring Foundation

Art is about something being seen, whether it is absorbed by the eyes of people in the subways or of people in galleries. In the subways, one needs total abandon; since the work only exists for a fleeting moment, it can and probably will be erased. The moment when it was seen may be all that is left of it. Objects, of course, have much less chance of disappearing, they will be protected, and this changes the value that is placed on them. But permanence and impermanence are both plausible outcomes to an activity. If I believed only in ephemeral things, that would be too hard a philosophy to live by; you have to believe in concrete things too, things that don't go away. There shouldn't be anything wrong with things that stay there and accumulate meaning by becoming part of someone's life. There *shouldn't* be anything wrong with that, although the situation which surrounds it does seem to pervert it. The Rockefeller wing at the Met is a perfect example of that kind of perversion, of the ability of people with money and resources to take things away which are vital to the lives of other people. The question is how good or important is it for us to see these extraordinary things compared to what those people had to lose for us to be able to do so; it's enlightening for me to see them, but it's awful for them. There is no answer, for it's a paradox; an answer would mean it was one way or the other, and anyway, it's the way things are.

I left home when I was 18. I ended up in Pittsburgh in a school for commercial art, but I hated it immediately and left. I decided to go to the School of Visual Arts in New York, where I studied with Joseph Kosuth and Keith Sonnier. I've always thought I didn't want to be paid a lot for what I do, just enough to keep things going—but there's no way to do that. If you sell your work cheaply, you just get used by the system; somebody else buys it and sells it for more, so you have to take it from them. I don't know of a way to control prices. Money's like a drug, I see it in every walk of life so far; I've not found any way to make a dent in, or alter that. In some sense, I'm already addicted. It's really hard not to be—it's such a basic idea of the world now, to always want more, to want bigger and better. And when you don't *have* to do something else to survive, it's hard to *want* to work for somebody else at $2.50 an hour, just to maintain your integrity. If *anyone* was given an alternative to that situation, they'd take it, obviously. If I say "things are going great, I guess," the response is "I'd give anything to be in your shoes." So that even if you can see that something is wrong, someone else would change places with you immediately. Even if your own thoughts about the situation haven't changed, you find the situation has changed you, and you can't reverse that. I'm just not in the same boat as I was when I was in nightclubs organizing shows which everybody just thanked me for, and there's nothing I can do to make it seem the same situation. I don't feel that different, but I'm forced to *be* different. It's made me conscious of being an exemplary person, of how to behave as a model for others.

Quoted in Suzi Gablik, "Report from New York: The Graffiti Question," *Art in America* (October 1982): 35.

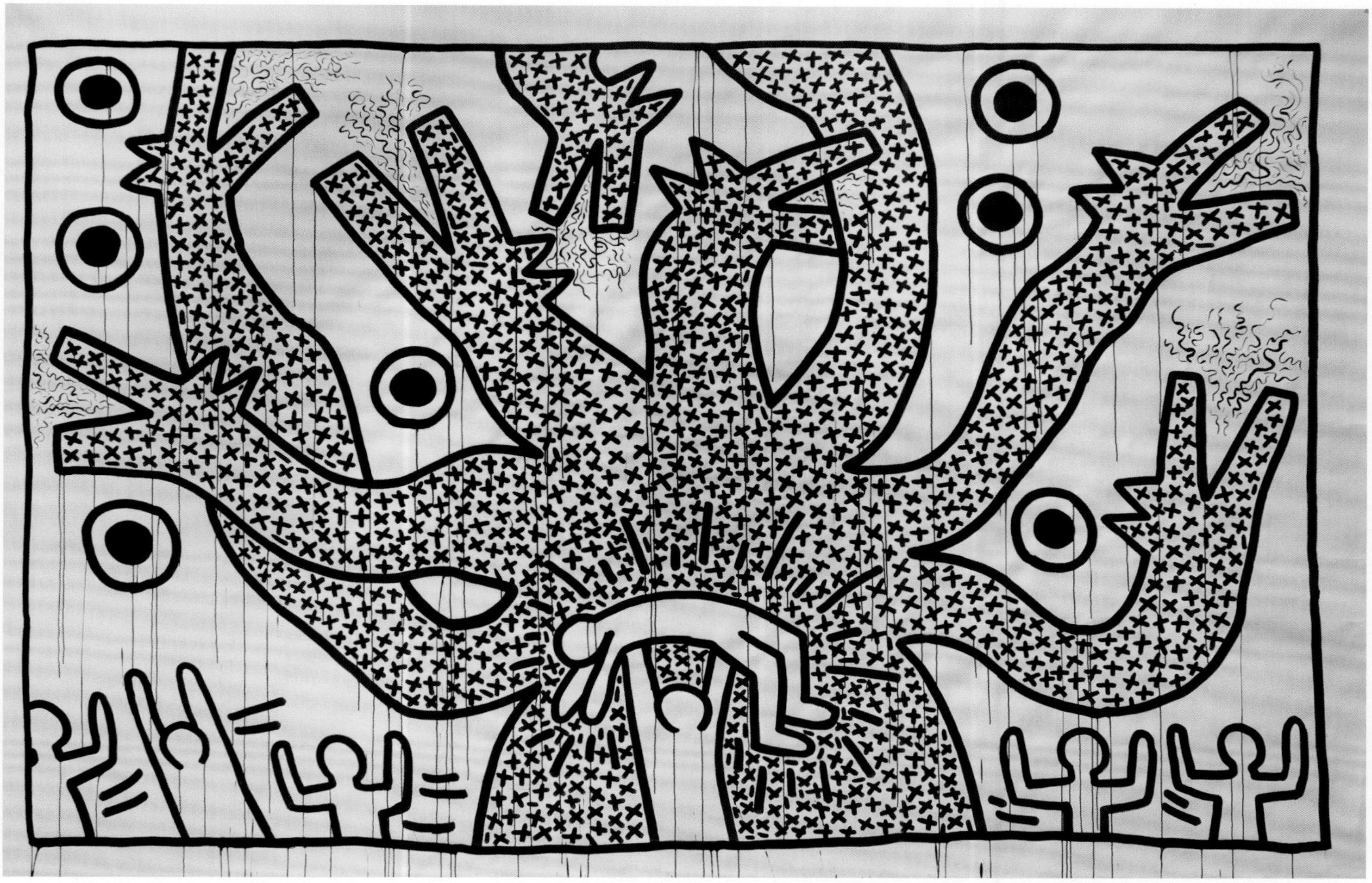

Keith Haring
Untitled, 1982
Sumi ink on paper
107 × 160 inches
Courtesy Collection of Scott and Yael Braun
Keith Haring artwork © Keith Haring Foundation

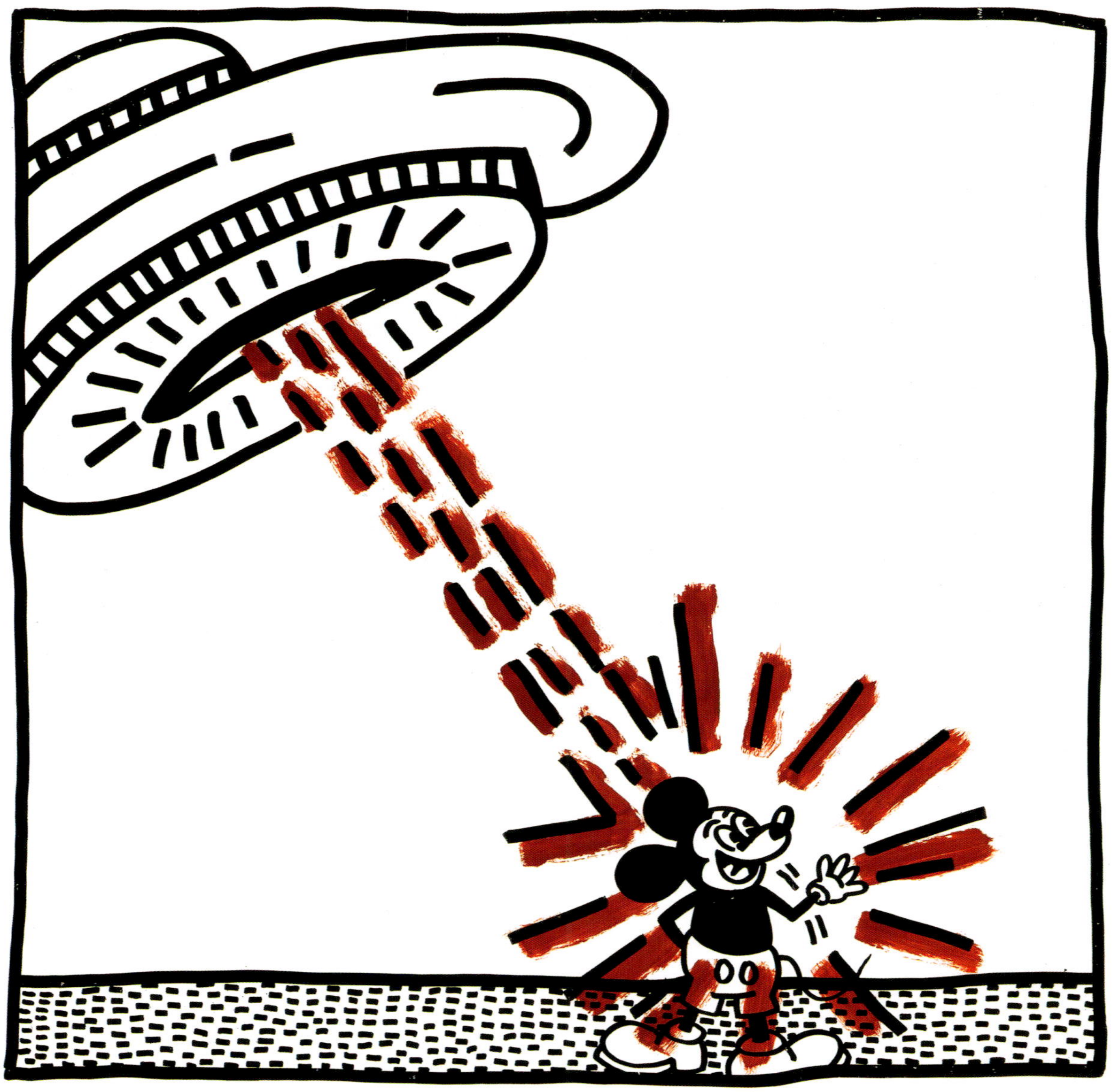

Keith Haring
Untitled, 1981
Enamel on fiberboard
48 × 48 inches
Rubell Family Collection, Miami

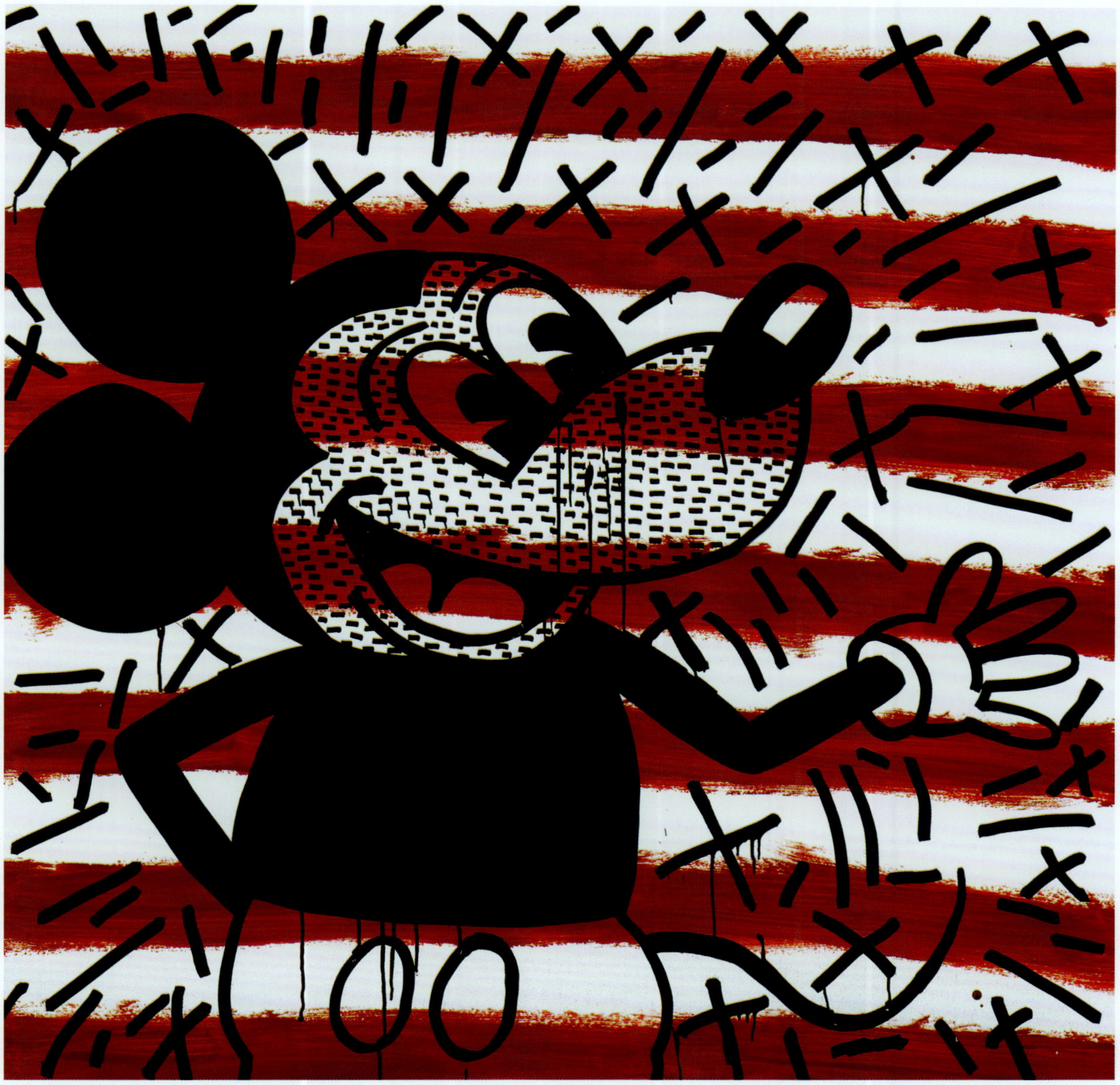

Keith Haring
Untitled, 1981
Enamel on fiberboard
48 × 48 inches
Rubell Family Collection, Miami

Jenny Holzer

New York in the '80s was not a "peaceful" place. There was so much you were confronted with. People were living high and dying low. Someone you knew would sell a work of art for what seemed like an incredulous amount, and then someone else you knew would die of AIDS. Throughout the decade, the momentum kept spiraling upward and downward.

When you talk about the '80s, it depended on which neighborhood you were talking about. The economics and geography of Manhattan were diverse. For some artists, money came fairly quickly. If you made paintings, you were at the front of the line. If you didn't get in the painting line, which I didn't, you gravitated to different fringe elements. Getting involved with a collection, like Co-Lab, was a survival technique. The galleries weren't yet interested in what we were doing, so we became our own audience. We also genuinely felt we could make a difference, promoting art that asked questions rather than just provided product.

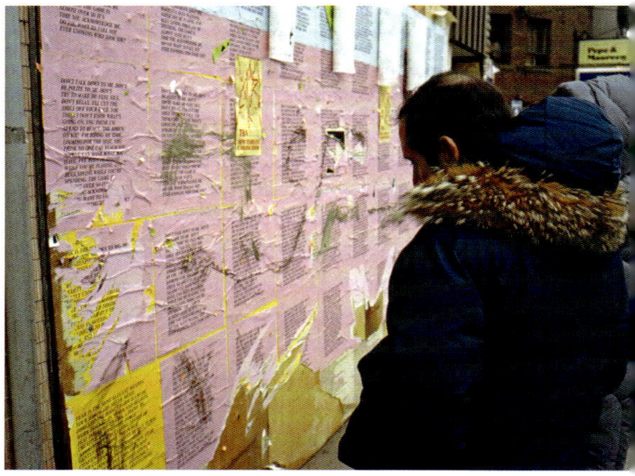

The economy was good in the '80s, but the politics, sometimes on both sides, was suspect. It wasn't hard to sort out right from wrong, but it was hard to stay calm enough to keep a focus. I think the *Truisms* were partly about that—making statements that forced you to focus, either in reaction to the statement or in support of it. For me, they were personal and political. They got more and more personal as the decade progressed. I think the titles of the later series—*Survival* and *Under a Rock*—say something about how I felt about the moment.

Art is always political, even when it is personal. To paint on canvas is political. I'd also say that using language as your medium, as I do, doesn't necessarily make you more political. I do think that language is more argumentative, and maybe that's why I've been attracted to it. An image can be ambiguous. A text can deliver a very specific image or content that makes you react.

Jenny Holzer, in a telephone conversation with Michael Auping, November 10, 2013

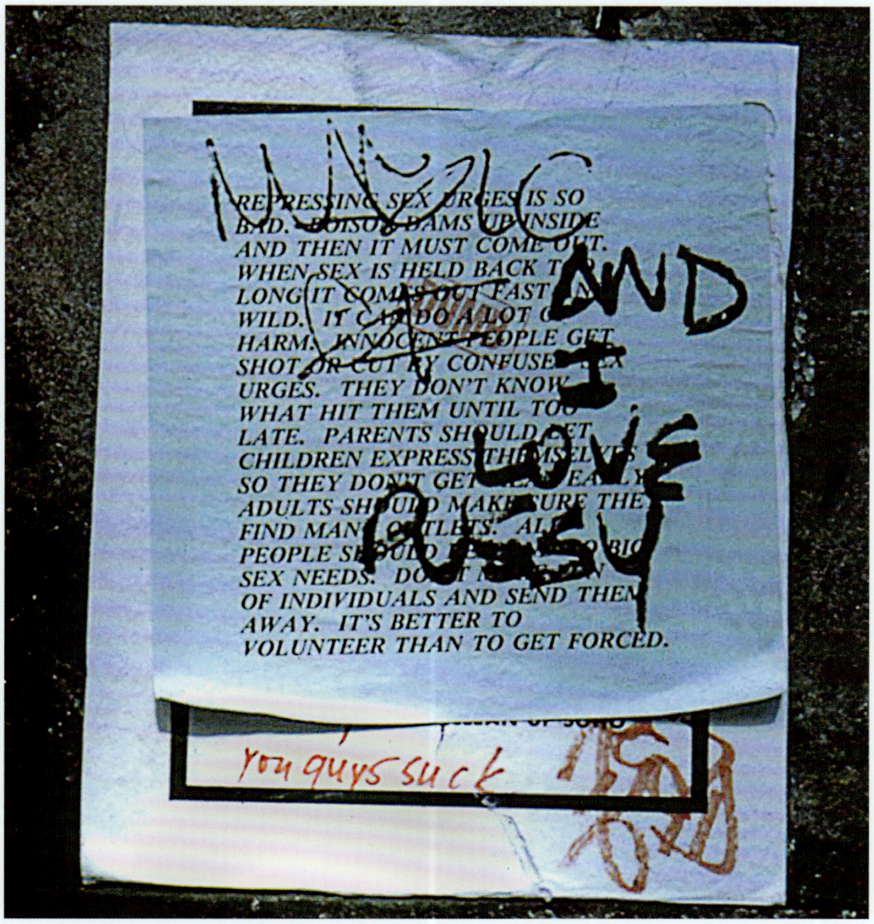

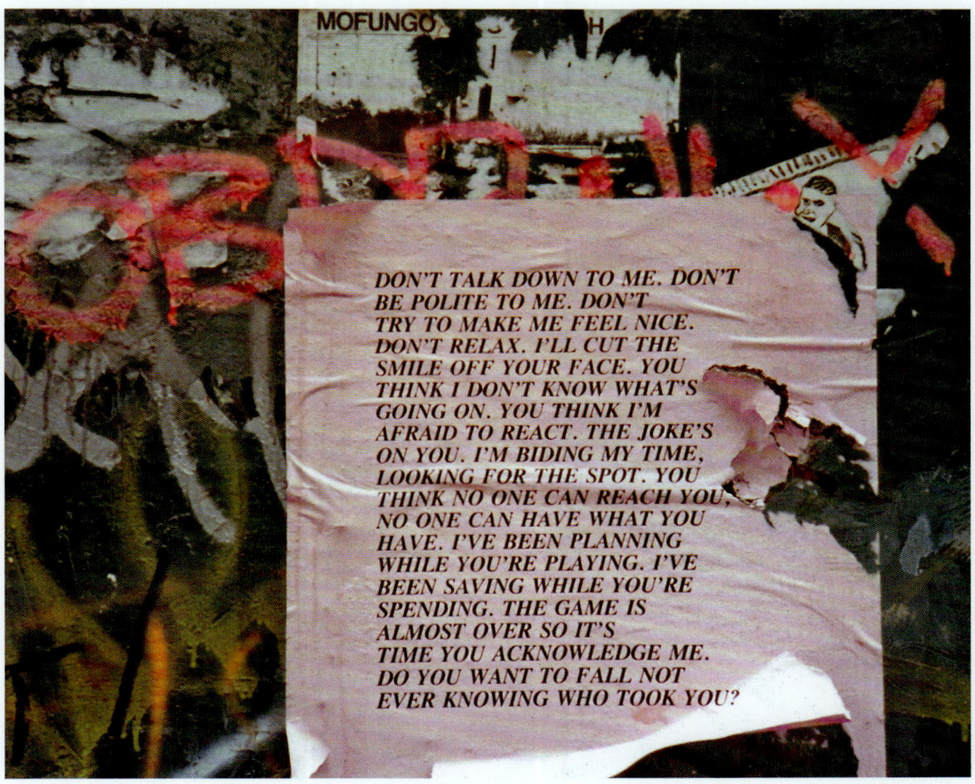

Jenny Holzer
Inflammatory Essays, 1979–82
Offset posters
Each 17 × 17 inches
Installation: New York, 1982 and 1983
Courtesy of the Artist

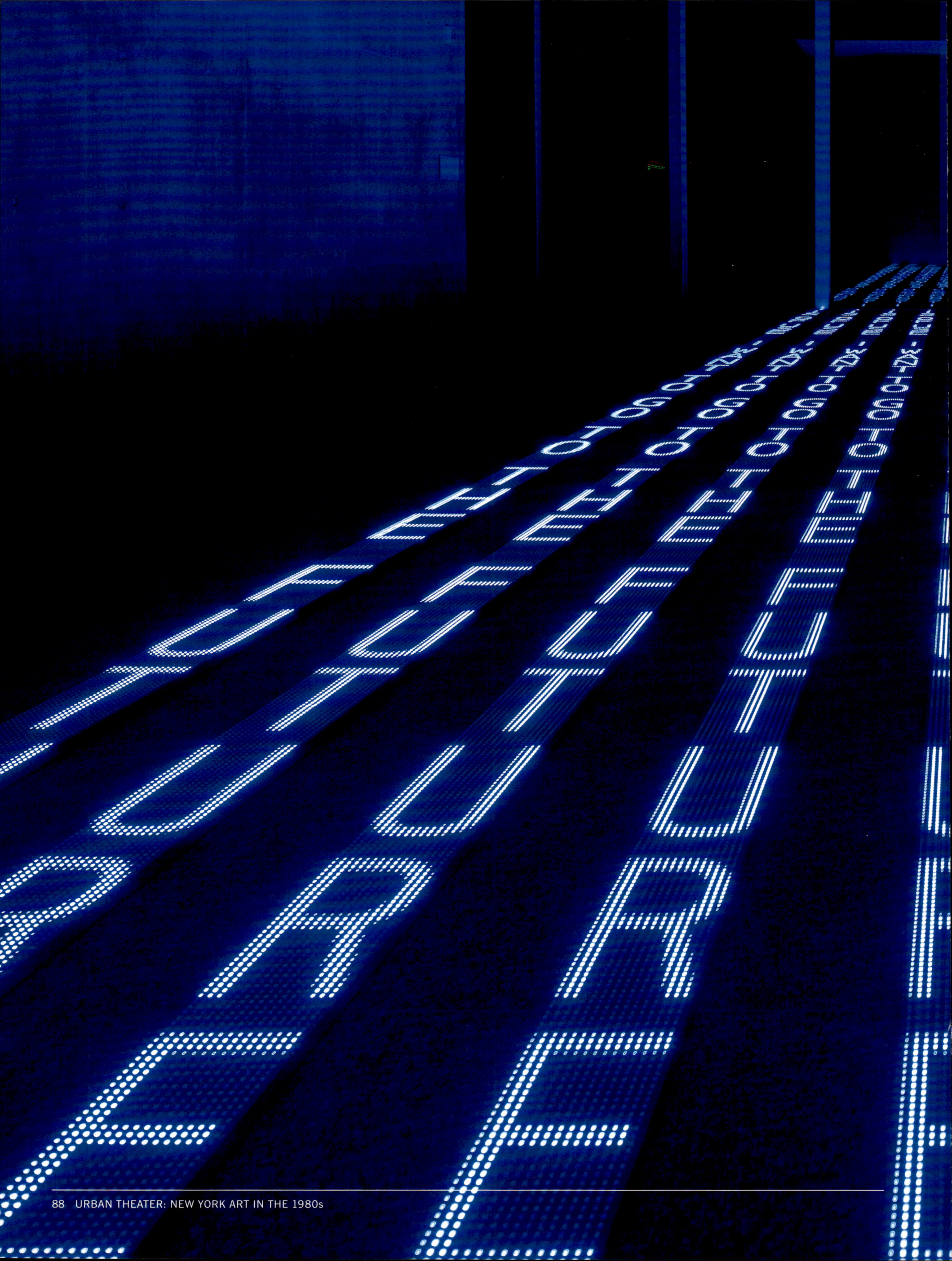
GO TO THE FUTURE
GO TO THE FUTURE
GO TO THE FUTURE
GO TO THE FUTURE

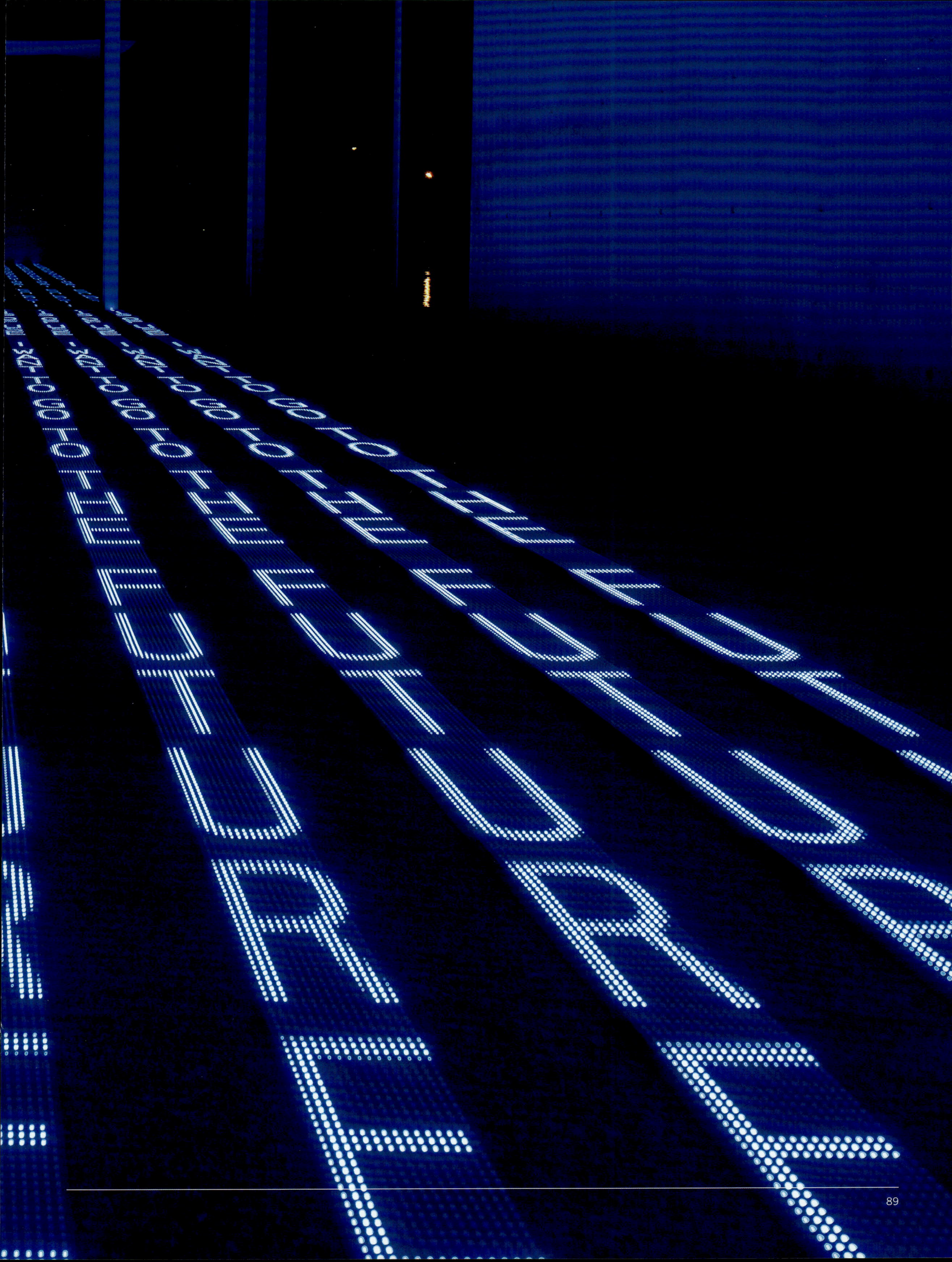
TO GO TO THE FUTURE

this page and previous spread:
Jenny Holzer
Kind of Blue, 2012
9 LED signs with blue diodes
9/10 × 120 × 576 inches
Text: *Truisms*, 1977–79; *Inflammatory Essays*, 1979–82;
Living, 1980–82; *Survival*, 1983–85;
Under a Rock, 1986; *Laments*, 1989;
Mother and Child, 1990; *Erlauf*, 1995; *Arno*, 1996
Collection of the Modern Art Museum of Fort Worth,
Museum purchase
 Photographs by Collin LaFleche

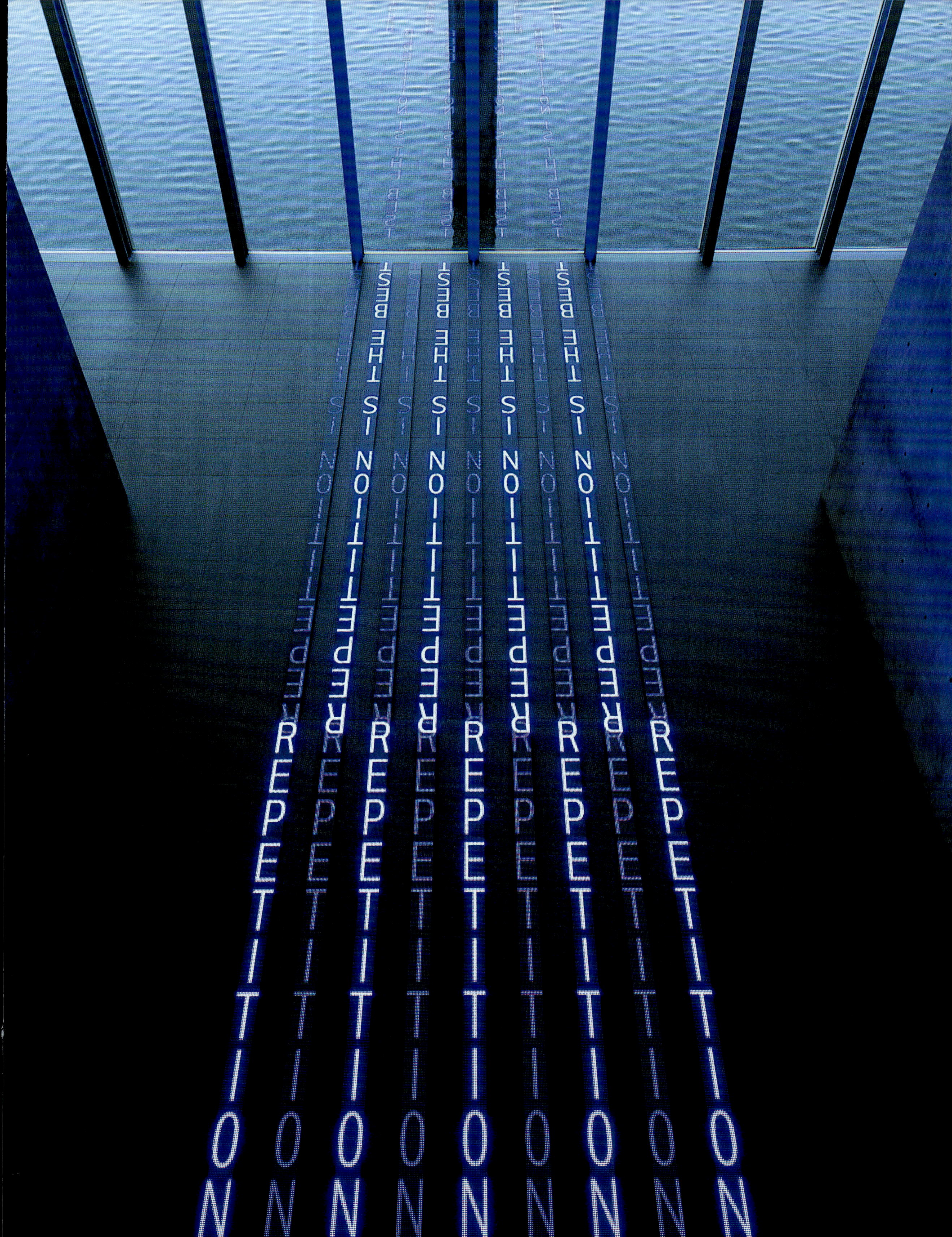
REPETITION

Jeff Koons

I transform the content of a chosen object by putting it in a specific context. I control the new content through the support mechanisms. I use billboard ads, the juxtaposition of the object with the other objects, as well as the actual process of transformation I put the object through. This recodifies the object so that it gives off the kind of information I would like people to view.

It stems from my need to perform art with a value that is not just masturbatory. I don't care to move a paintbrush across a canvas and think "Oh, this is right, this feels good." I don't seek to make consumer icons, but to decode why and how consumer objects are glorified. The *Equilibrium* body of work was in part based on physics, think of the basketballs suspended in a fifty-fifty tank, because the tools of science, such as the tank, are seen as purely analytical, not as commodities. The basketballs denote social mobility particularly for urban blacks and, more removed, those who practice art for that reason rather than live it as a philosophical way of life. The accompanying Nike ads are the sirens of "go for it," they are the great deceivers who tell you "I've achieved the state of equilibrium. You can do it too. You'll be a star."

Quoted in Daniela Salvoni, "Interview with McCollum and Koons," *Flash Art* 131 (December 1986/January 1987): 66–68. Originally published in *Flash Art International*. Courtesy Flash Art International and Giancarlo Politi Editore, Milan

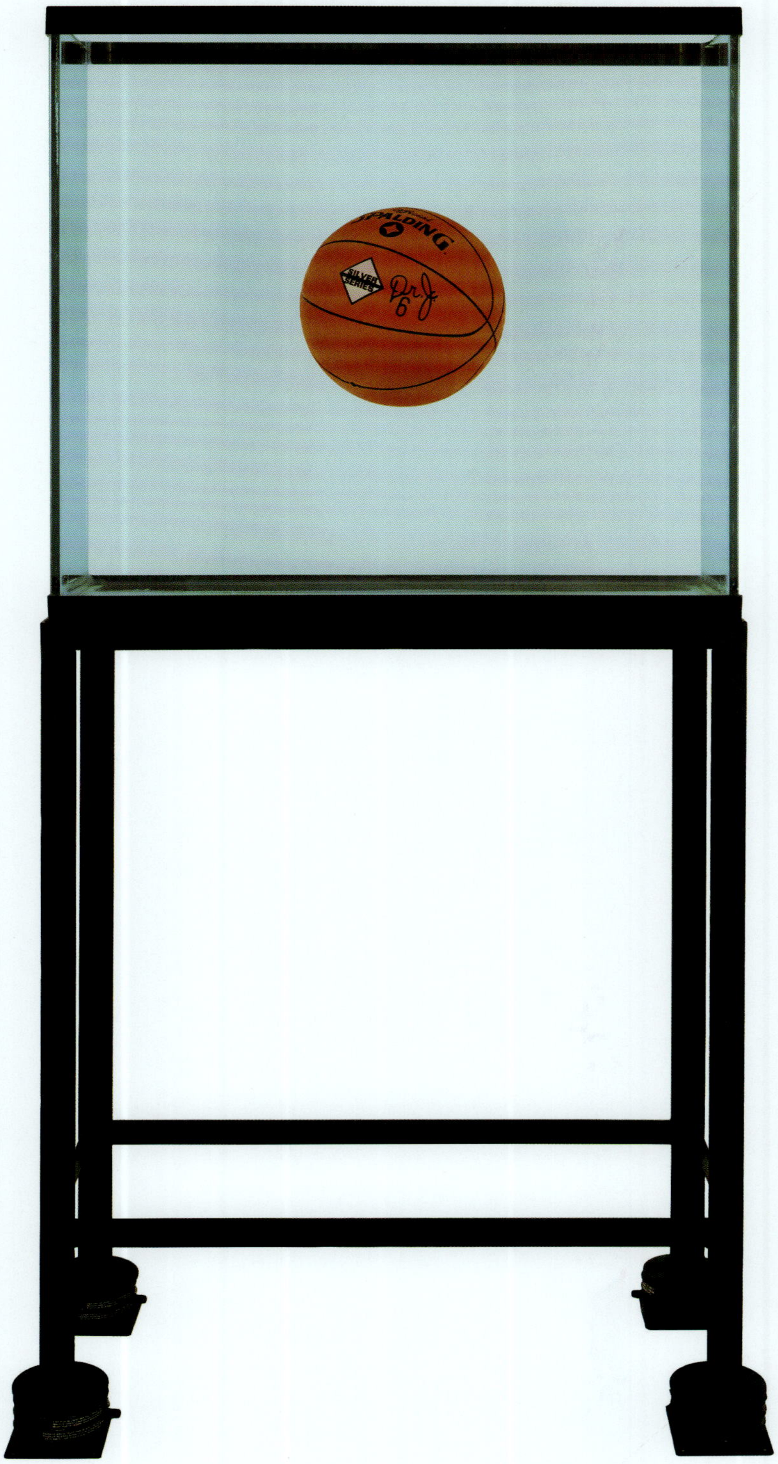

Jeff Koons
One Ball Total Equilibrium Tank
(Spalding Dr. J Silver Series), 1985
Glass, steel, sodium chloride reagent,
distilled water, and basketball
$64\frac{3}{4} \times 30\frac{3}{4} \times 13\frac{1}{4}$ inches
Collection of Jeffrey Deitch

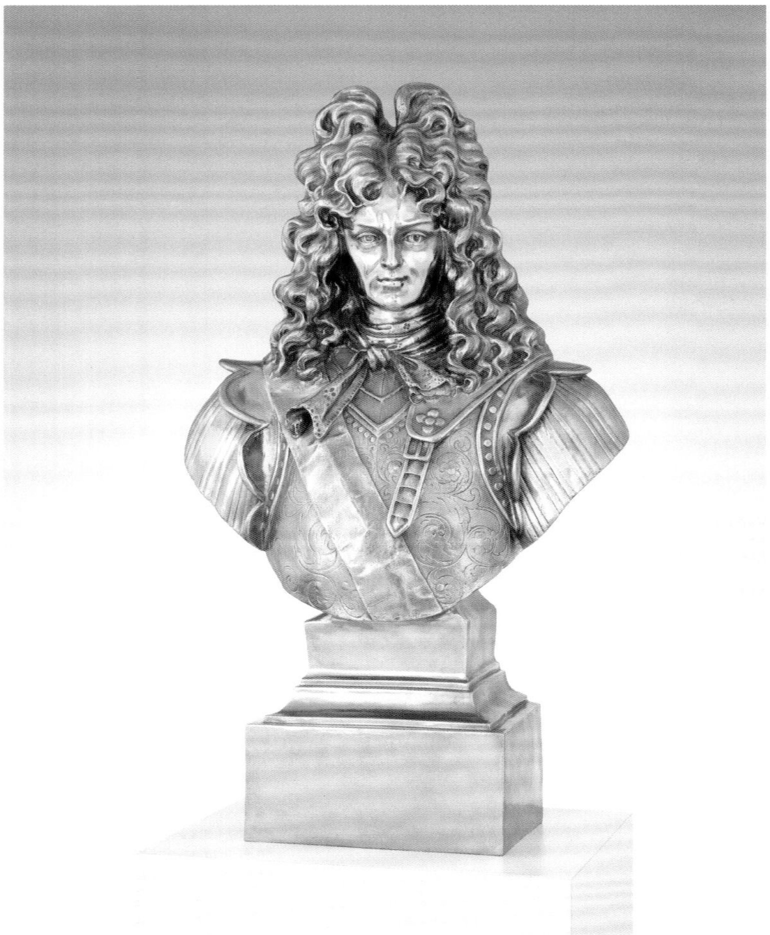

Jeff Koons
Louis XIV, 1986
Stainless steel
46 × 27 × 15 inches
Raymond and Patsy Nasher Collection,
Nasher Sculpture Center, Dallas
© Jeff Koons

opposite page:
Jeff Koons
New Hoover Convertibles, Green, Red, Brown, New Hoover Deluxe Shampoo Polishers, Yellow, Brown Doubledecker, 1981–87
Three vacuum cleaners, two shampoo polishers, and fluorescent lights in Plexiglas casing
82 5/8 × 54 × 28 inches
Glenstone
© Jeff Koons
Photograph by Tim Nighswander

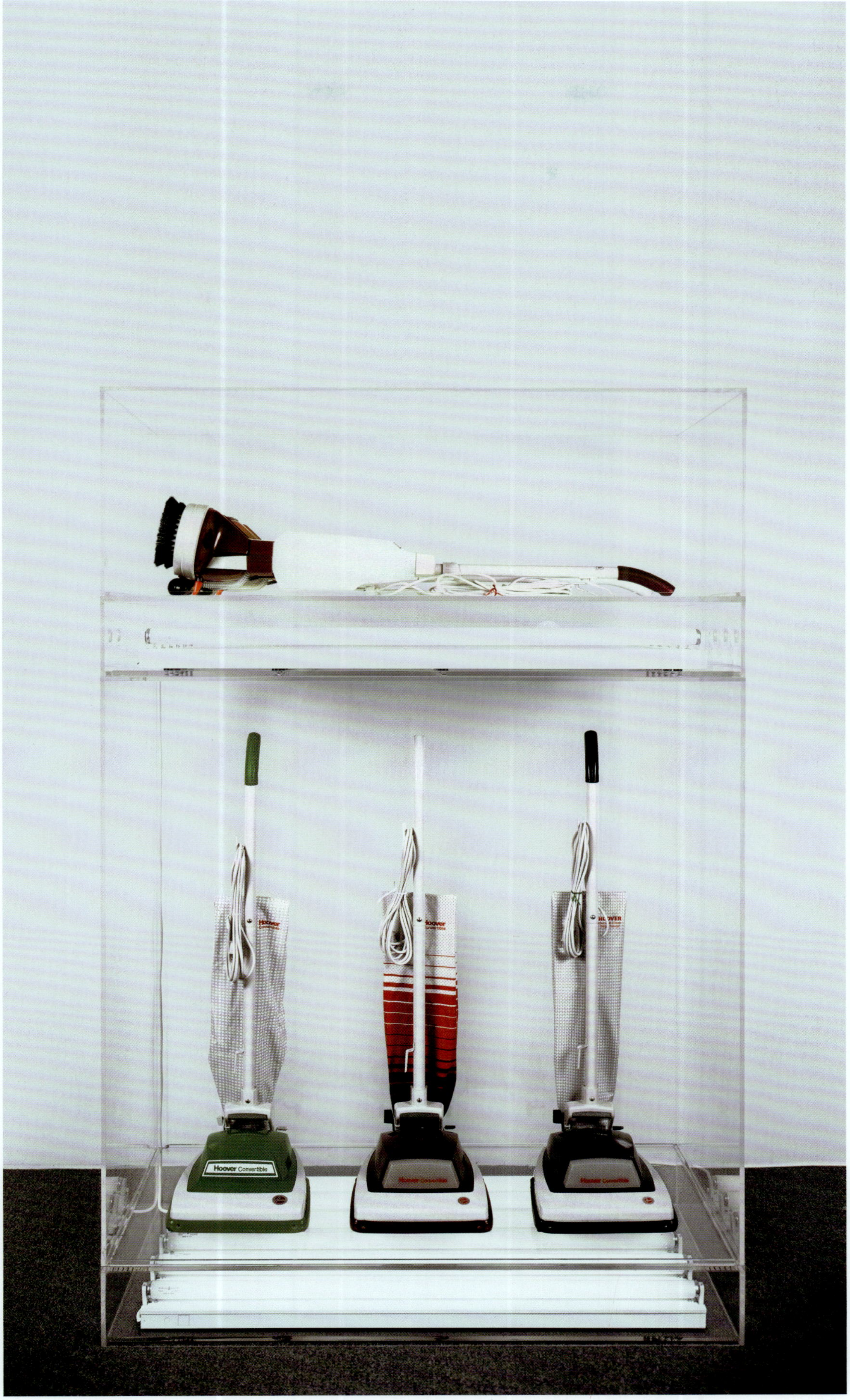
Hoover Convertible

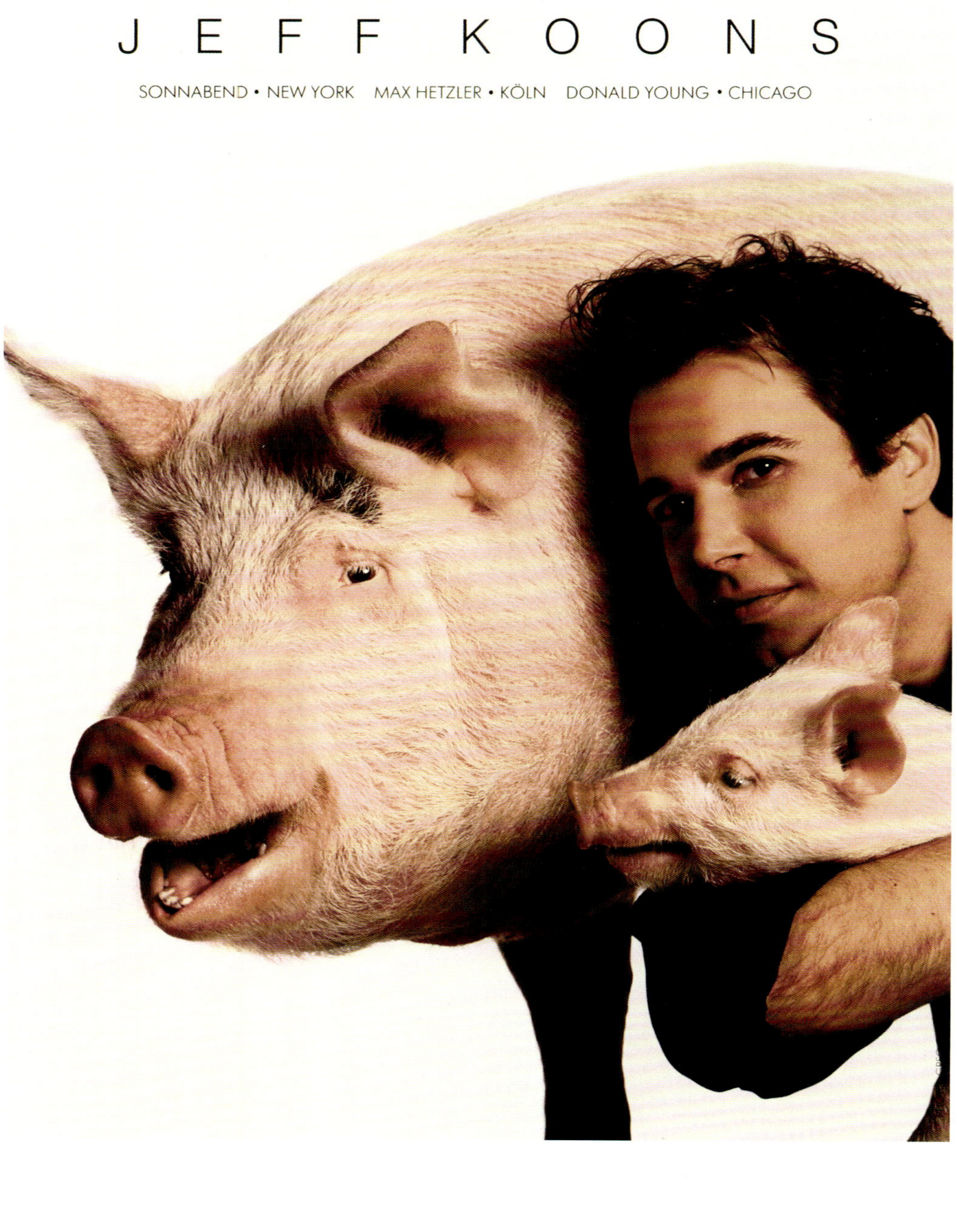

Jeff Koons
Art Magazine Ads (Flash Art), 1988–89
Lithograph, edition of 50 plus 10 artist proofs
45 × 37 1/4 inches
Collection of the Modern Art Museum of Fort Worth,
Anonymous Gift
© Jeff Koons

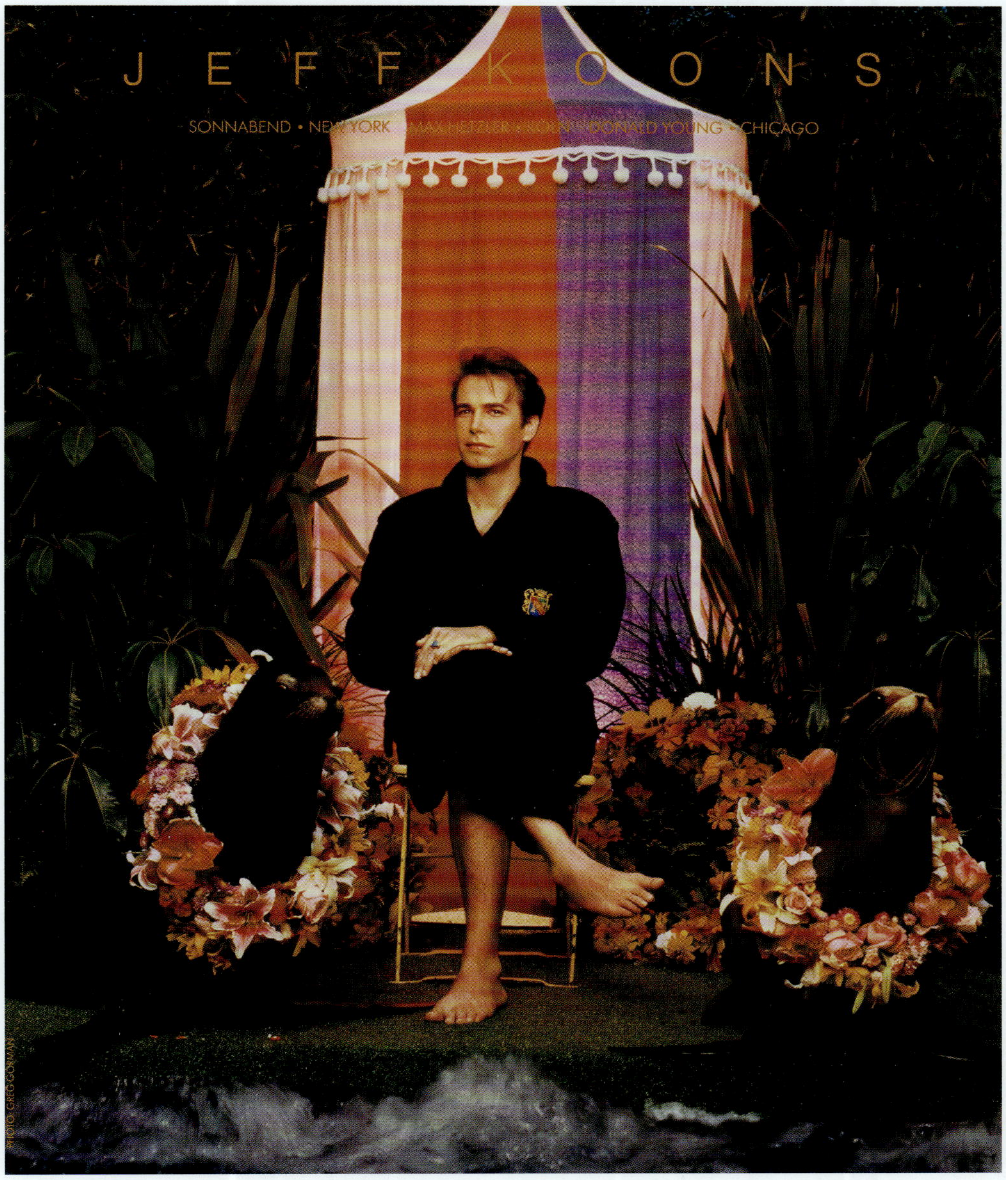

Jeff Koons
Art Magazine Ads (Arts), 1988–89
Lithograph, edition of 50 plus 10 artist proofs
45 × 37¼ inches
Collection of the Modern Art Museum of Fort Worth,
Anonymous Gift

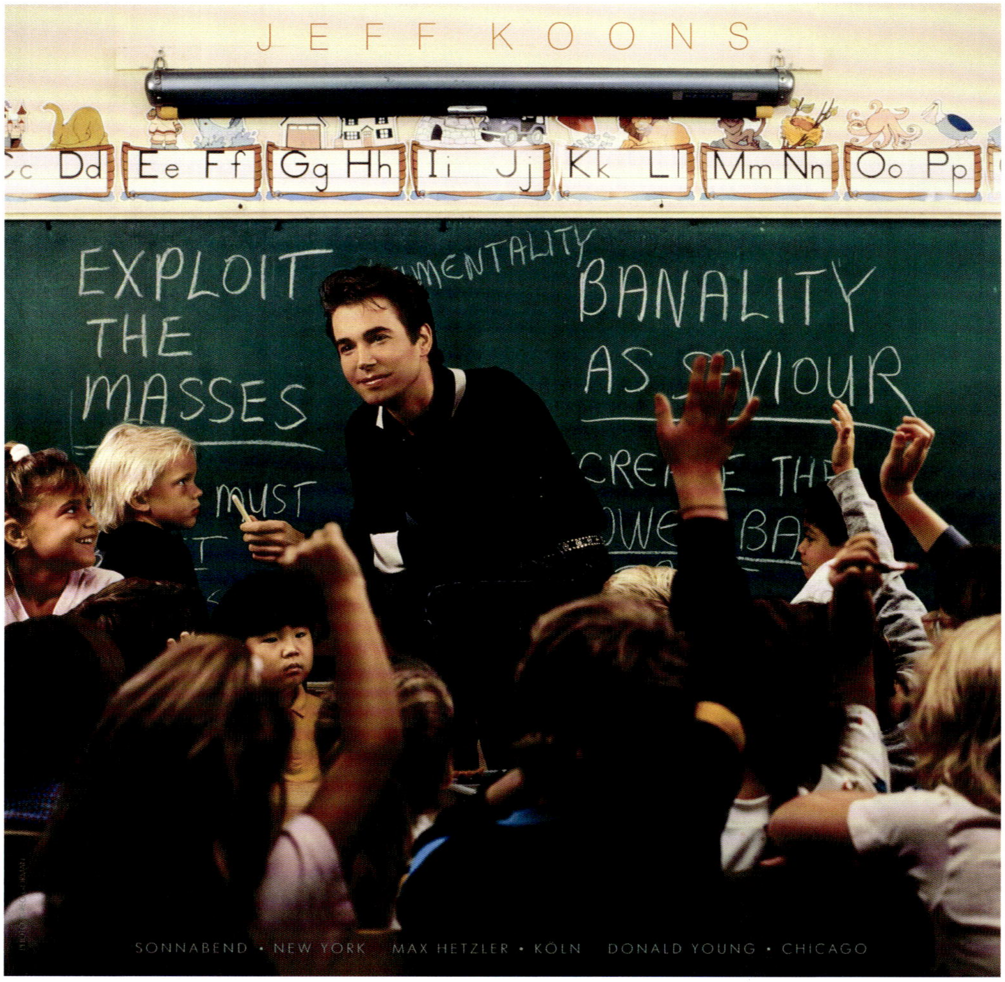

Jeff Koons
Art Magazine Ads (Artforum), 1988–89
Lithograph, edition of 50 plus 10 artist proofs
37 1/4 × 45 inches
Collection of the Modern Art Museum of Fort Worth,
Anonymous Gift
© Jeff Koons

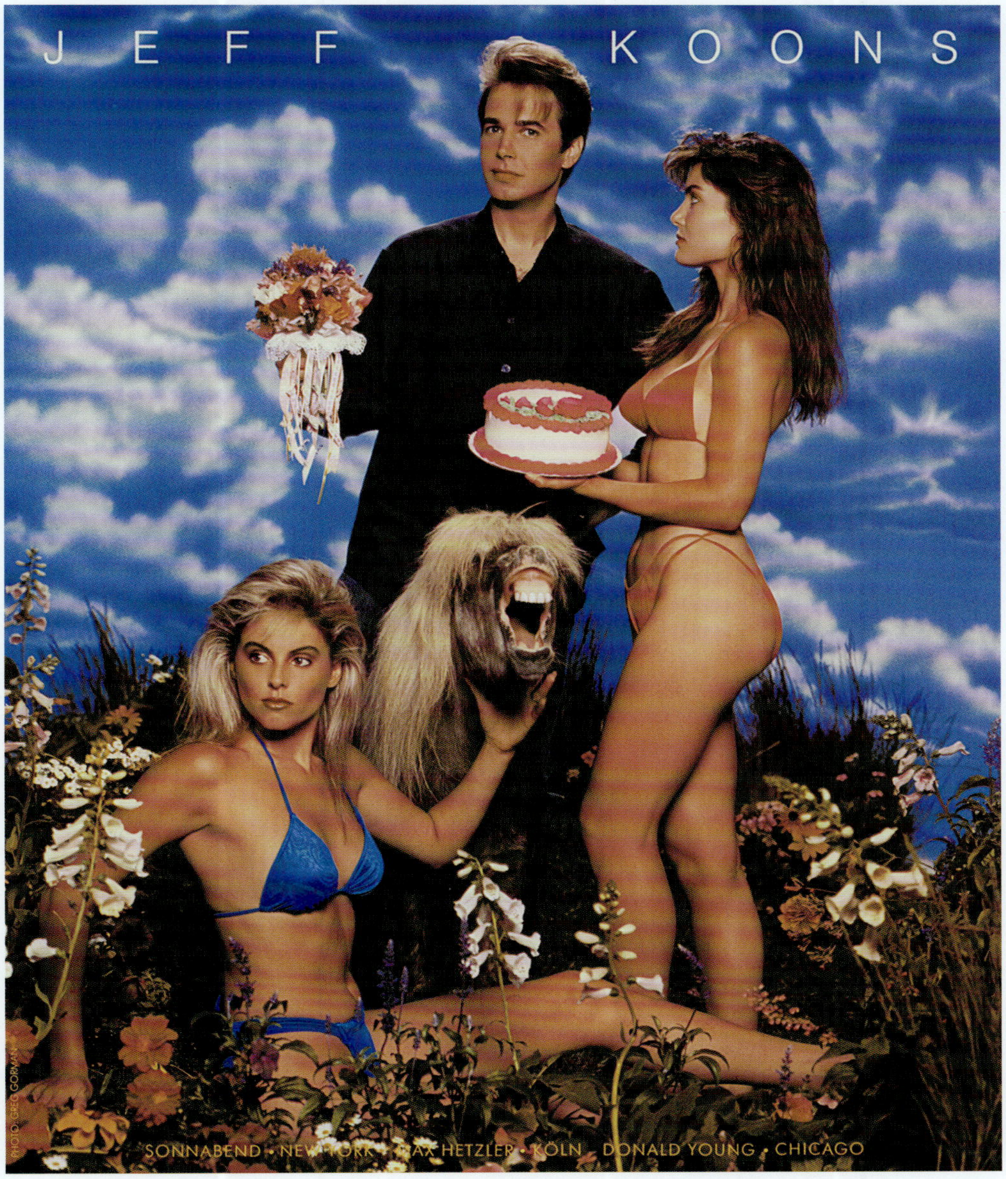

Jeff Koons
Art Magazine Ads (Art in America), 1988–89
Lithograph, edition of 50 plus 10 artist proofs
45 × 37 ¼ inches
Collection of the Modern Art Museum of Fort Worth,
Anonymous Gift

Barbara Kruger

I think I developed language skills to deal with threat. It's the girl thing to do—you know, instead of pulling out a gun.

Direct address has been a consistent tactic in my work, regardless of the medium that I'm working in.

I think what I'm trying to do is create moments of recognition. To try to detonate some kind of feeling or understanding of lived experience.

Quoted in Thyrza Nichols Goodeve, "The Art of Public Address," *Art in America* 85 (November 1997): 92–99.

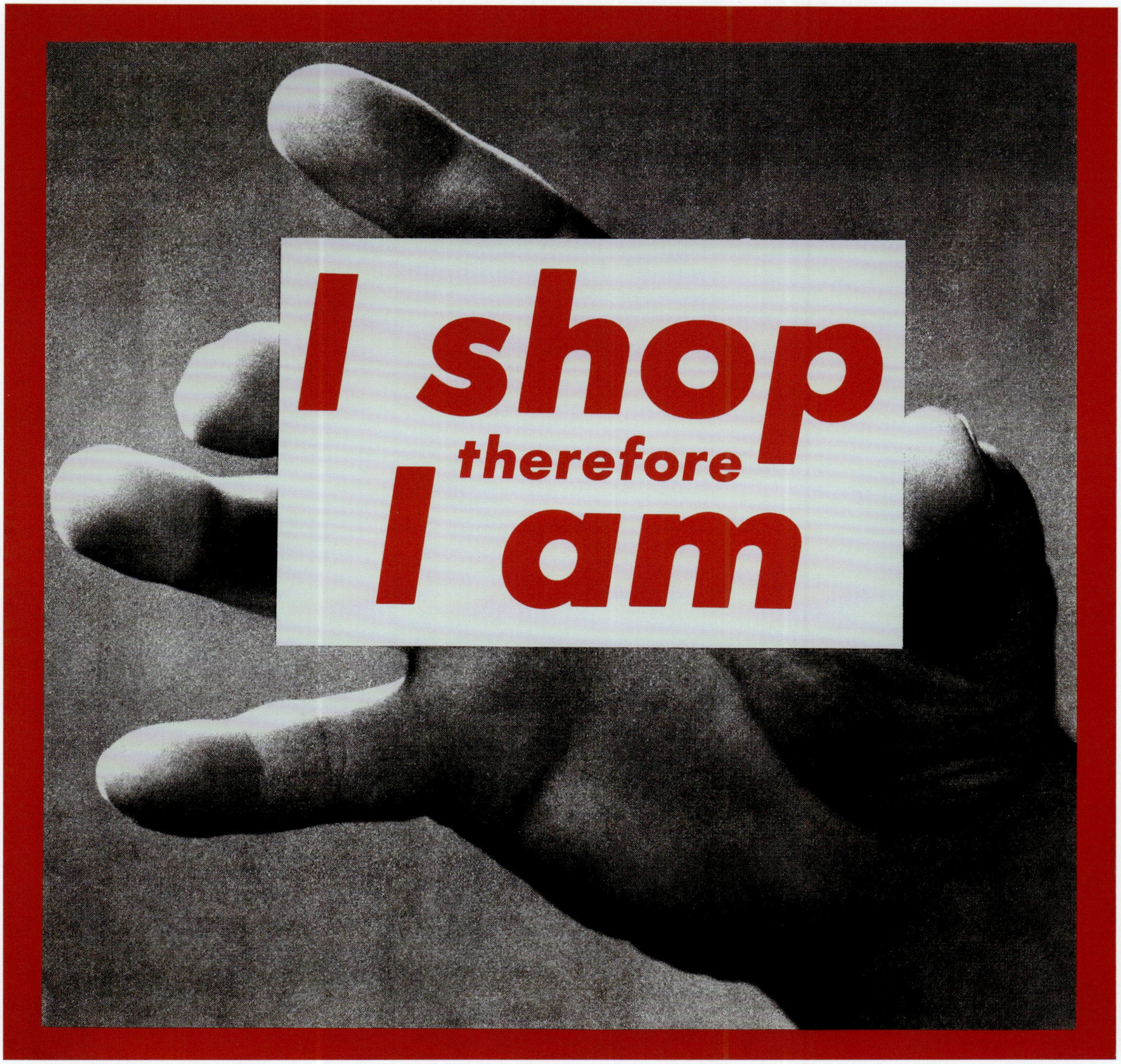

Barbara Kruger
Untitled (I shop therefore I am), 1987
Photographic silkscreen on vinyl
111 5/8 × 113 1/4 × 2 1/2 inches
Glenstone

Photograph by Tim Nighswander

Sherrie Levine

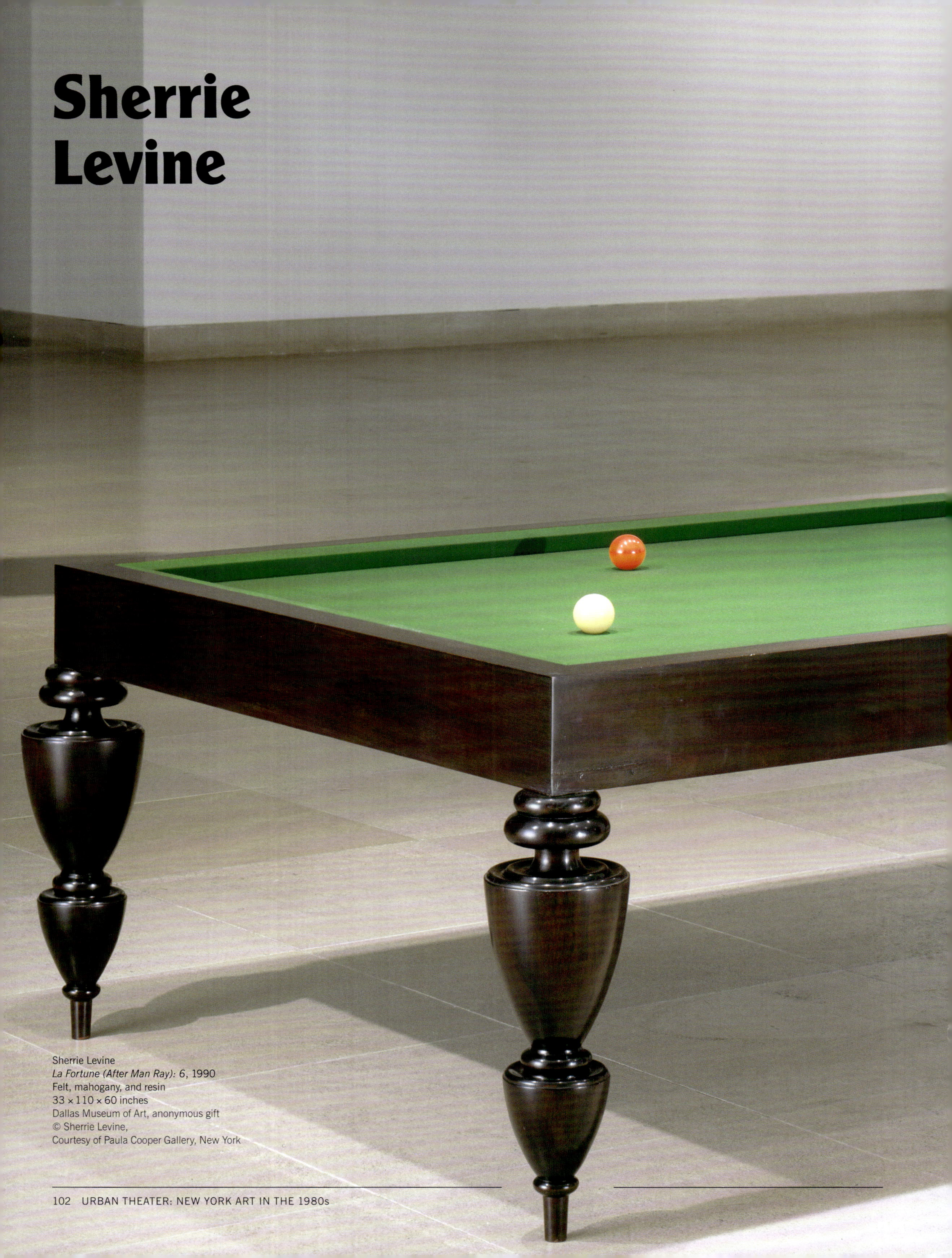

Sherrie Levine
La Fortune (After Man Ray): 6, 1990
Felt, mahogany, and resin
33 × 110 × 60 inches
Dallas Museum of Art, anonymous gift
© Sherrie Levine,
Courtesy of Paula Cooper Gallery, New York

Sherrie Levine: I am interested in making a work that has as much aura as its reference. For me the tension between the reference and the new work doesn't really exist unless the new work has an auratic presence of its own. Otherwise, it just becomes a copy, which is not that interesting.

Constance Lewallen: You're turning Benjamin's theory in on itself. A lot of your work has the effect of taking ideas one step further than one would expect.

SL: To create a conundrum.

I think it's the auratic quality that's built into it. There's a level of seduction in the work that keeps you. . . . It's a visceral, sensual seduction that always draws you back. That's where the hook is. Otherwise it would be an idea as opposed to . . . I want it to be an experience.

CL: A work of art.

SL: A work of art. Something you experience in a visceral sense, because I believe that intellectual experiences are stronger when related to sensual experiences, a sense of the world.

CL: I imagine you knew Man Ray's *La Fortune* from the Whitney. Did you just see it one day and then get the idea for your installation?

SL: I had seen it a million times at the Whitney, but it was in the Man Ray show that was traveling around the country and was in Los Angeles when I was there and then I happened to see it in Philadelphia as well. That's the wonderful thing about moving art around, that you can see it new, as if for the first time. And when I saw the painting again, I thought, "Wouldn't it be incredible to build this table?"

CL: But your billiard tables are not really billiard tables.

SL: No, they're sculptures.

CL: In fact, they are not exactly the right size.

SL: They are actually to scale but the tops aren't Levineate and there are no works underneath. The painting has very exaggerated proportions, the legs are more delicate and more unstable than they would be in reality; they would never be able to sustain the weight of a game.

Quoted in Constance Lewallen,"Sherrie Levine," *Journal of Contemporary Art* 6.2 (1993): 59–83

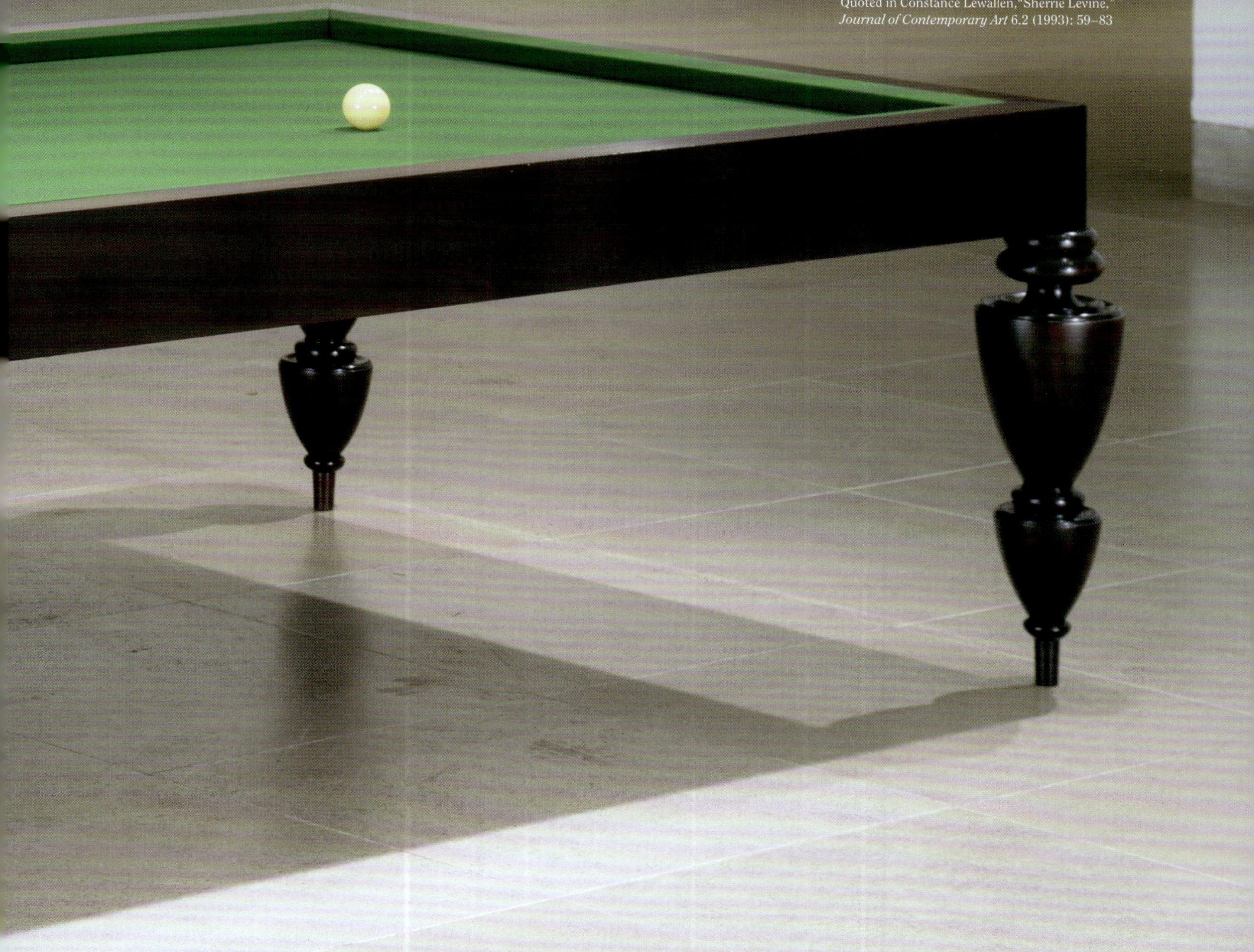

Robert Longo

When Metro Pictures [Longo's New York gallery] first opened, the atmosphere in SoHo was almost like a street fight. Artists should have been wearing leather jackets with the name of their gallery on the back and walking around with baseball bats. But the early to mid-'80s was an extraordinary time: the art-music scene, the clubs, the drugs, the camaraderie of artists, the night. I was playing in bands with Rhys Chatham, Glenn Branca, and Richard Prince, collaborating on performances with Bill T. Jones and Eric Bogosian. At the same time I was making my work with total abandonment and intensity—"make work, make work, make work."

One thing that became difficult in the '80s was that we went into Metro Pictures as a group, but once the gallery opened and shows started to happen, it became clear who was going to get more attention and the group started to disintegrate. Friendships were strained. There was an excitement, even if it was a competitive excitement.

Unfortunately the greed-is-good mentality overrode it, but it was a blossoming moment—so much about art had been taken apart and rearranged and given back to us with new parts to work with. It was our time to shine; little did I know burnout would be the next stage.

I had an ego that was totally out of control, but if I hadn't had that ego I couldn't have made many of the things I did. My work wasn't about modesty at that point; it was about living in America, I was making "big" art because I thought that was a way of critiquing what was American. I wanted to take an aggressive position in a culture that I thought was sick. The bombastic nature of the work, particularly the combines, I felt was a language of our time. In hindsight, one risks becoming what one critiques.

Quoted in Mary Haus, "'80s Then: Robert Longo Talks to Mary Haus," *Artforum* 41, no. 7 (March 2003): 238–39. © Artforum

Robert Longo
Untitled, 1981
Charcoal, graphite, and dye on paper
98 × 48 inches
Courtesy of the Artist

Image Courtesy of the Artist and Metro Pictures

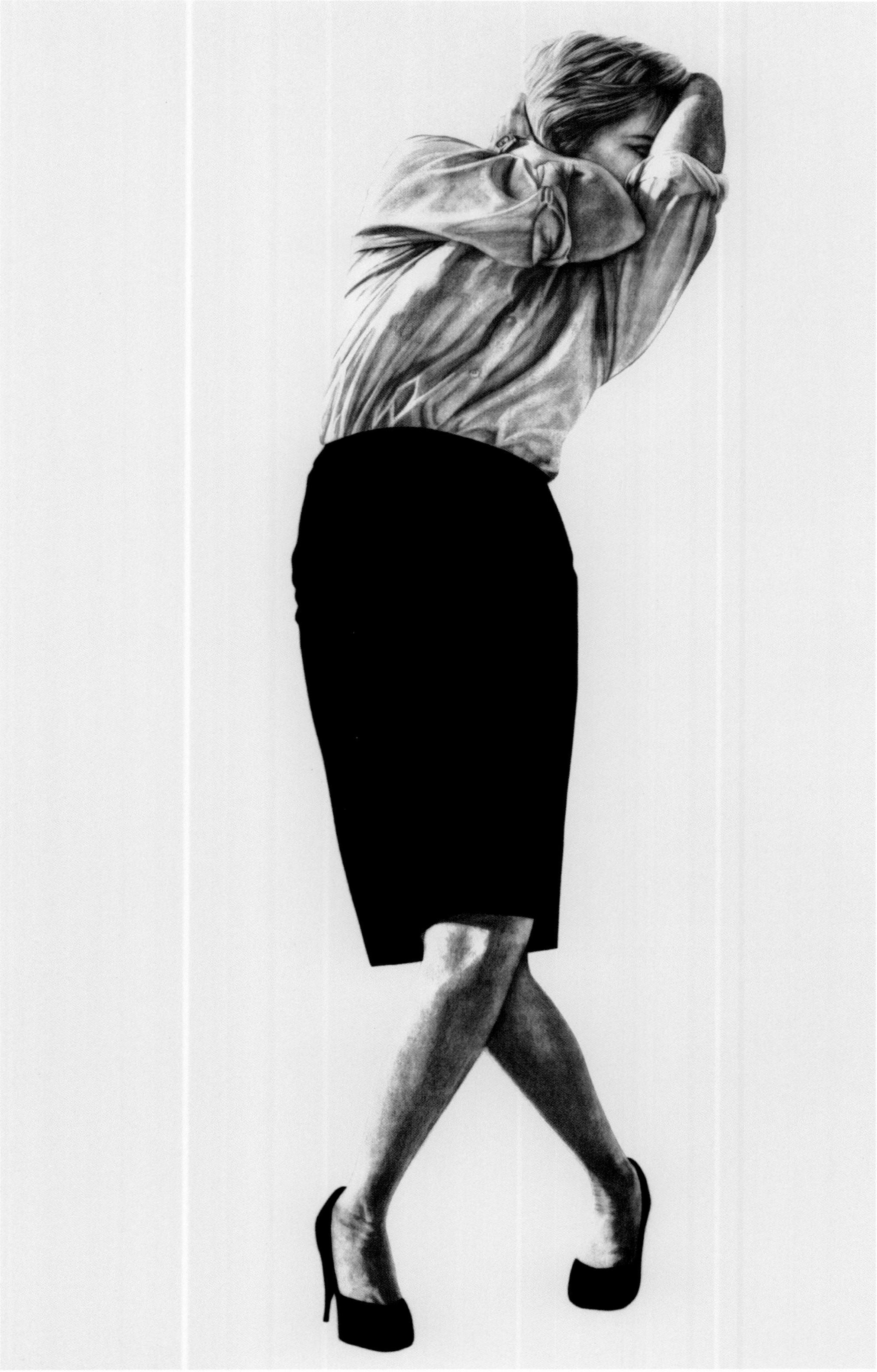

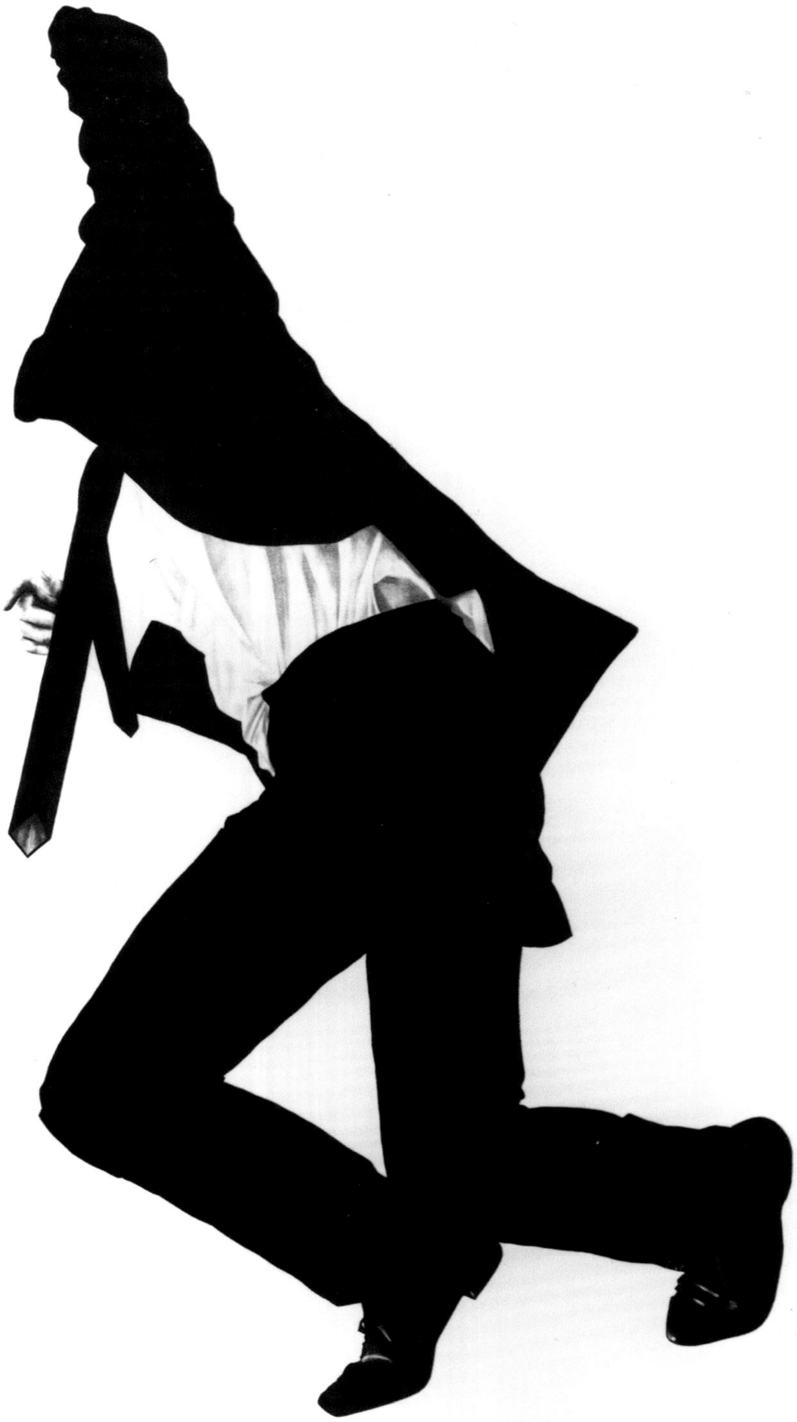

Robert Longo
Untitled, 1981
Charcoal and graphite on paper
96 × 60 inches
Collection Metro Pictures

Image Courtesy of the Artist and Metro Pictures

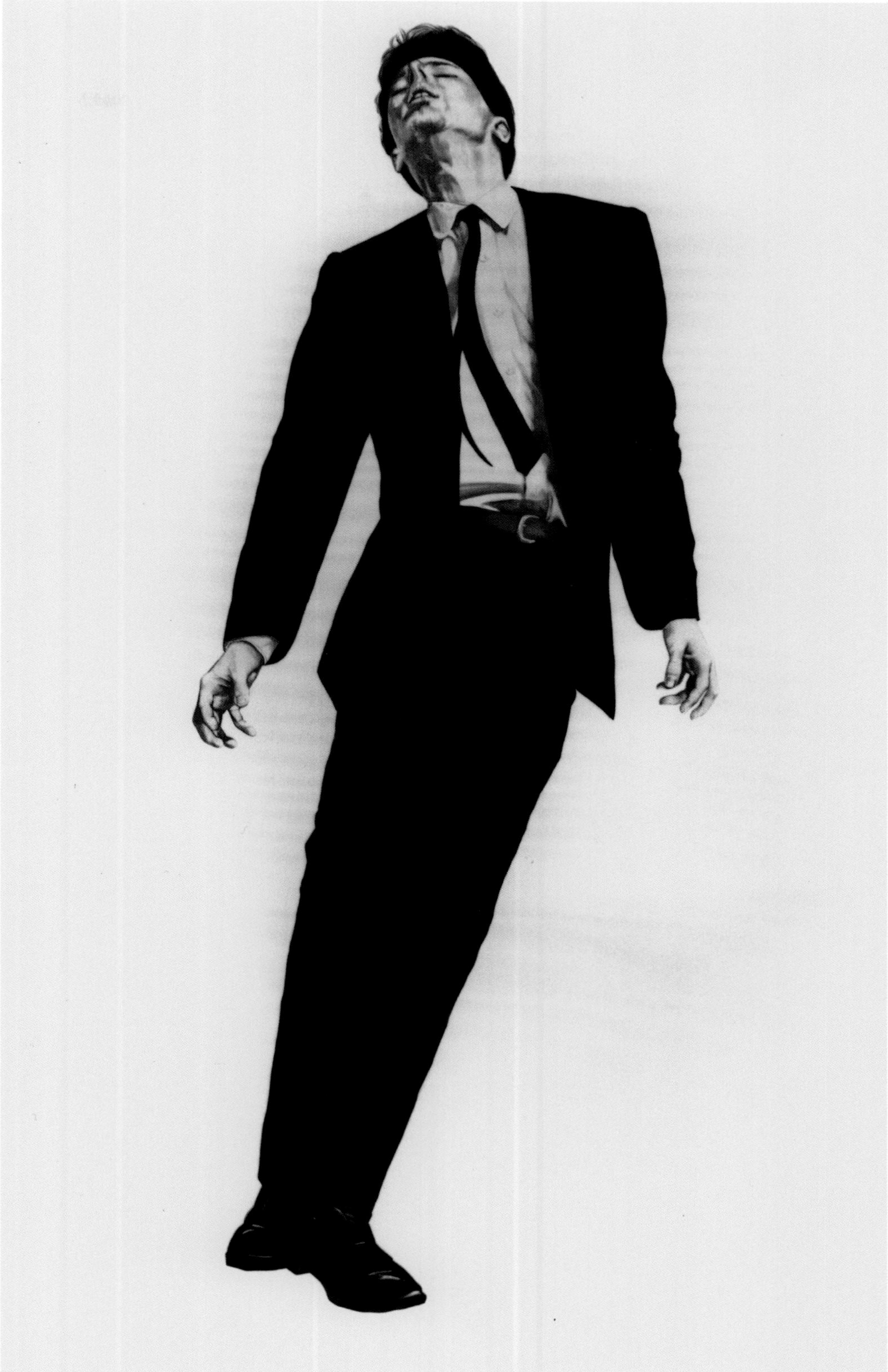

Robert Longo
Untitled, 1981
Charcoal and graphite on paper
96 × 60 inches
UBS Art Collection

Image Courtesy of the Artist and Metro Pictures

Robert Mapplethorpe

My whole point is to transcend the subject. … Go beyond the subject somehow, so that the composition, the lighting, all around, reaches a certain point of perfection. That's what I'm doing. Whether it's a cock or a flower, I'm looking at it in the same way … in my own way, with my own eyes.

Quoted in Lawrence Chua, "Interview with Robert Mapplethorpe," *Flash Art*, no. 145 (January/February 1989). Originally published in *Flash Art International*. Courtesy Flash Art International and Giancarlo Politi Editore, Milan

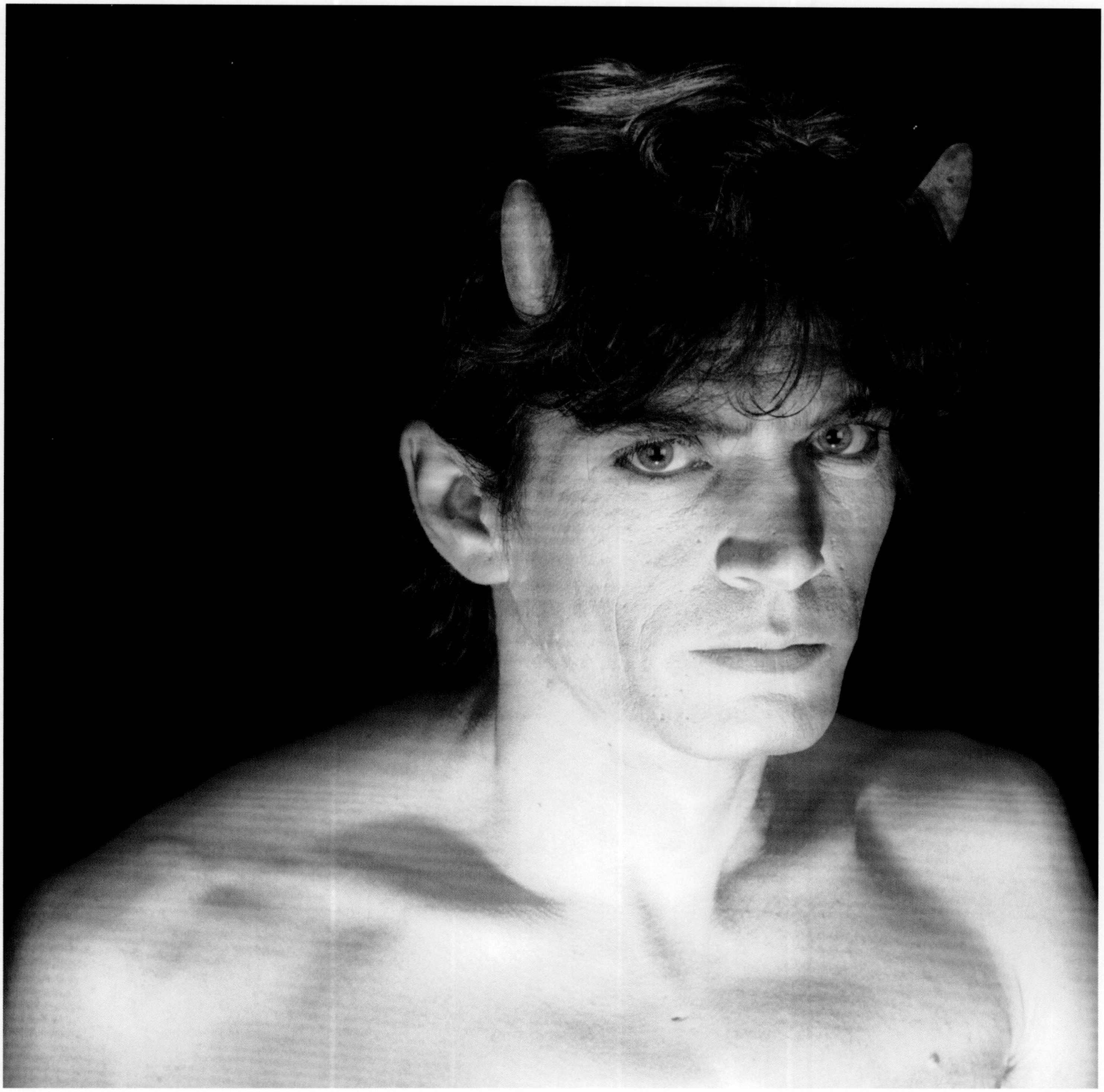

Robert Mapplethorpe
Self Portrait, 1985
Silver gelatin print
20 × 16 inches
All Mapplethorpe Works

Patti Smith: Much has been said about Robert, and more will be added. Young men will adopt his gait. Young girls will wear white dresses and mourn his curls. He will be condemned and adored. His excesses damned or romanticized. In the end, truth will be found in his work, the corporeal body of the artist. It will not fall away. Man cannot judge it. For art sings of God, and ultimately belongs to him.

Patti Smith, *Just Kids* (New York: Ecco, 2010), ix.

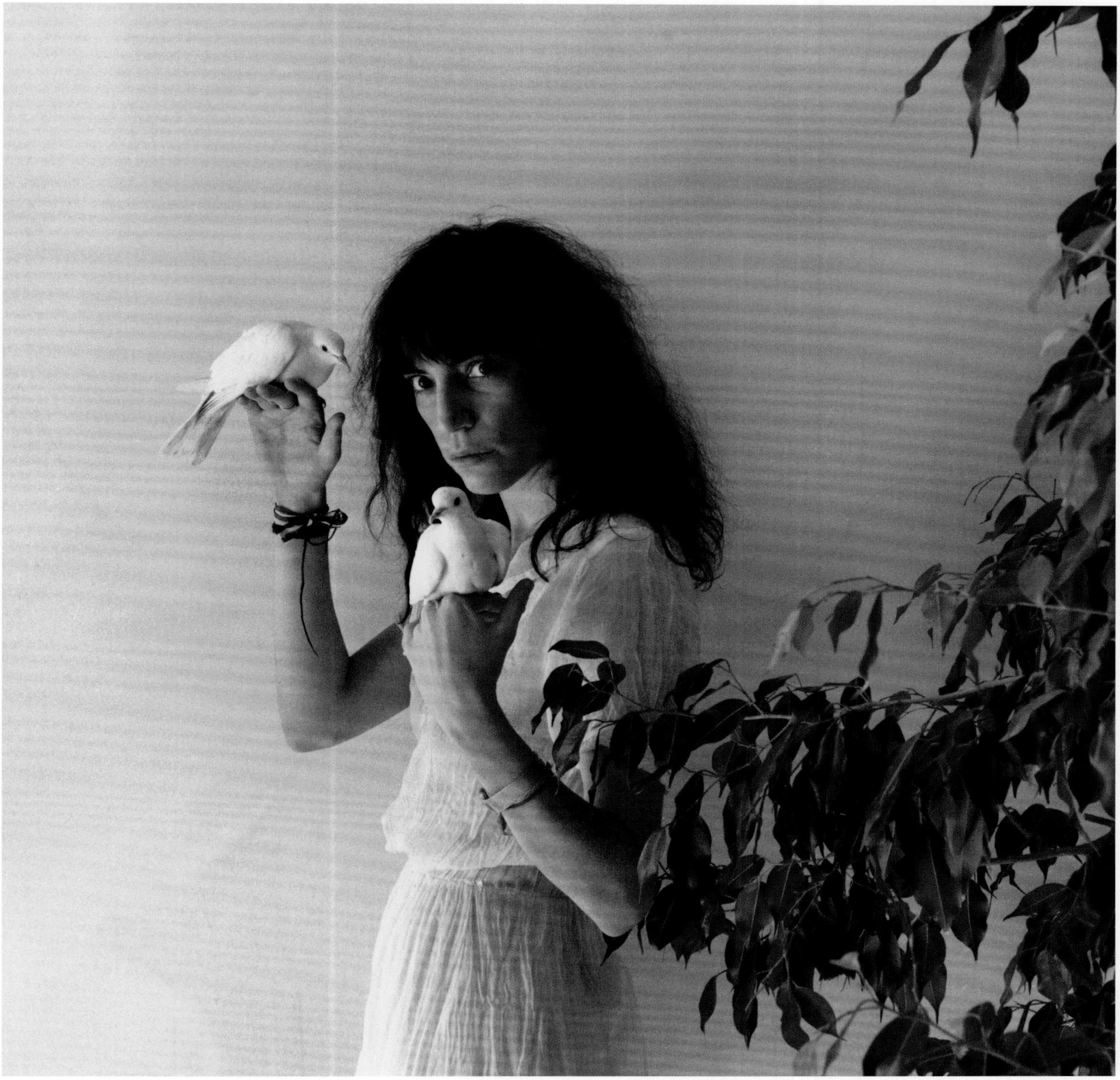

Robert Mapplethorpe
Patti Smith, 1979
Silver gelatin print
20 × 16 inches
All Mapplethorpe Works

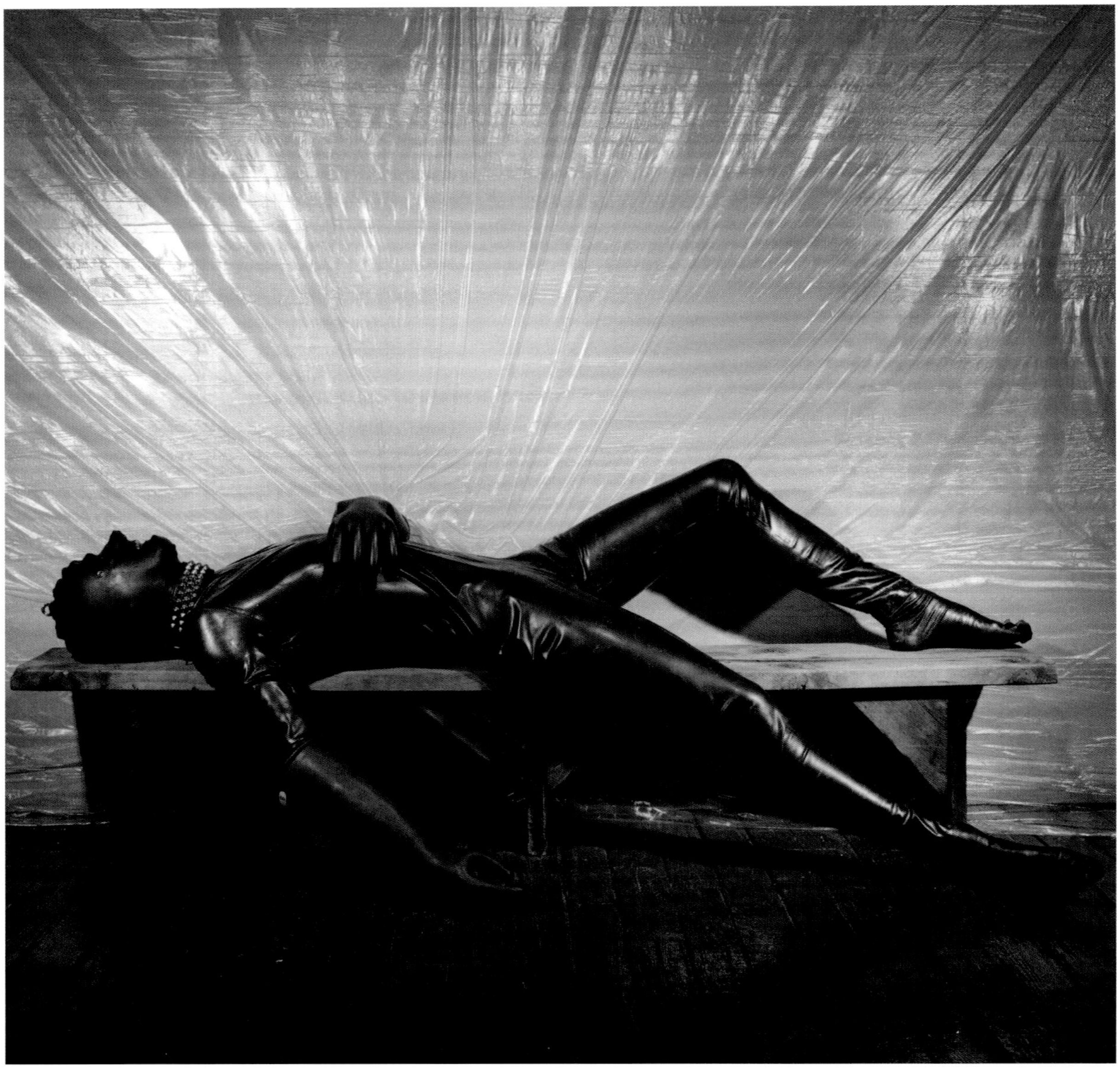

Robert Mapplethorpe
Joe / Rubberman, 1978
Silver gelatin print
20 × 16 inches
All Mapplethorpe Works

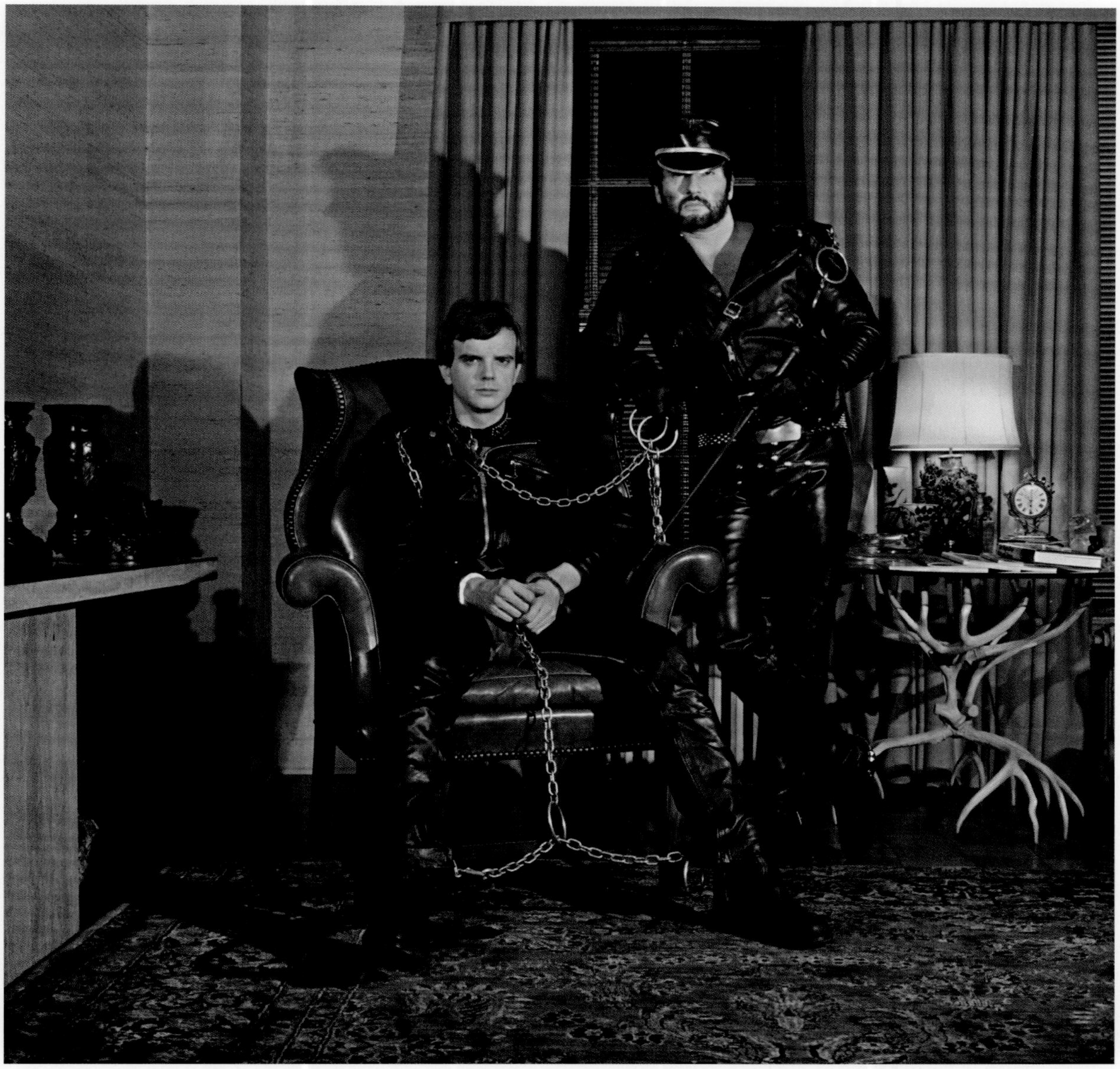

Robert Mapplethorpe
Brian Ridley and Lyle Heeter, 1979
Silver gelatin print
20 × 16 inches
All Mapplethorpe Works

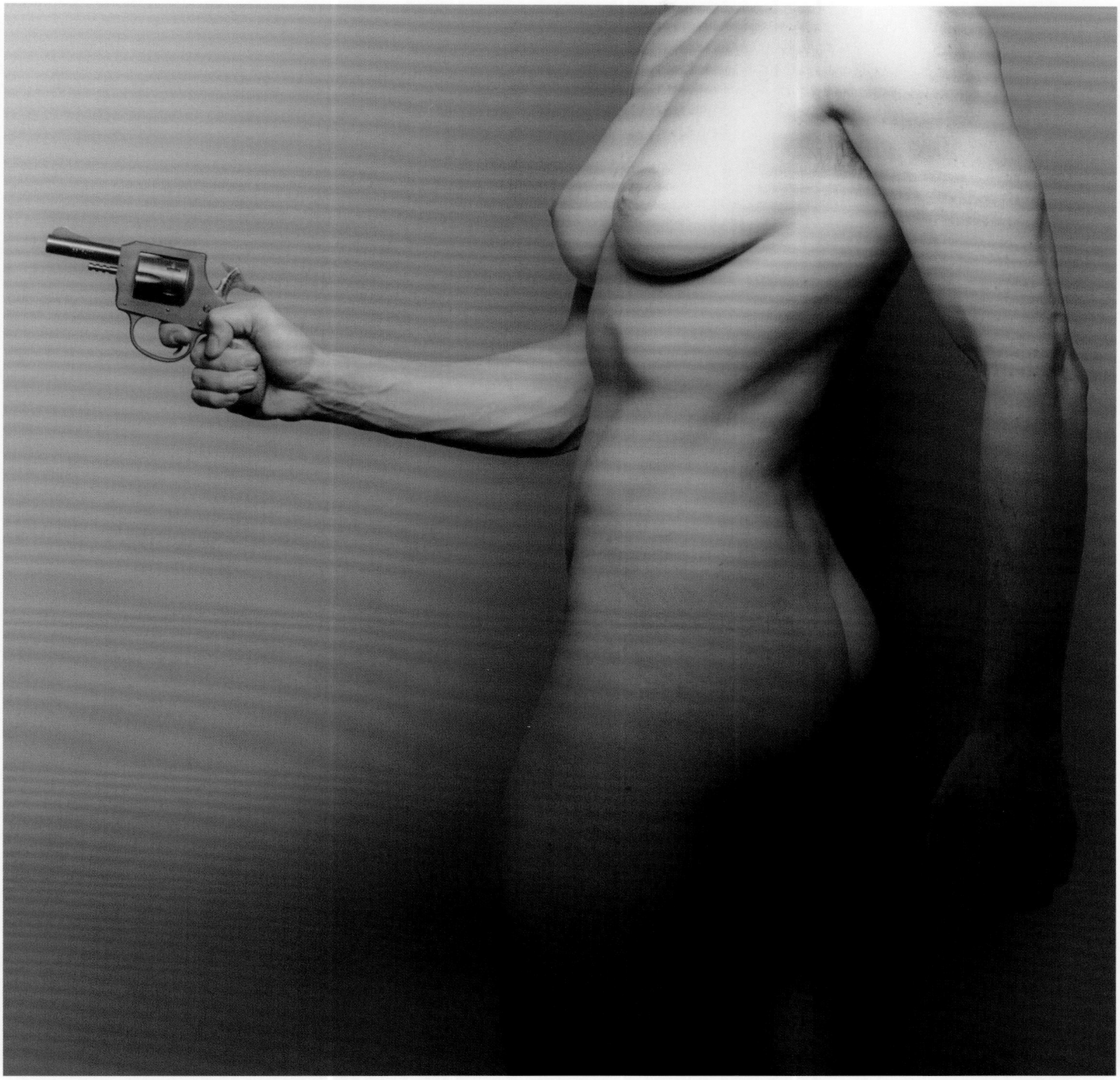

Robert Mapplethorpe
Lisa Lyon, 1982
Silver gelatin print
20 × 16 inches
All Mapplethorpe Works

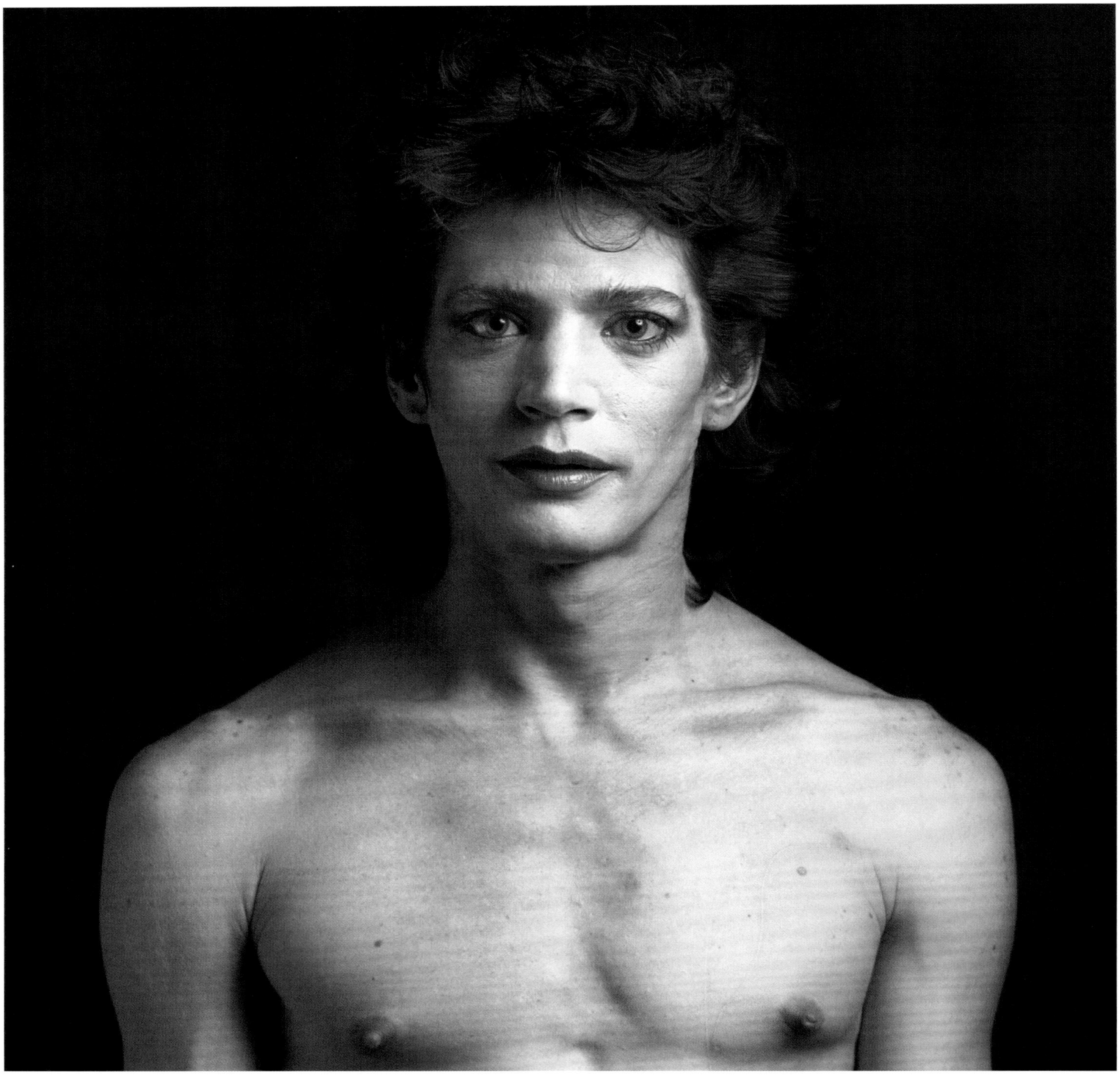

Robert Mapplethorpe
Self Portrait, 1980
Silver gelatin print
20 × 16 inches
All Mapplethorpe Works

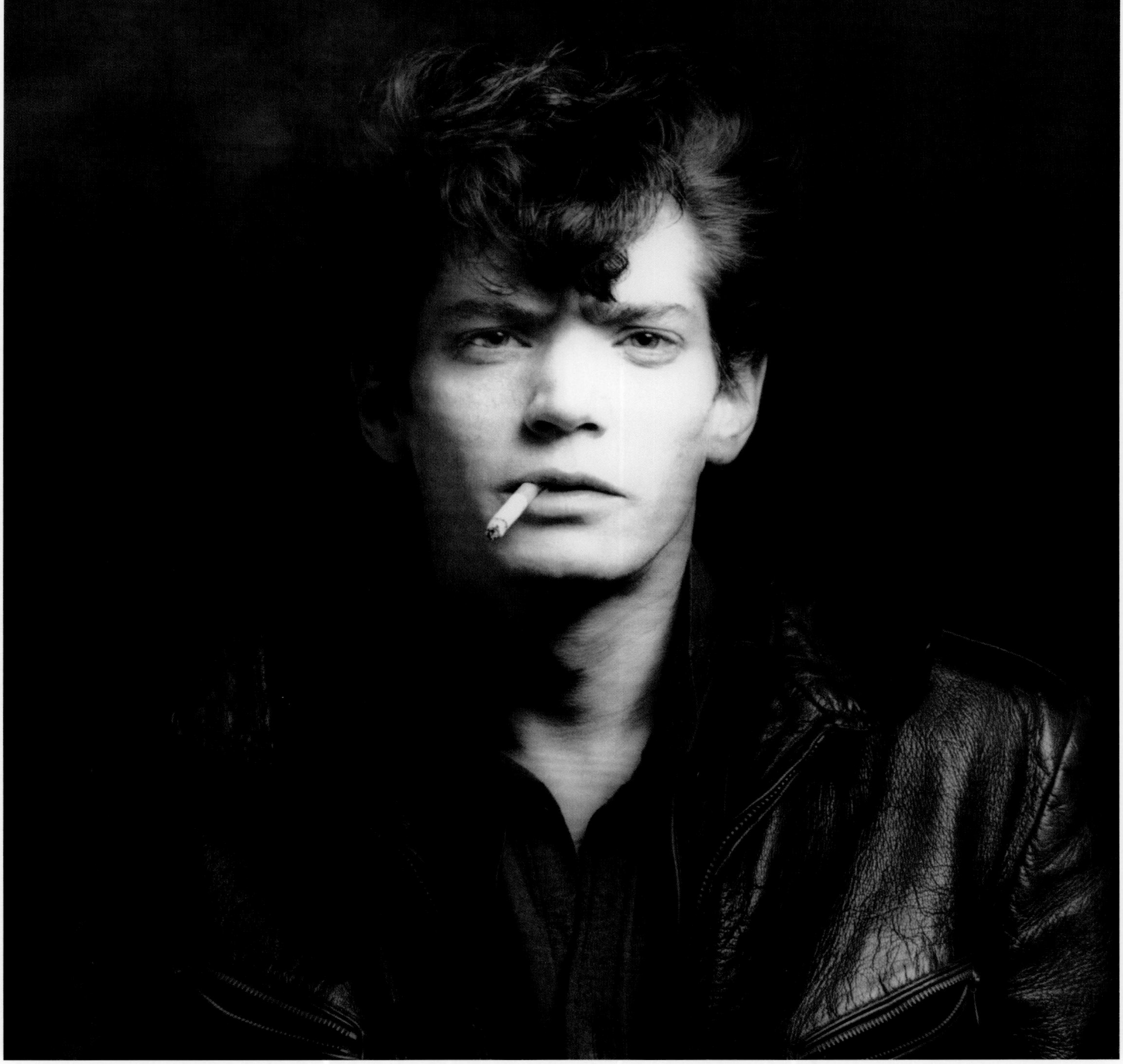

Robert Mapplethorpe
Self Portrait, 1980
Silver gelatin print
20 × 16 inches
All Mapplethorpe Works

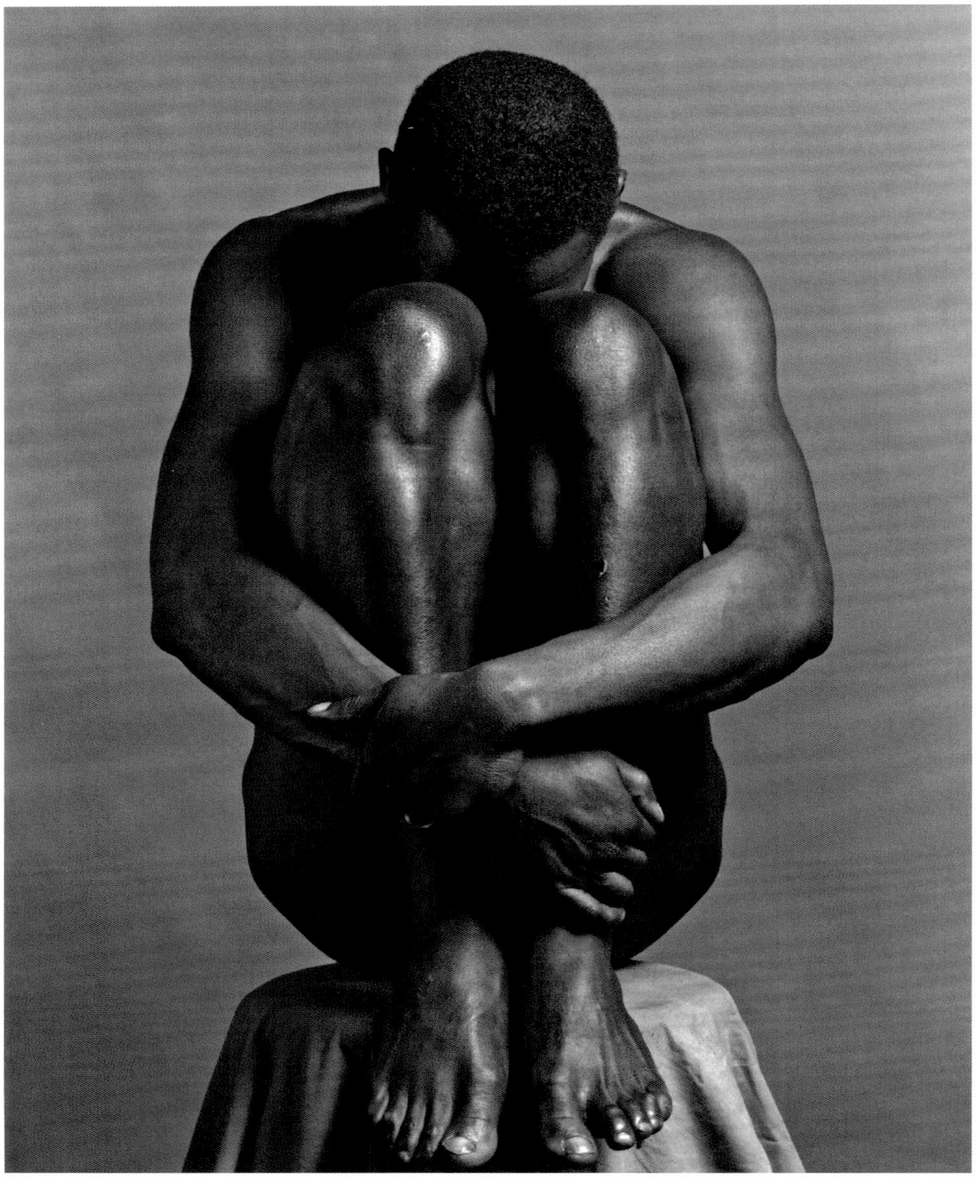

Robert Mapplethorpe
Ajitto, 1981
Silver gelatin print
20 × 16 inches
All Mapplethorpe Works

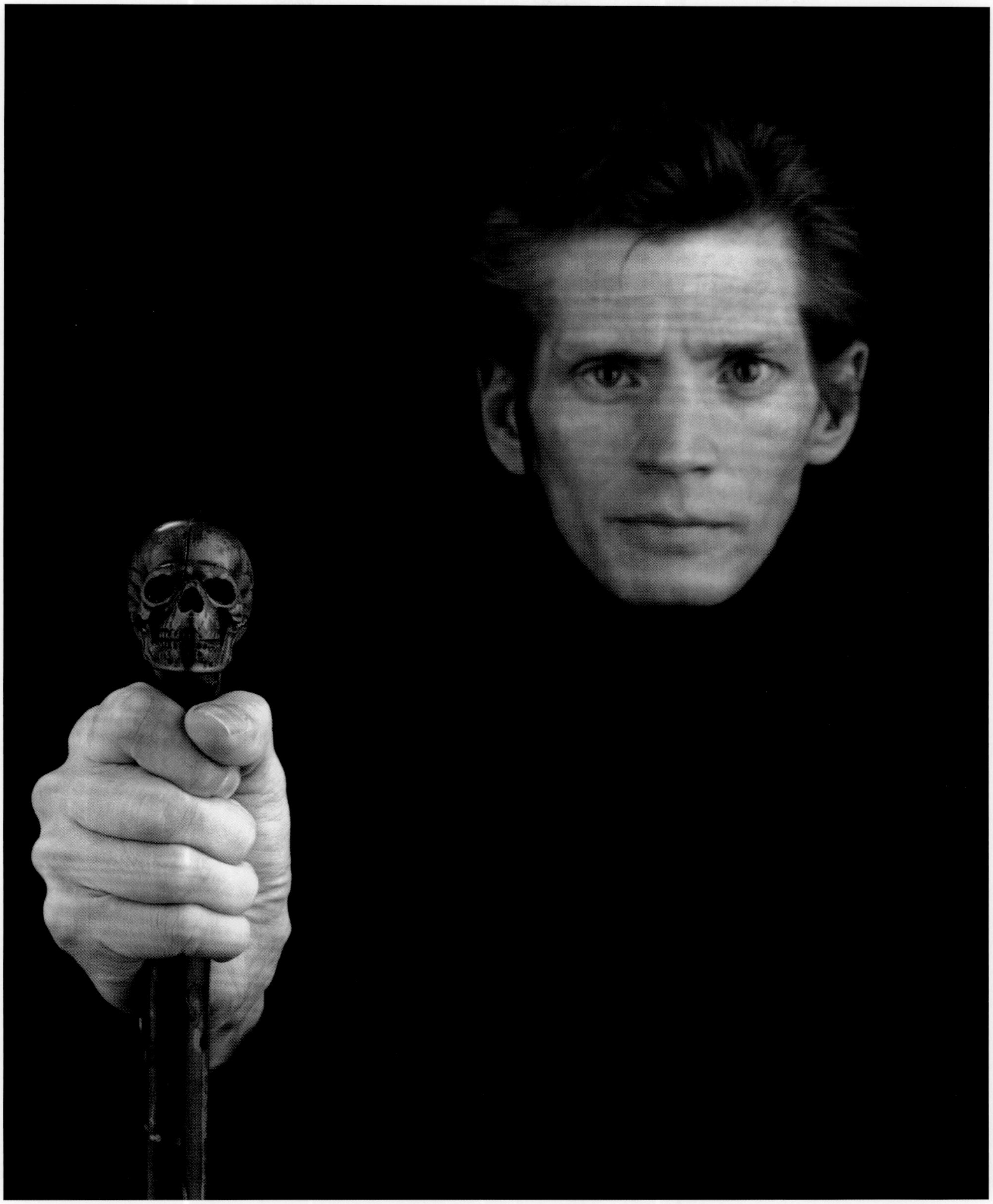

Robert Mapplethorpe
Self Portrait, 1988
Silver gelatin print
24 × 20 inches
All Mapplethorpe Works

Allan McCollum

In a world without mass-produced symbolic objects, we would have little need for the contrary concept of the unique artwork. But in our world, we are always working to protect the integrity of the unique against its debasement by the replica, to make defense against the threat of plenitude by retreating into the solace of scarcity. But if we could come to embrace the mechanisms that drive our passions, and understand these along with the passions that animate our machines—maybe then we could begin to look for an art which is both repetitive and expressive, both copy and original, both abundant and precious: an art to embody both the horror and the promise of modern life, without shrinking from either.

It's fascinating and touching that people work so hard to build an immanent meaning into things; that they pursue their desire to produce symbolic objects for themselves to keep, and to exchange with others. In our culture, an artwork is an object of this kind; and whatever specific meaning the artist works to put into it, it will always retain its promise as a gift, its destiny as a keepsake. This is the artwork I am interested in making: an object filled with the absence of certain meaning, and yet rich with the quality of meaningfulness in and of itself.

Quoted in Tricia Collins and Richard Milazzo, "Double Talk. Quantity and Immanence. Allan McCollum," *Tema Celeste*, no. 22–23 (October/December 1989)

this page and the following spread:
Allan McCollum
Collection of Two Hundred Plaster Surrogates, 1982/1983–85
Enamel on cast Hydrostone
Dimensions variable
The Rachofsky Collection
Photograph by Chad Redmon

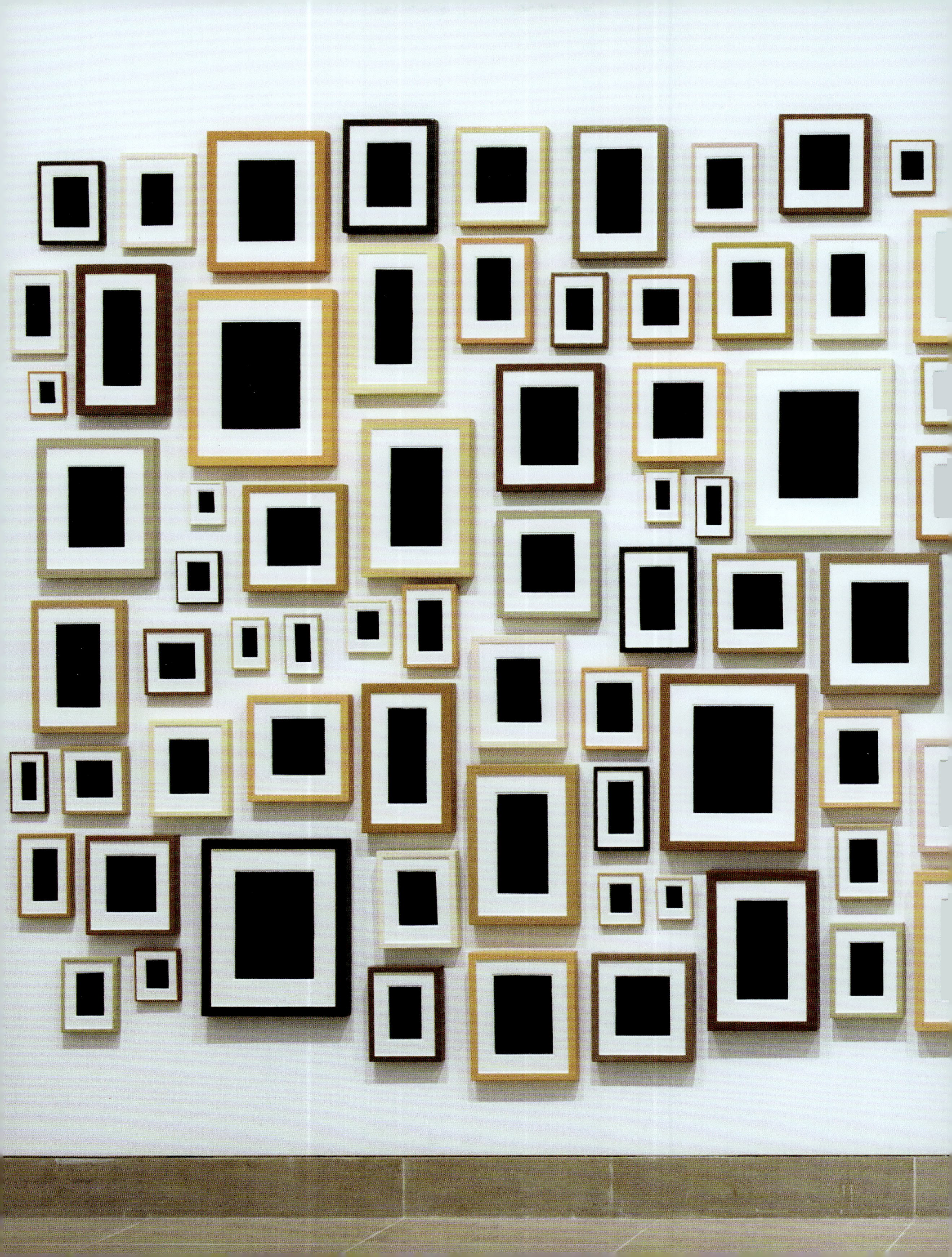

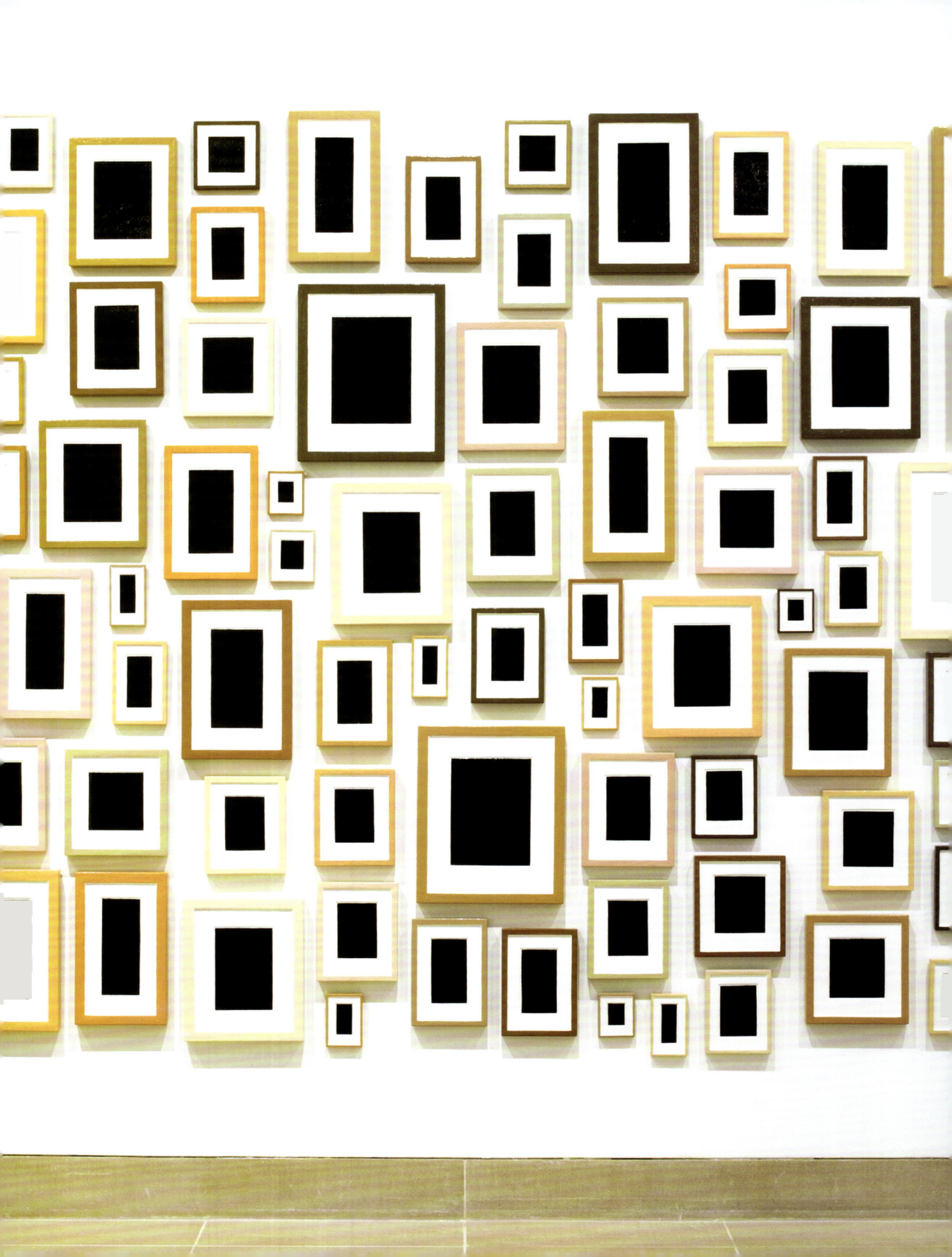

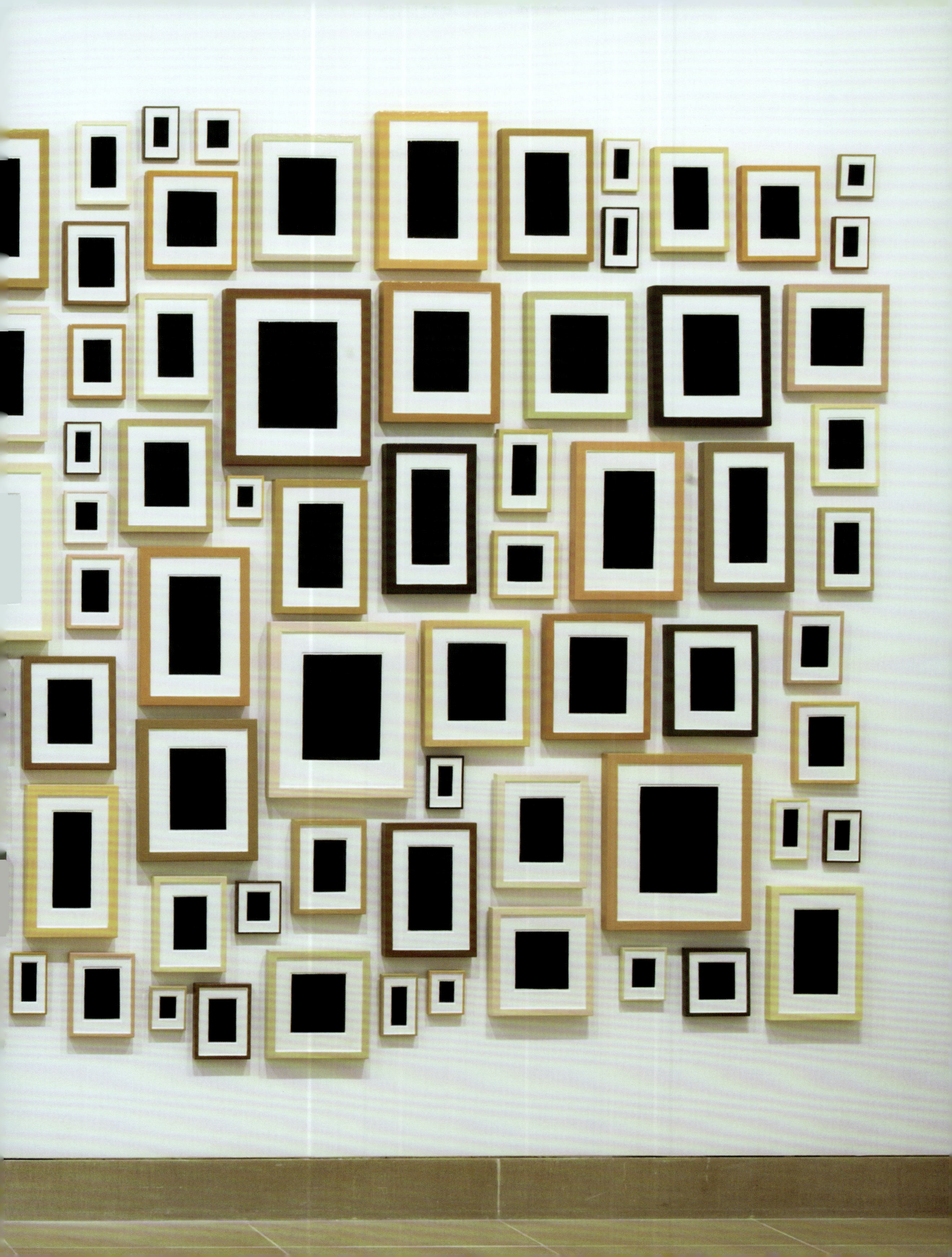

Richard Prince

Prior Availability 1977, West 11th St. NYC

The material I appropriate is available to anyone who cares to use it. The fact that the material has possibly been observed or unconsciously collected by persons other than myself, in effect defines its desires and threats. It's this "prior availability" that verifies the fictional transformation and helps cool down any reference to an observable reality.

To de-referentialize the material is not to take it out of context. The great thing about an appropriation is that even though the transformation reads as fiction, everybody knows that the source of the appropriation was at some point non-fiction, (magazine, movie, etc.), and it's these sources, or elements of non-fiction, that gives the picture, no matter how questionable, its believable edge.

Appropriation is a theoretical procedure, and like any other procedure, interesting only to a point. (The point being that we're all pretty intelligent, but are we smart enough to stop paying attention to how intelligent we are?) I'm wondering if appropriation as procedure will become the supplementary sweetheart for gallery toughs. I have a funny feeling it's the stuff of which art/writing is made. Personally, I think it would be far more entertaining to continue to customize the built-in elements that appropriation provides, and concentrate on why certain records sound better when someone on the radio station plays them, than when we're home alone, and play the same records ourselves.

The Picture Kit 1978, West 11th St. NYC

By cropping and taking a photograph from an already existing picture, you're in a sense fragmenting the real and attempting to add on, or "annex" it to something more real.

Another way and perhaps another step toward this pseudo-reality, is to make a photograph that has the effect of being sent away for. Not in the literal sense of course, but having the spirit of having been commercialized.

This commercialization of the picture requires a sophisticated attitude or at least the permission of letting oneself work on a pairing or fifty-fifty partnership where something of another personality or emotion or product signs the work.

The idea is to promote a "where the fuck did you get those" kind of take.

This questioning reaction could in many respects become the point of seduction.

It's kind of early to tell, but I'm assuming it would require a spectator with a willingness to be a sucker. And if not a sucker, at least someone who wanted some fun and who spent a lot of times in the movies, and didn't pay any attention to the credits.

Richard Prince, statements on the artist's website, http://www.richardprince.com/writings/prior-availability/

Richard Prince
Spiritual America, 1983
Cibachrome print
24 × 20 inches
Courtesy of the Artist
© Richard Prince

following spread:
Richard Prince
Untitled (Cowboy), 1995
Ektacolor print, edition 1 of 2
48 × 72 inches
Collection of the Modern Art Museum of Fort Worth, Museum purchase made possible by a grant from The Burnett Foundation
© Richard Prince

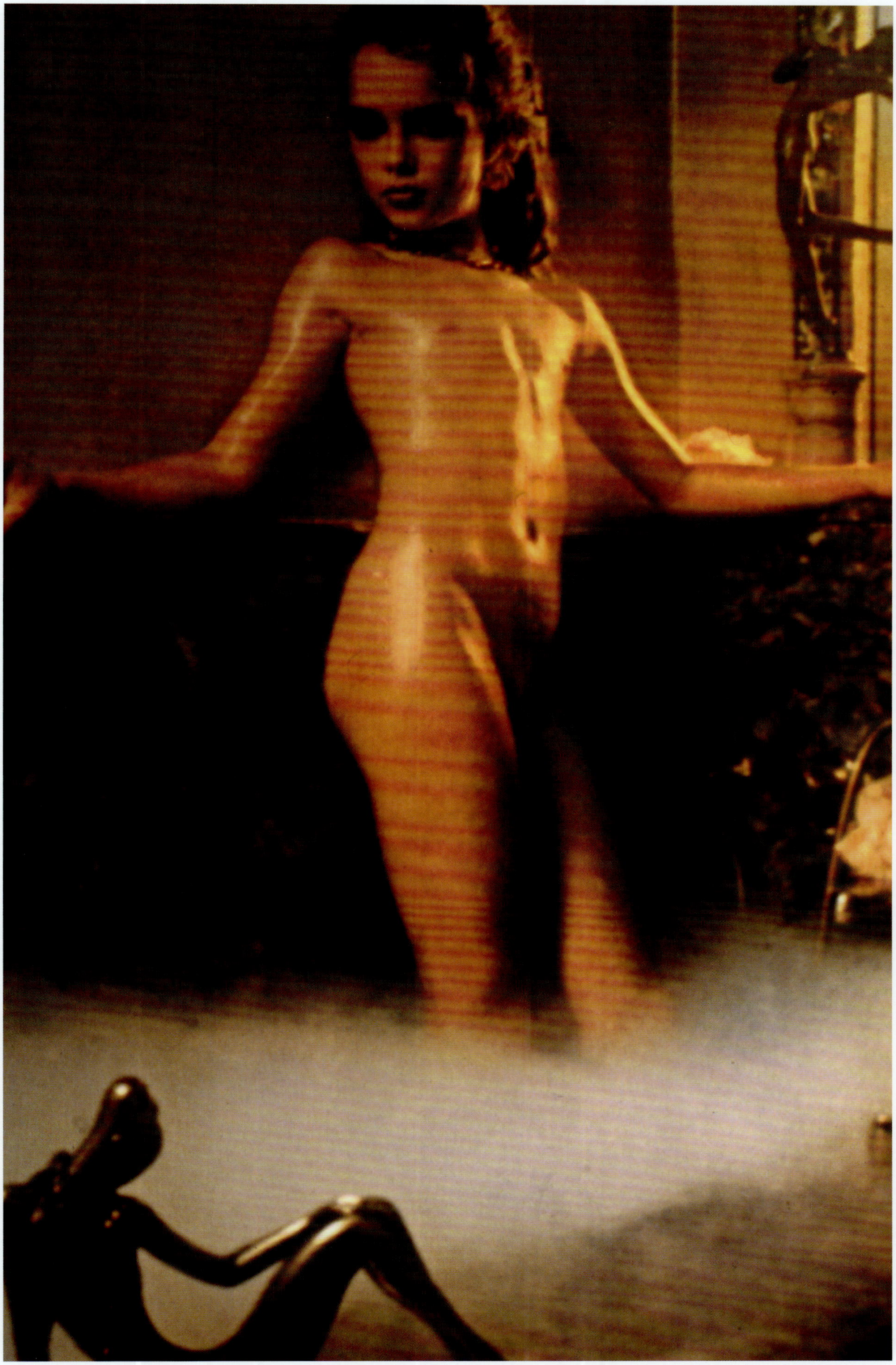

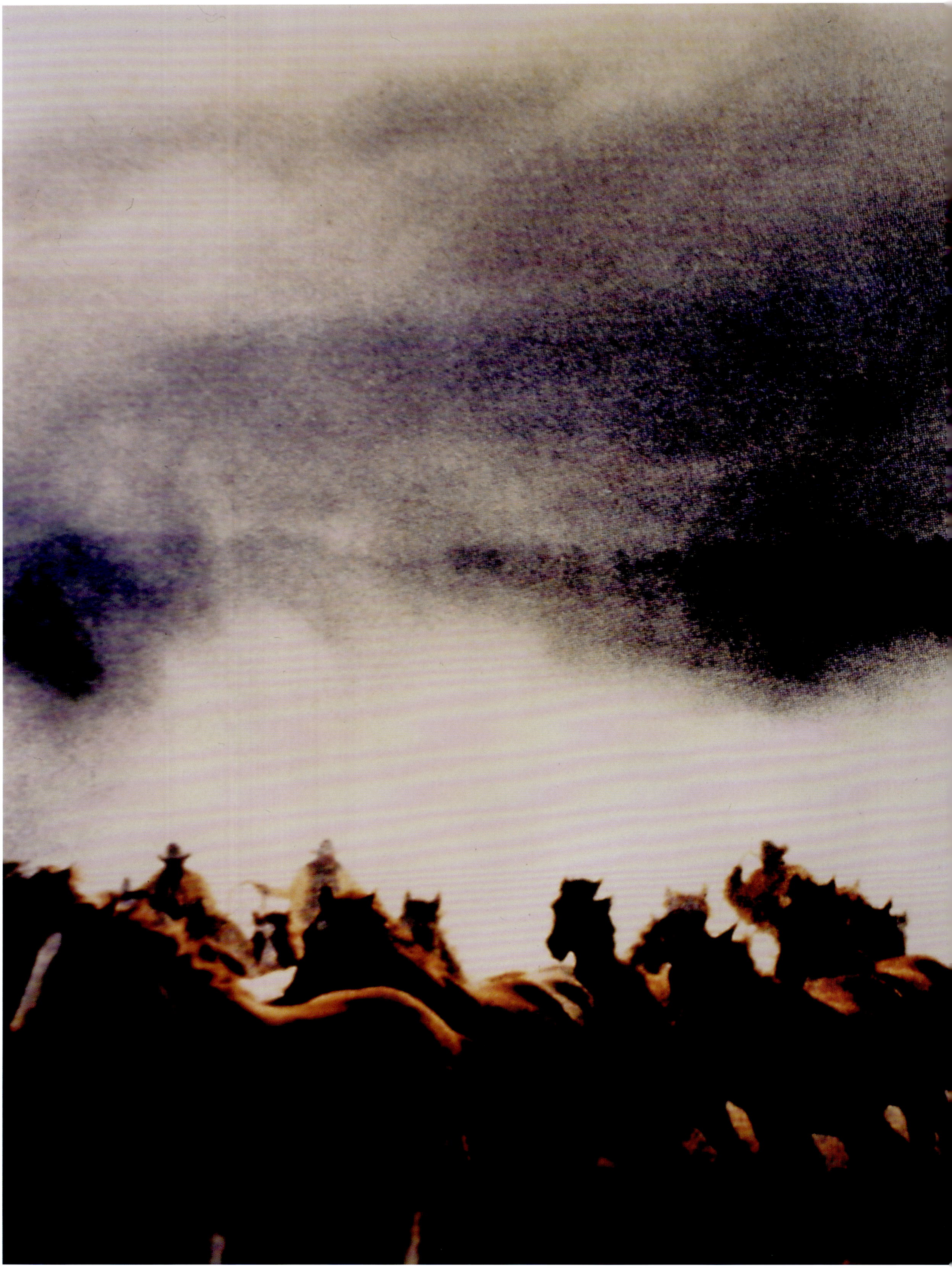

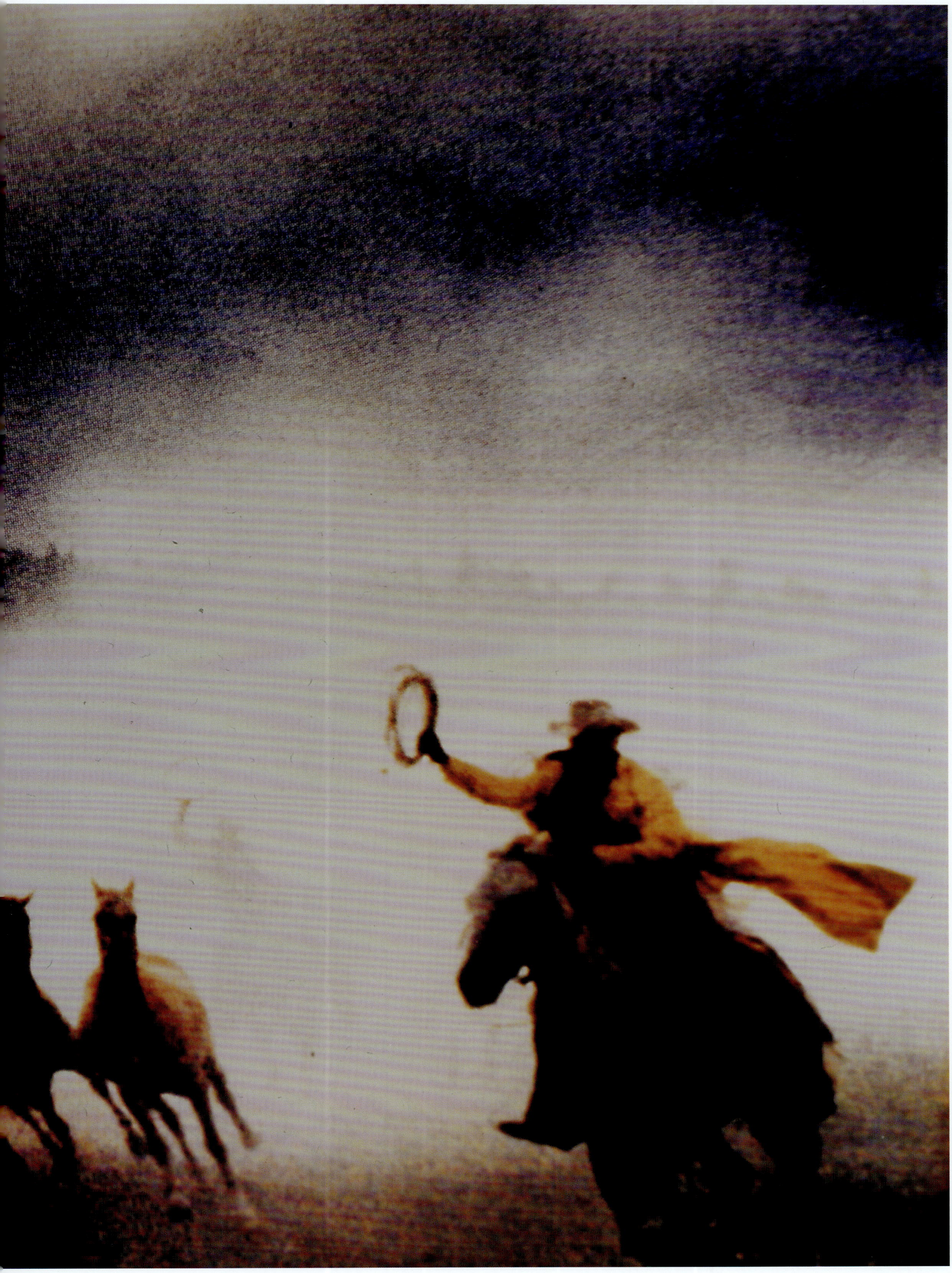

David Salle

There is a murky, misunderstood area—the notion of popular culture. It's assumed my work is a commentary on popular culture, you know. For years I have been saying the opposite. At least in my mind, my work has absolutely nothing to do with popular culture. Not only does it have nothing to do with popular culture in any kind of didactic, deliberate way, it simply doesn't have popular culture on its mind.

I think about a couple of different things which appear, which have lived out their lives in the arena of popular culture, but I don't think of them as popular. One is a comedy, the other is pornography. Those are two things that are important to me . . . for themselves. Not as a comment on the society that produces them, but in their own mechanistic ways, you know, how they operate.

Quoted in Robert Pincus-Witten, "Pure Pinter: An Interview with David Salle," *Arts Magazine* (November 1985): 78–81

I think of a lot of images I use as having a real sweet emotional texture. The kind of soft, satiny, feathered sheen of a duck's head. I think that the predominant feeling is a tender one. In almost all the works.

I wanted to make pictures that had that quality of unassailable identity, but I also wanted to make pictures that you could look at for a long time.

Underneath human frailty you probably find perversion. That's an important painting [Leonardo's *St. John the Baptist*], an important gesture in painting. But that range of feelings in paintings was so successfully eradicated . . .

The kind of classicism I'm thinking about now is something which I think admits great emotional depth. Just right underneath the surface of the very self-assured, there is great emotional depth. The two are visible simultaneously. And you feel one through the other. Really, the point of classicism is to experience one through the other, not to seal one off from the other.

One thing that I've always thought about my paintings, regardless of how similar they look after they're done, my opinion about them when I'm working on them is that there's very little carry-over from one painting to the next, each painting is closer to starting over from scratch.

That was the program for several generations of artists, to make personal necessity and historical necessity identical. That was the job. But once you've done that, then you're absolutely stuck with it. The point is to have a working process that is that intuitive and chancey and have results that are still able to live within this postwar American painting aesthetic.

Quoted in Georgia Marsh, "David Salle," *Bomb Magazine*, no. 13 (Fall 1985): 20–25.

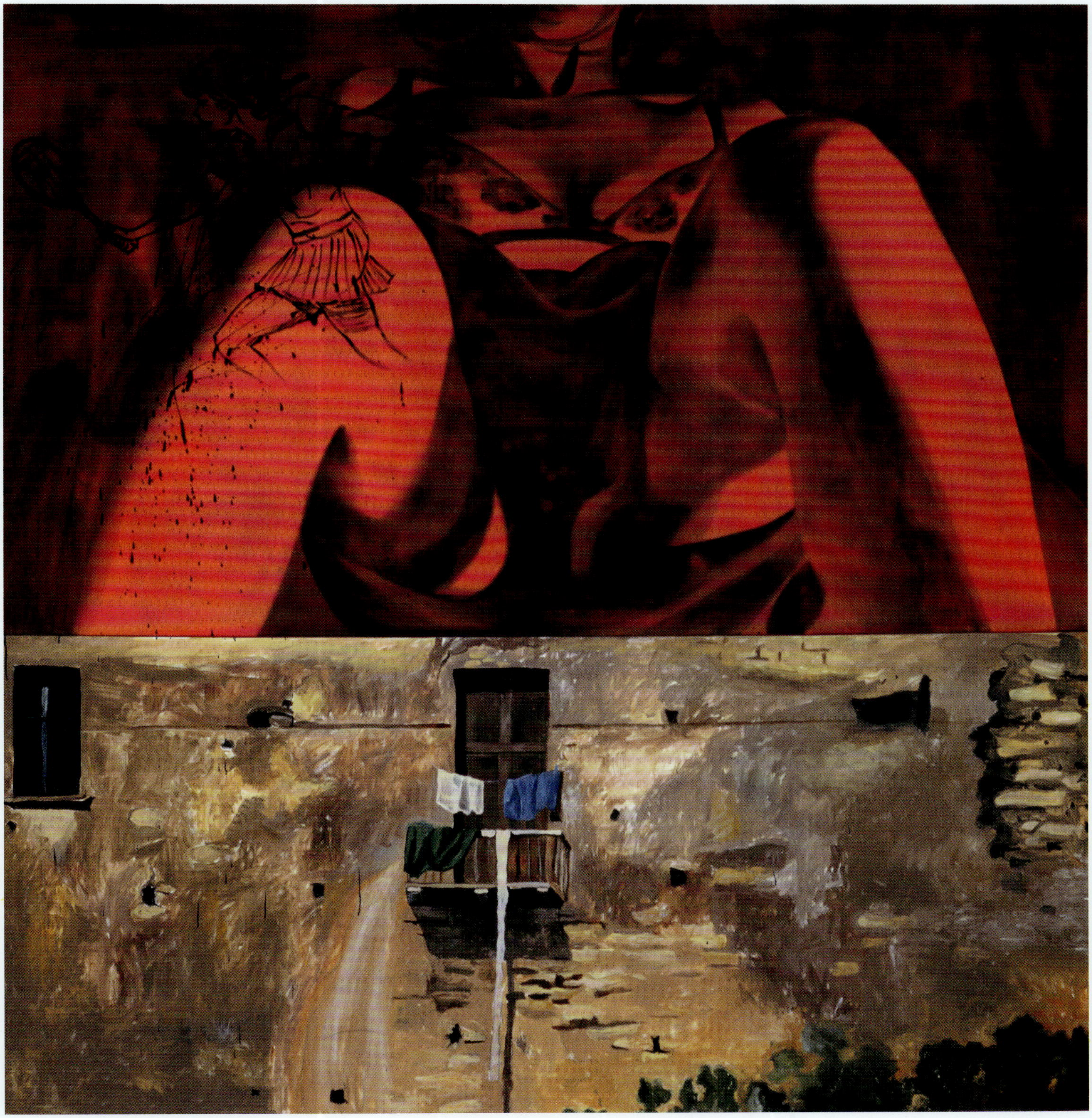

David Salle
Clean Glasses, 1985
Acrylic and oil on two canvas panels
105 × 100 inches
The Broad Art Foundation, Santa Monica

Photograph by Douglas M. Parker Studio, Los Angeles

Kenny Scharf

I remember learning about Andy Warhol and that whole scene. And I said, like, Wow! That guy is really great. That's something I'm really interested in. And I want to go there. And I knew that it wasn't like it used to be. But I thought maybe—I didn't know. That was one of the reasons why I came to New York. Learning about pop art, Andy inspired me. And I knew that in Santa Barbara, California, there was nothing going on, so I went to New York to attend the School of Visual Arts.

But I never wanted to do photorealism. I thought, what a great idea to learn how to do photorealist technique, but make up your own reality. I never understood why they would do photorealist painting if they were just copying from photographs, why not just do the photograph? But if you could do a painting of something you could never take a photograph of, that made more sense to me.

Kenny Scharf, "A Talk with Keith Haring," *Flash Art* (January 1985): 14–17.
Originally published in *Flash Art International*. Courtesy Flash Art International and Giancarlo Politi Editore, Milan

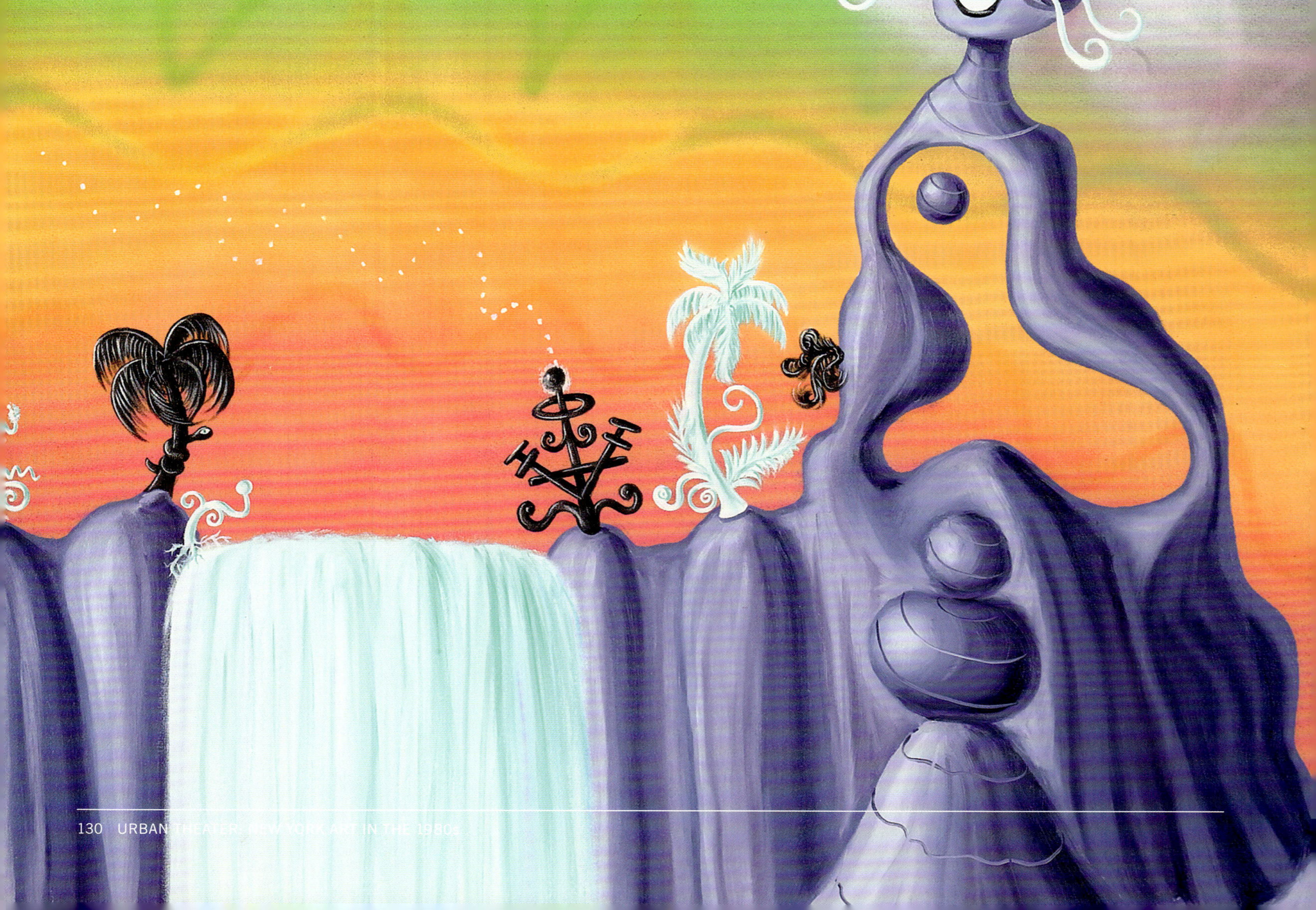

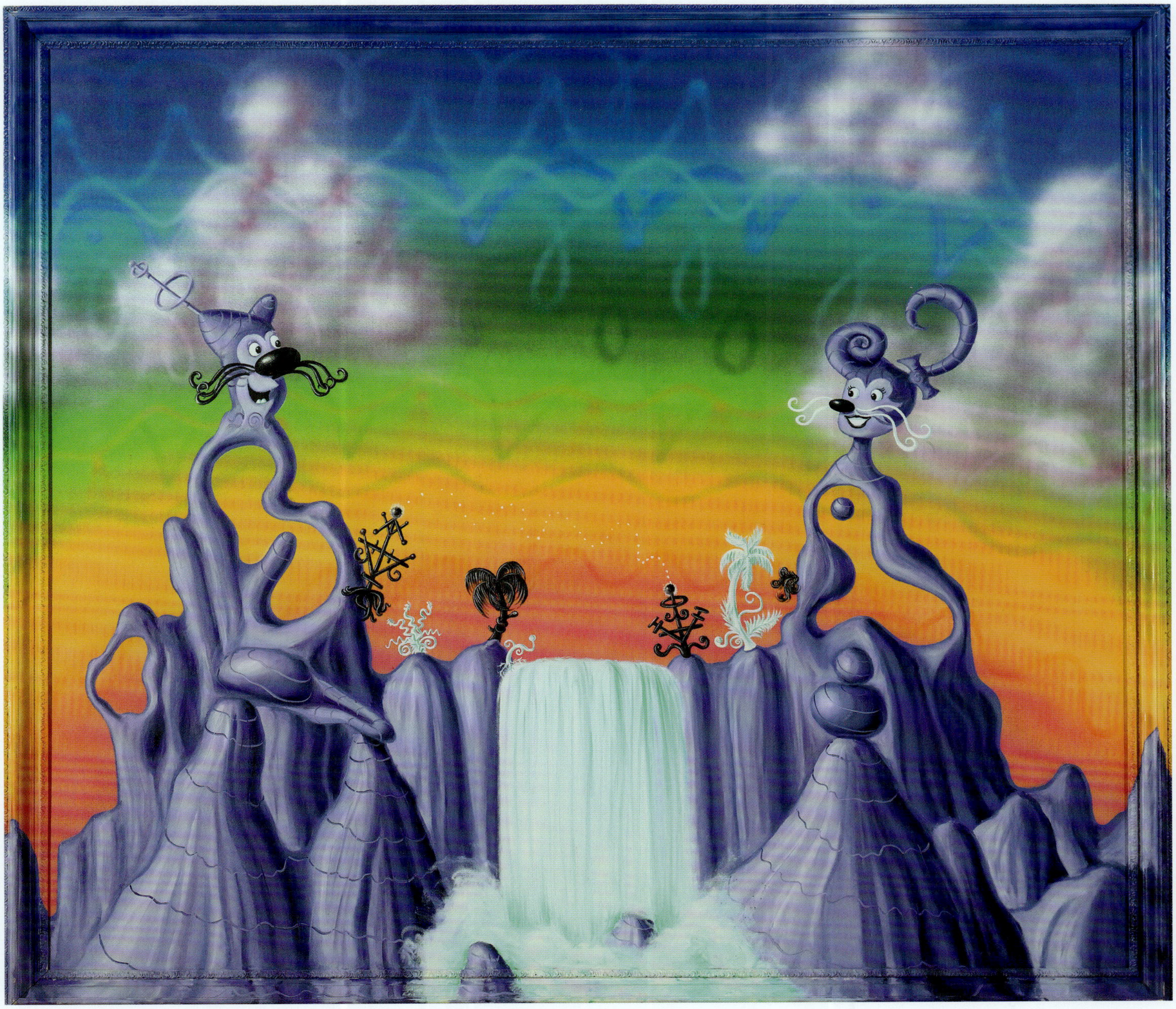

Kenny Scharf
Agua Pollination, 1983
Oil and spray paint on canvas
91 ½ × 103 ½ inches
Courtesy of Paul Kasmin Gallery, New York
and Honor Fraser Gallery, Los Angeles

Julian Schnabel

Most of my paintings have some kind of drawing in them, mostly drawing with paint. Without the plates the drawing usually has more clarity. The gesture is more naked. Sometimes I want drawing or gesture to declare itself in as clear or big a way as possible. I like the large gesture. When I use the plates, the gesture gets broken up. The gesture has to fight through the surface. It's two different ways of animating the image. The big gesture creates the movement or the broken surface.

The plates make the surfaces flicker ... that's the effect the plates give me. Without the plates, the gesture or whatever image I put down just sweeps through the space of the painting.

I like artists that are not afraid to use a lot of material. I think painting today should be about adding, not taking away. Painting has to start doing more things. That's what my generation needs to be about. We need to put more in painting. Every painter that I'm interested in is putting more things in their art—more ideas, more images, more gestures. Minimalism cleaned everything out and now we have to start filling it up again.

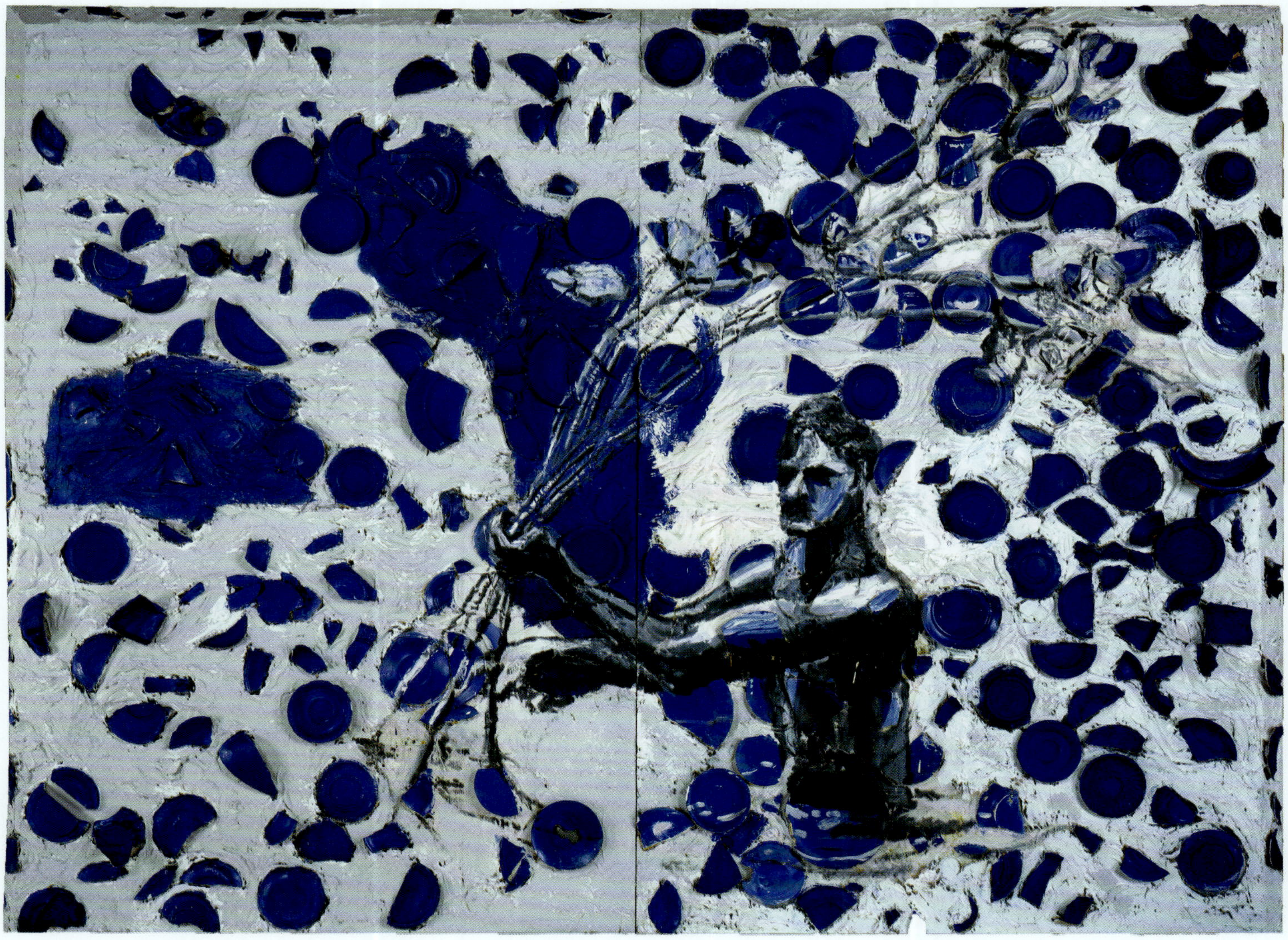

Julian Schnabel
The Jute Grower, 1980
Oil, plates, and Bondo on wood
90 × 120 inches
Ara Arslanian

I try to get my ideas from as many different realities as possible. To be honest, sometimes when I'm painting I'd rather go to see a film, even rather than going to an exhibition. . . . I think about these weird instances when an image is still and about to move or when something is moving and you want it to stop. . . . Film doesn't want to stop. It's always moving. And painting doesn't want to move, physically I mean. A painting has weight and mass so it's hard to get it moving. It fights against that. I think every image has some kind of momentum. I've actually had some ideas about making paintings about film—American films versus European films. I think all good painting moves in some way. It's just a matter of how fast. Great painting never just sits there. That's part of the drama. It's all about drama.

Julian Schnabel, in an unpublished interview with Michael Auping, New York, 1979

Julian Schnabel
Zum Solitaire, 1988
Oil on carpet
138 × 104 inches
Collection of Joseph Mizzi

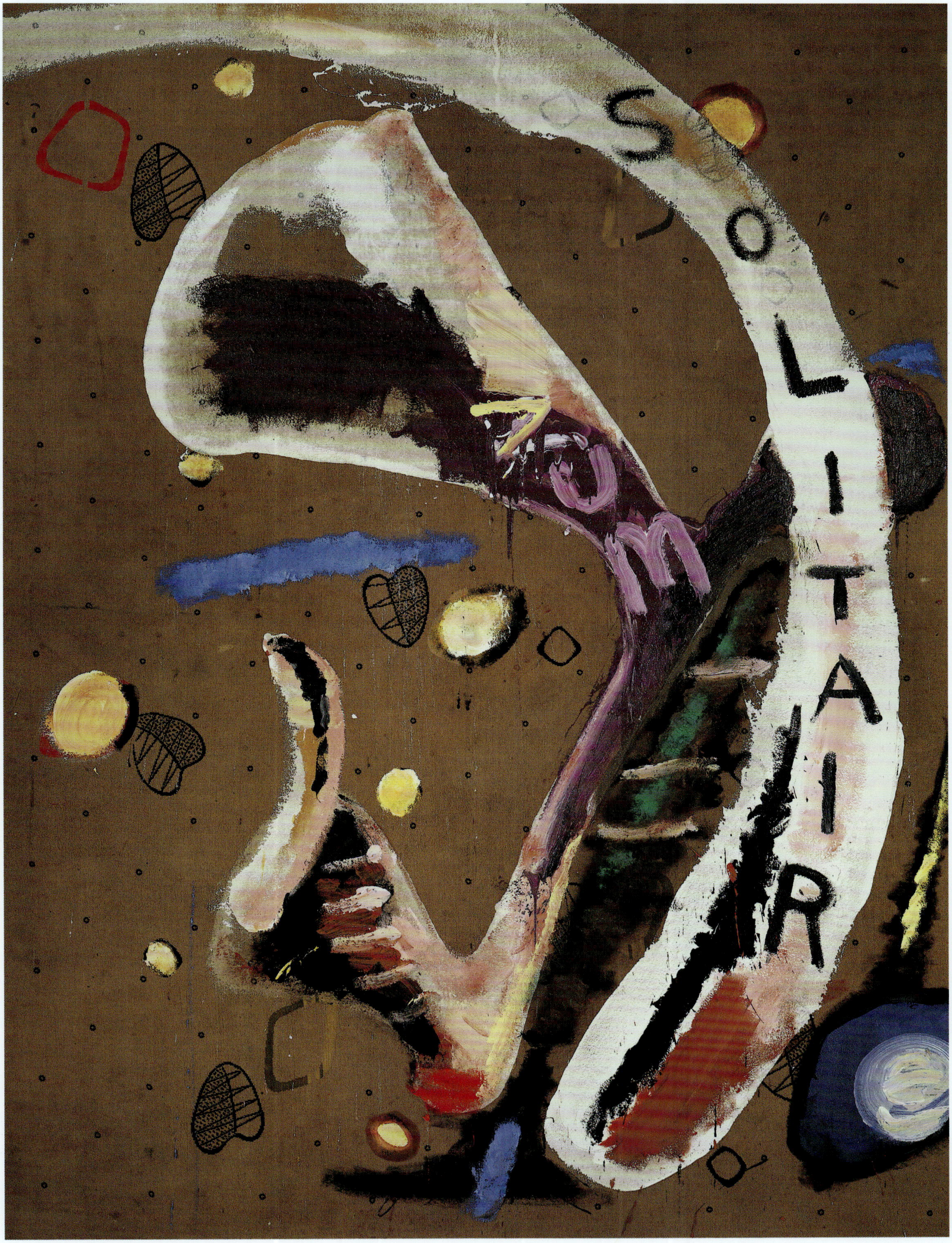
SOLITAIR

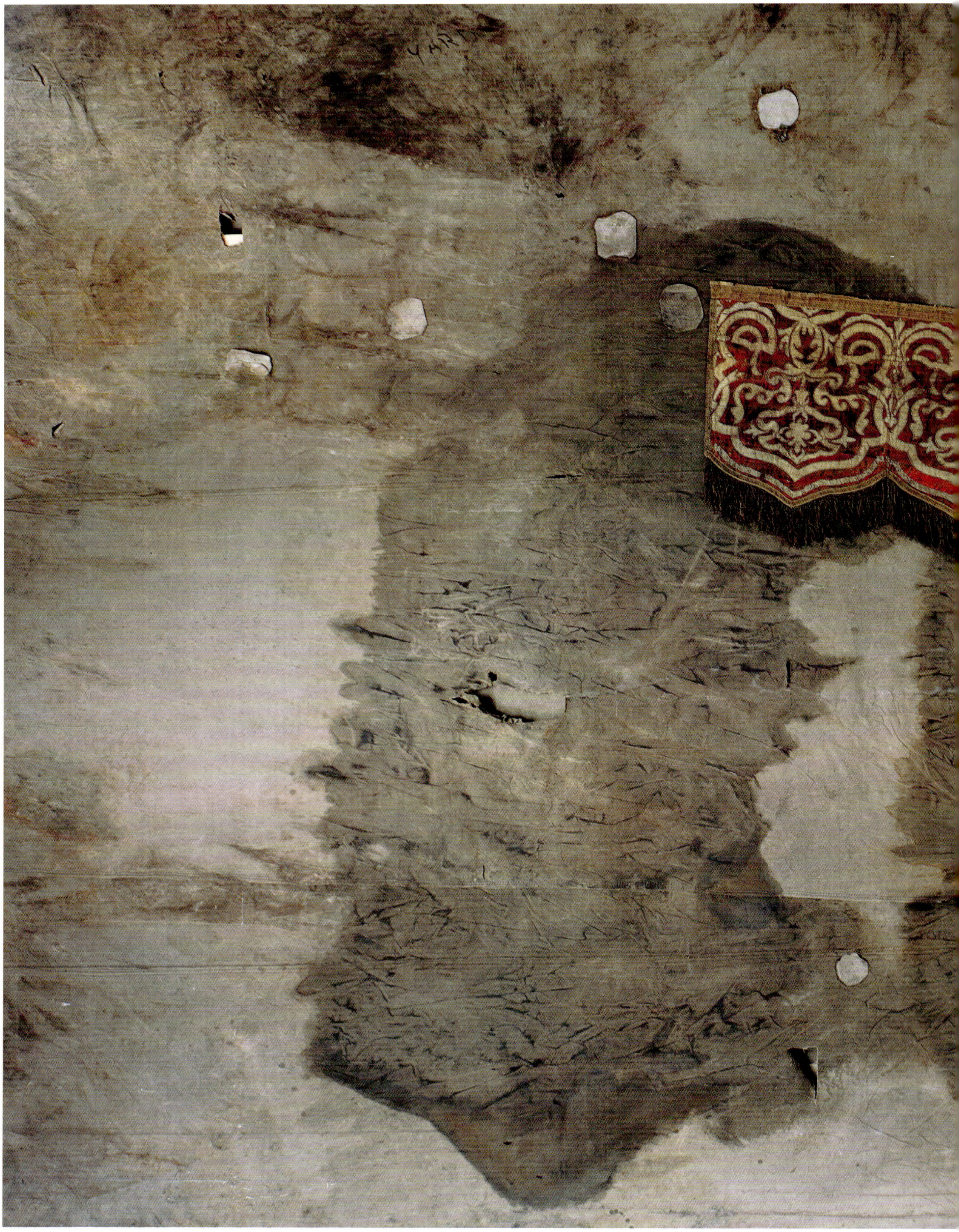

Julian Schnabel
Cortes, 1988
Oil and velvet on
drab tarpaulin
132 × 228 inches
Collection the Artist

Cindy Sherman

I never thought I was acting. When I became involved with close-ups I needed more information in the expression. I couldn't depend on background or atmosphere. I wanted the story to come from the face. Somehow the acting just happened.

I think of *becoming* a different person. I look into a mirror next to the camera ... it's trance-like. By staring into it I try to become that character through the lens. It seems to work out, it sounds like meditation. But something happens that makes it more fun for me because I have no control over it. Something *else* takes over.

I think people are more apt to believe photographs, especially if it's something fantastic. They're willing to be more gullible. Sometimes they want fantasy. Even if they know it's fake they can believe anything. People are accustomed to being told what to believe in.

[My first approach to art was] painting in school, but realistically. I went into photography because it seemed like a fast way to say what you want rather than laboriously making something *look* real. And here we go again about reality. (*laughter*) I have never had a very good abstract sensibility. My mind needed organization so when I started photography it was out of a conceptual art vein making projects for myself.

Quoted in Betsy Sussler, "Cindy Sherman," *Bomb Magazine*, no. 12 (Spring 1985).

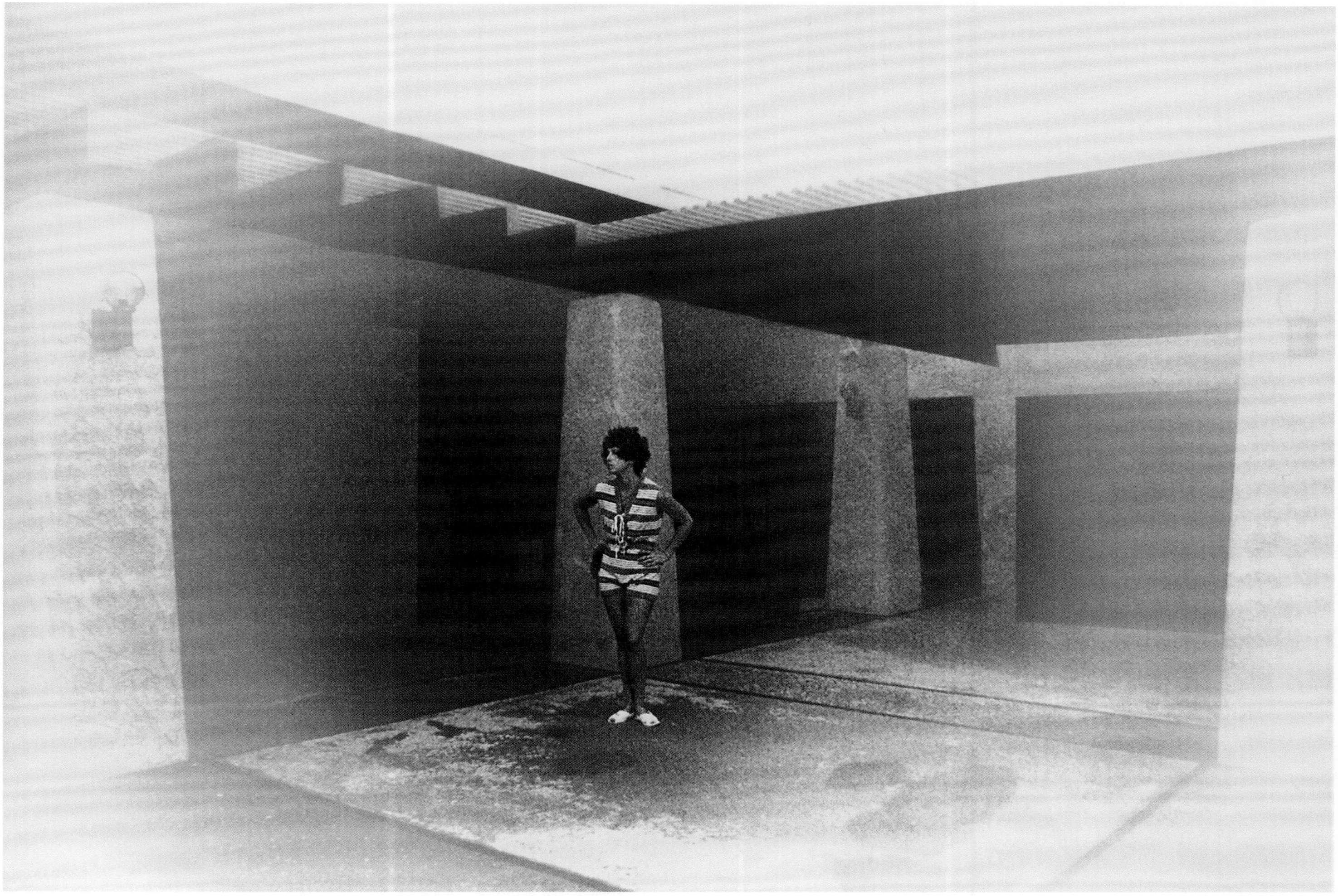

Cindy Sherman
Untitled Film Still #41, 1979
Gelatin silver print
30 × 40 inches
Barbara and Michael Gamson
Image Courtesy of the Artist and Metro Pictures

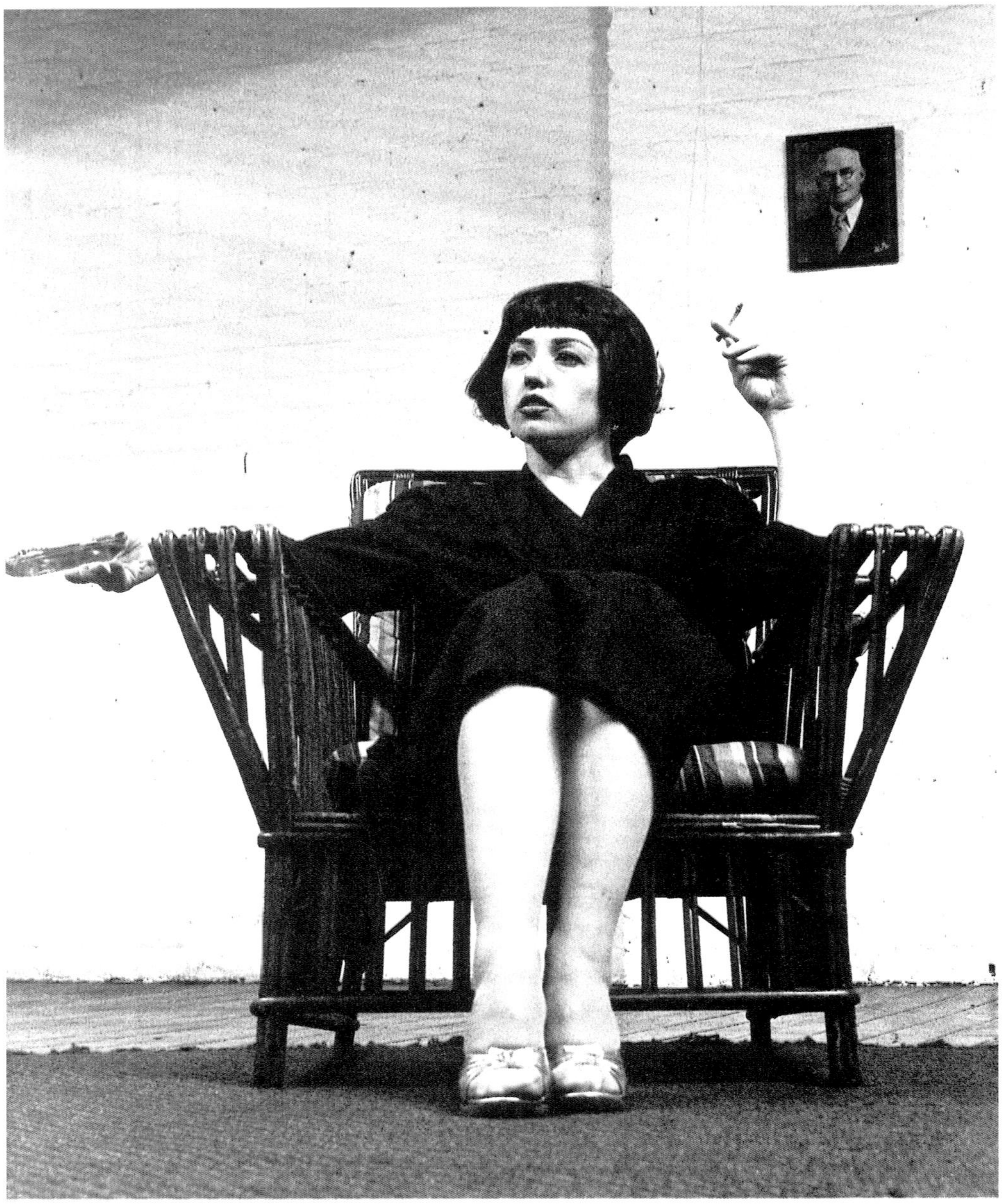

Cindy Sherman
Untitled Film Still #16, 1978
Gelatin silver print
40 × 30 inches
Aaron and Leslee Cowen, NY, NY
Image Courtesy of the Artist and Metro Pictures

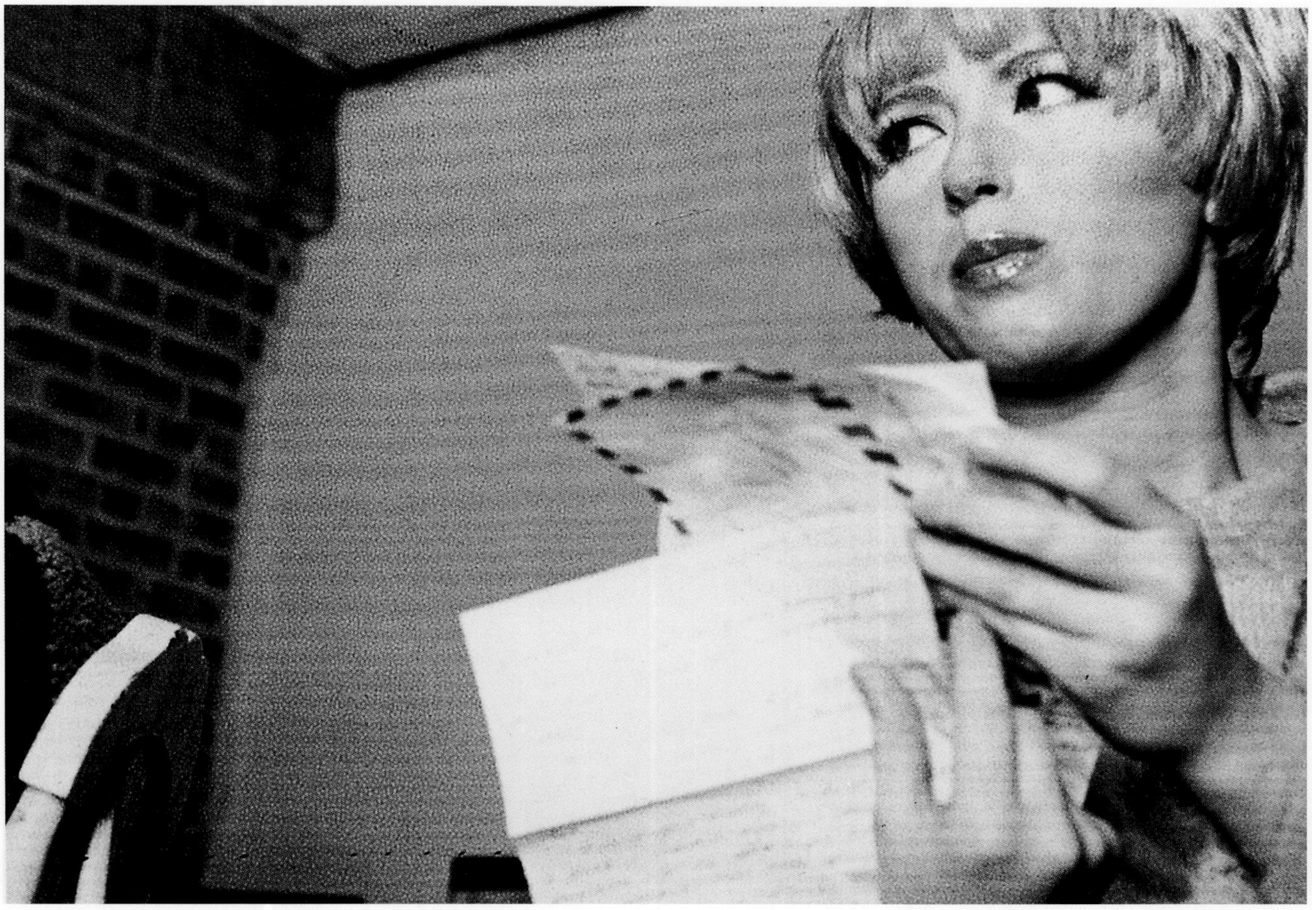

Cindy Sherman
Untitled Film Still #5, 1977
Gelatin silver print
30 × 40 inches
Gayle and Paul Stoffel
Image Courtesy of the Artist and Metro Pictures

When I moved to New York, in the summer of '77, I was trying to think of a new way to take pictures and tell a story. David Salle had been working at some sleazy magazine company where they had lots of shots of half-clothed women around, for those photo-novellas, like a cartoon but with photos. Slightly racy. It got me thinking, this cheap, throw-away image—if you just look at one, you make up your own story.

Back then, it was more the guys who were studio-visiting each other, and I wasn't interested in that sort of male-bonding thing. And there weren't that many other women artists who had discovered themselves. That was about to happen. But one interesting thing—there was much more crossover between different mediums. Robert Longo was in a band; Kim Gordon from Sonic Youth, she was an artist as well as starting to play music. Instead of just feeling, "Oh, we have to go to these galleries to see some art," we would also be saying, "Oh, we have to go hear so-and-so perform," or watch a movie at Max's Kansas City.

I like characters who are not smiling—they're sort of blank. It makes the viewer come up with the narrative.

Quoted in Mark Stevens, "How I Made It: Cindy Sherman on Her 'Untitled Film Stills,'" *New York*, April 7, 2008

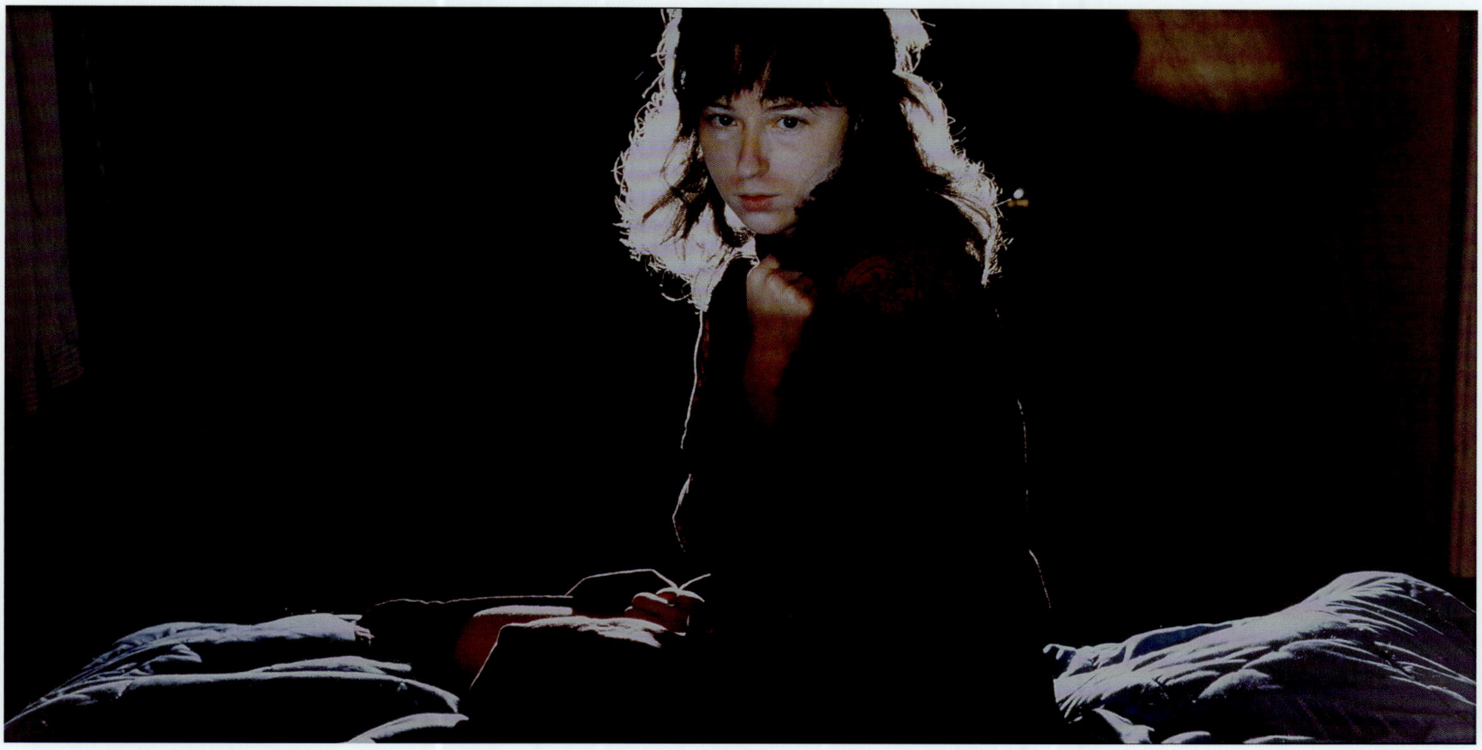

Cindy Sherman
Untitled, 1981
Cibachrome print
24 × 48 inches
Collection of the Modern Art Museum of Fort Worth,
Museum purchase made possible by a grant from
The Burnett Foundation

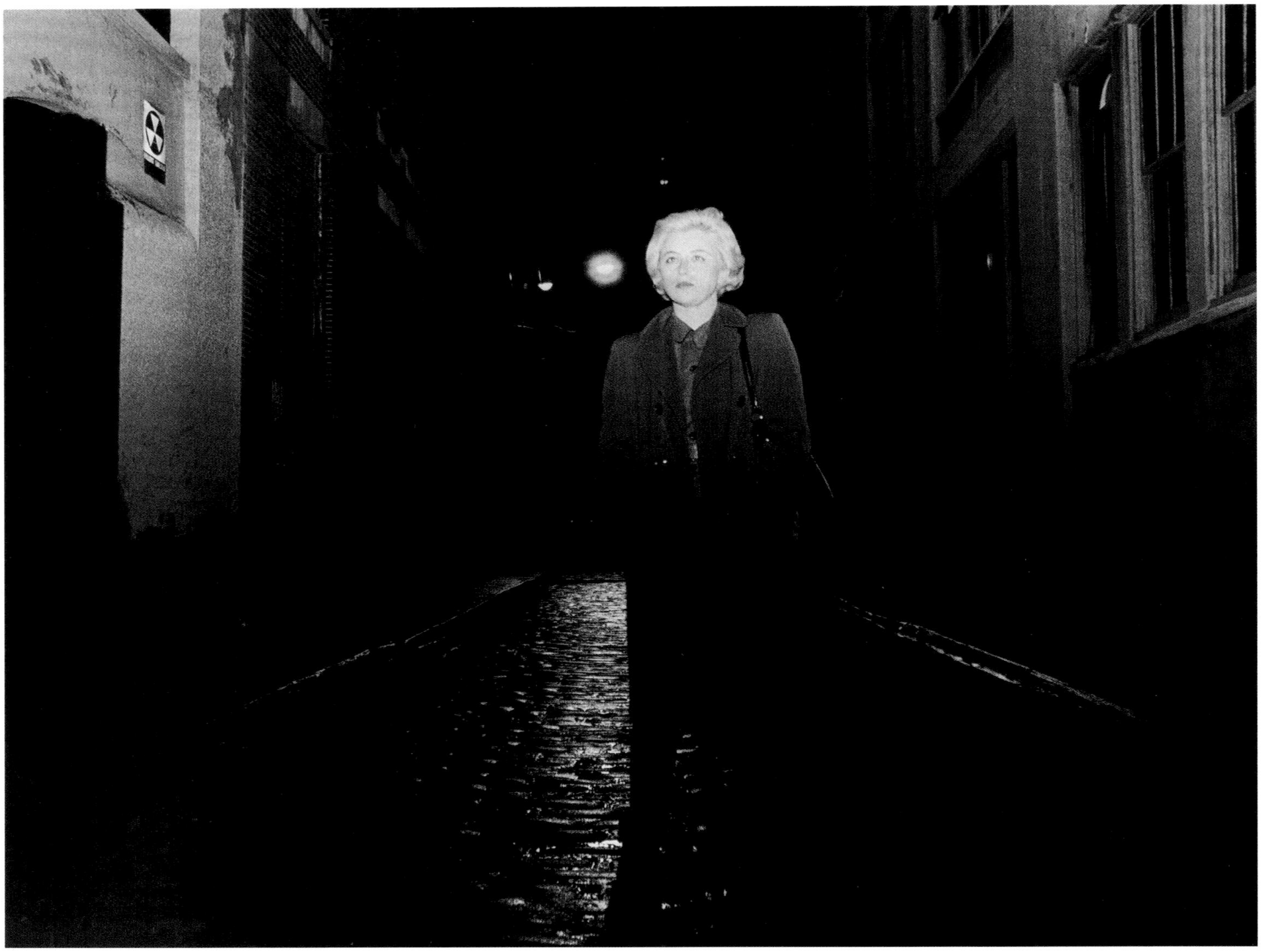

Cindy Sherman
Untitled Film Still #55, 1980
Gelatin silver print
30 × 40 inches
Collection of the Modern Art Museum
of Fort Worth, Museum purchase
made possible by a grant from
The Burnett Foundation

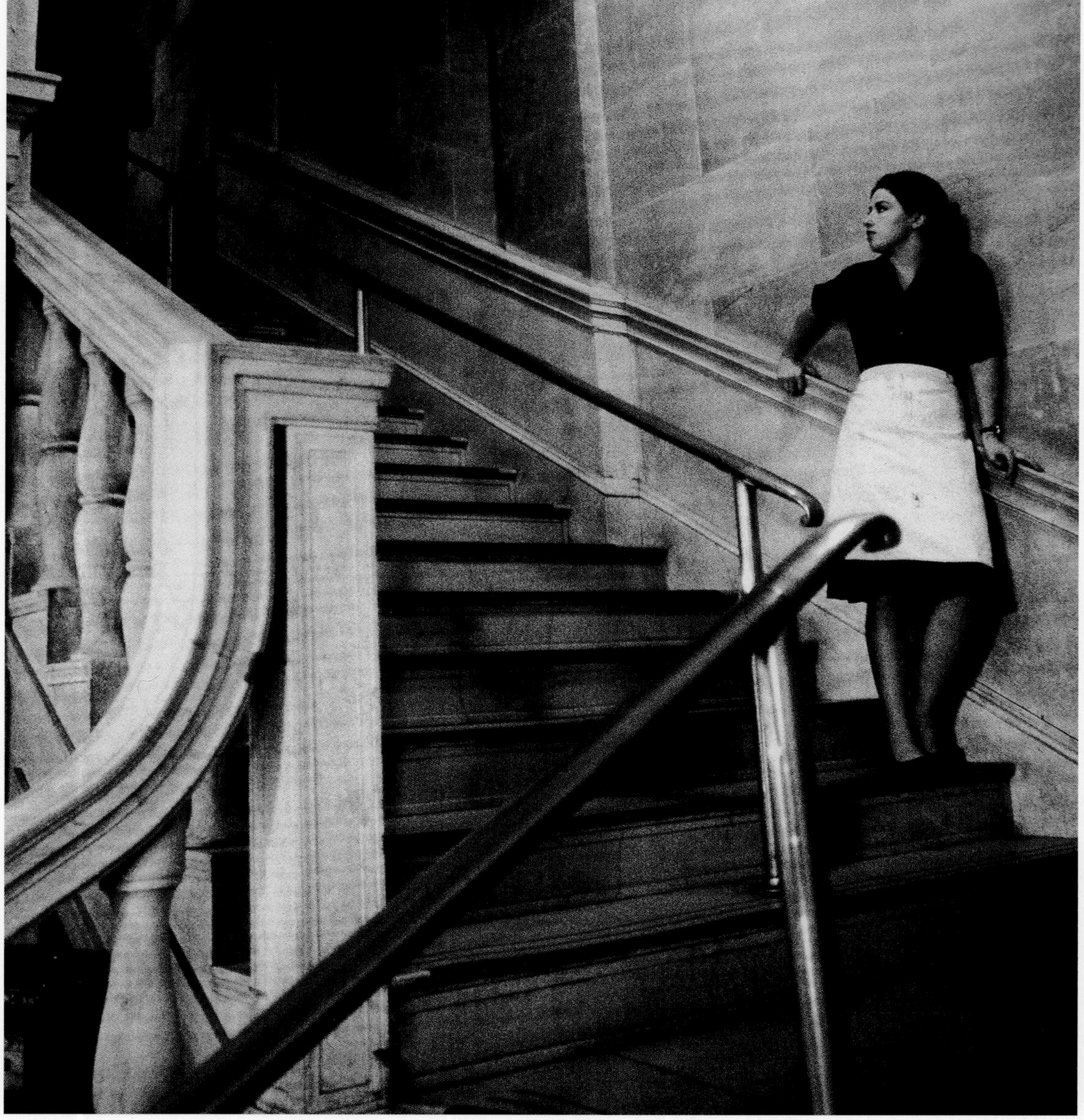

Cindy Sherman
Untitled Film Still #65, 1980
Gelatin silver print
40 × 30 inches
Collection of the Modern Art Museum of Fort Worth, Museum purchase made possible by a grant from The Burnett Foundation

Donald Sultan

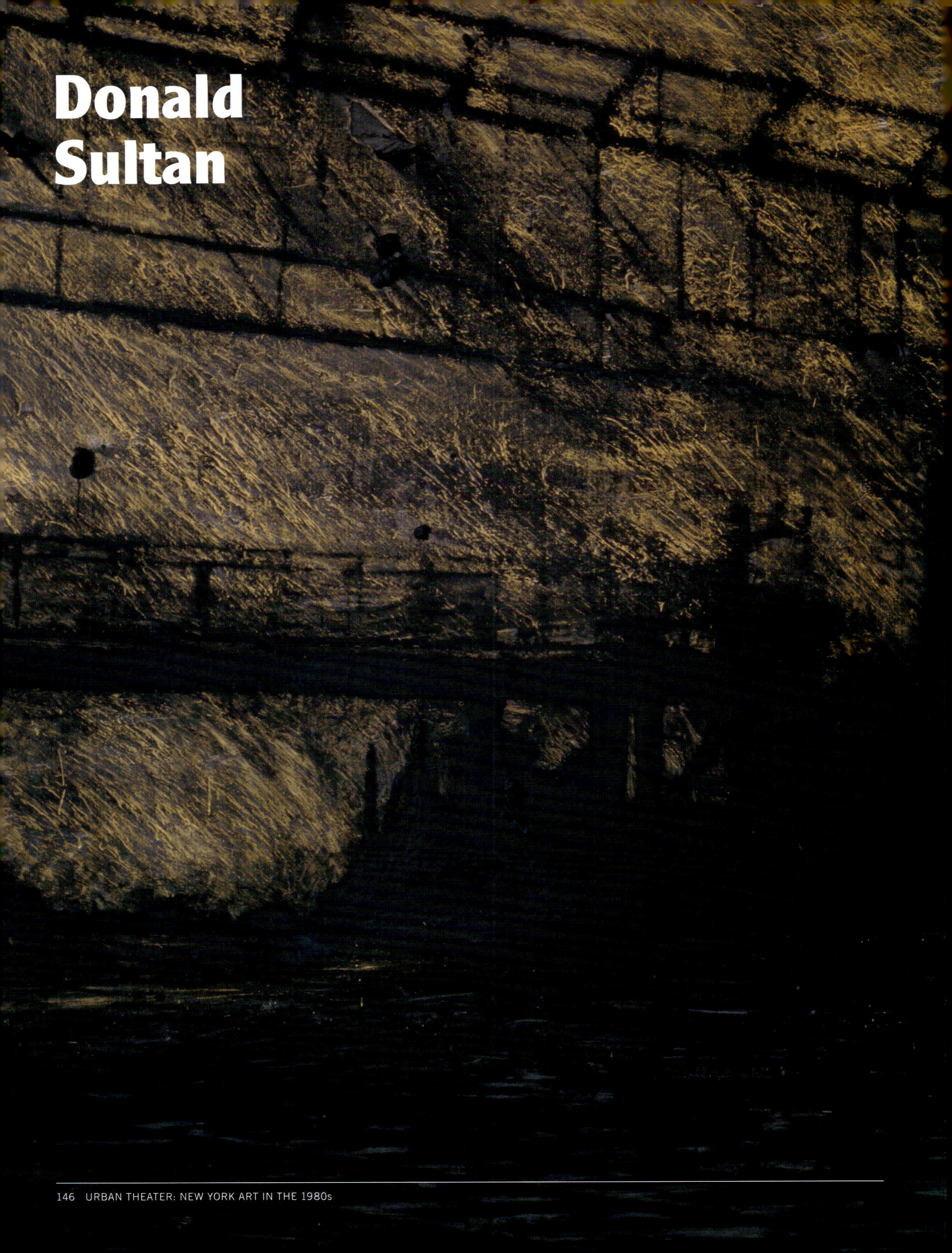

Most of my work deals with the idea of passing. *Dead Plant* is part of a series in which the image is meant to convey a kind of systemic passing by recognizing the impermanence of seemingly permanent structures. The plant symbolizes the changing of ostensibly unchanging aspects of life. It also points to the unseen impact of emotional and economic distress.

Quoted in Andrea Karnes, "Donald Sultan," in *Modern Art Museum of Fort Worth 110* (Fort Worth: Modern Art Museum of Fort Worth in association with Third Millennium Publishing, 2002), 306

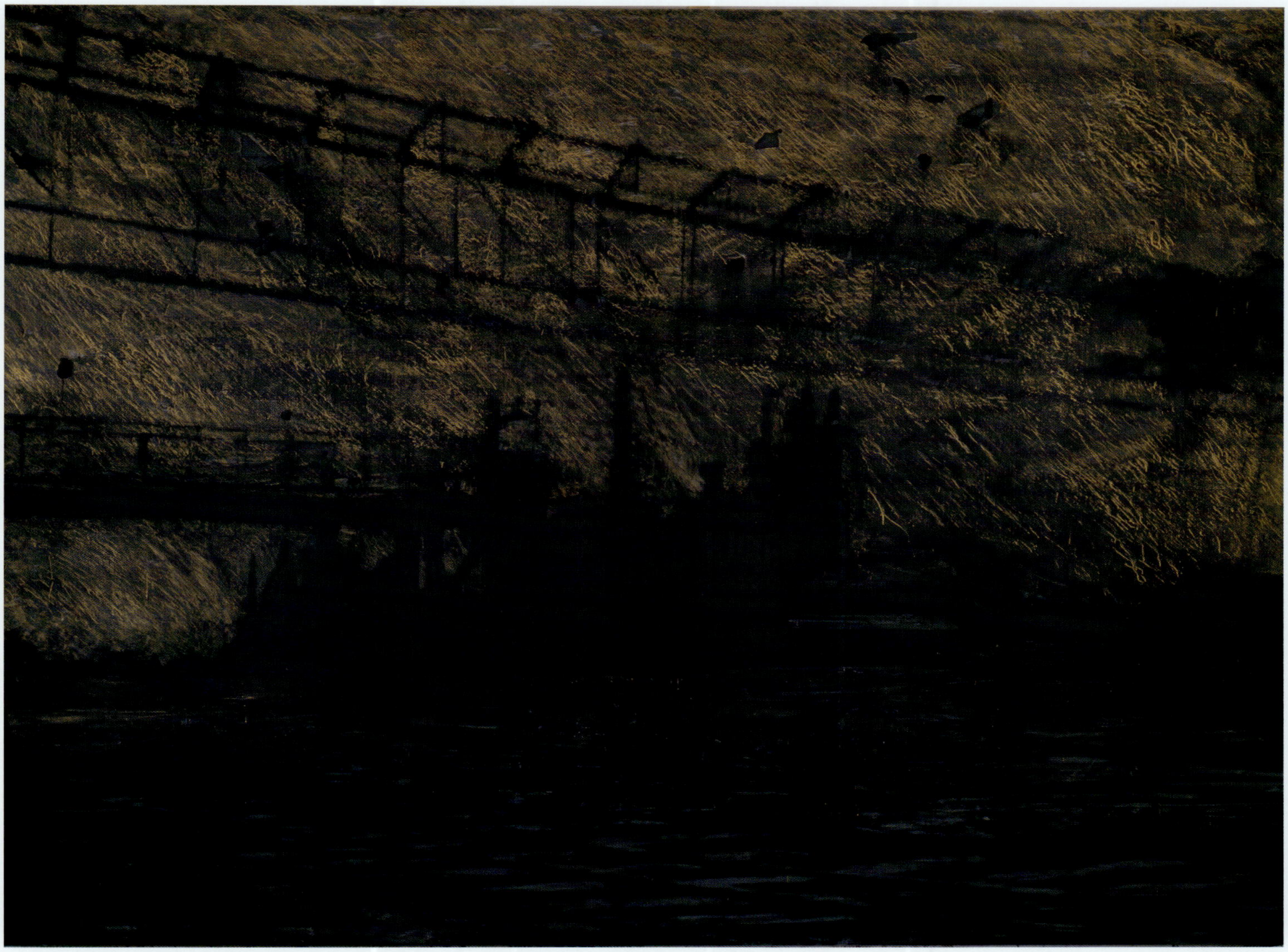

Donald Sultan
Dead Plant November 1 1988, 1988
Tar and latex paint on canvas
108 1/8 × 144 1/4 × 6 3/8 inches
Collection of the Modern Art Museum of Fort Worth,
Museum purchase made possible by a grant from
The Burnett Foundation

Philip Taaffe

Toward the end of the "picture binding series" I had wanted to expand the scale and do an allover picture. The visual tension, the play with positive and negative space in these works, and the opticality and the sharpness of the lines led to a reconsideration of op art. I thought it would be a logical next step. Going around the galleries I was seeing what Mike Bidlo and Sherrie Levine and Richard Prince were doing, so this whole idea of shifting one's historical perspective, one's relationship to the immediate past of art history was a very interesting prospect.

In the meantime, I'd been going to wastepaper-disposal plants in Newark, New Jersey, in this big old '57 Chevy. I would drive to these plants where printers get rid of their end runs for various rolls and samples of things like lightbulb-packaging paper, and bring them back to my apartment in Jersey City. I had always wanted to surgically dissect a Bridget Riley painting, just take it apart and put it back together. I had all these rolls of paper, and I decided to make linoleum carvings and print and collage the lines on this found paper. I dissected the wave in one of her paintings, and then another, and then a third, and I made the carvings based on projections of these waves. They were very carefully engineered and surgically constructed, even if they ended up having a strange topography.

I think a lot of people felt that some of the photo-based, appropriative work was a little dry, and that mine was concerning itself with the romance of painting, the facture of painting and craft. I think it was intriguing to people that someone could have a strong conceptual bias and yet make something that held up as a crafted painting.

Quoted in Bob Nickas, "'80s Then: Philip Taaffe talks to Bob Nickas," *Artforum* 41, no. 8 (April 2003): 180–81. © Artforum

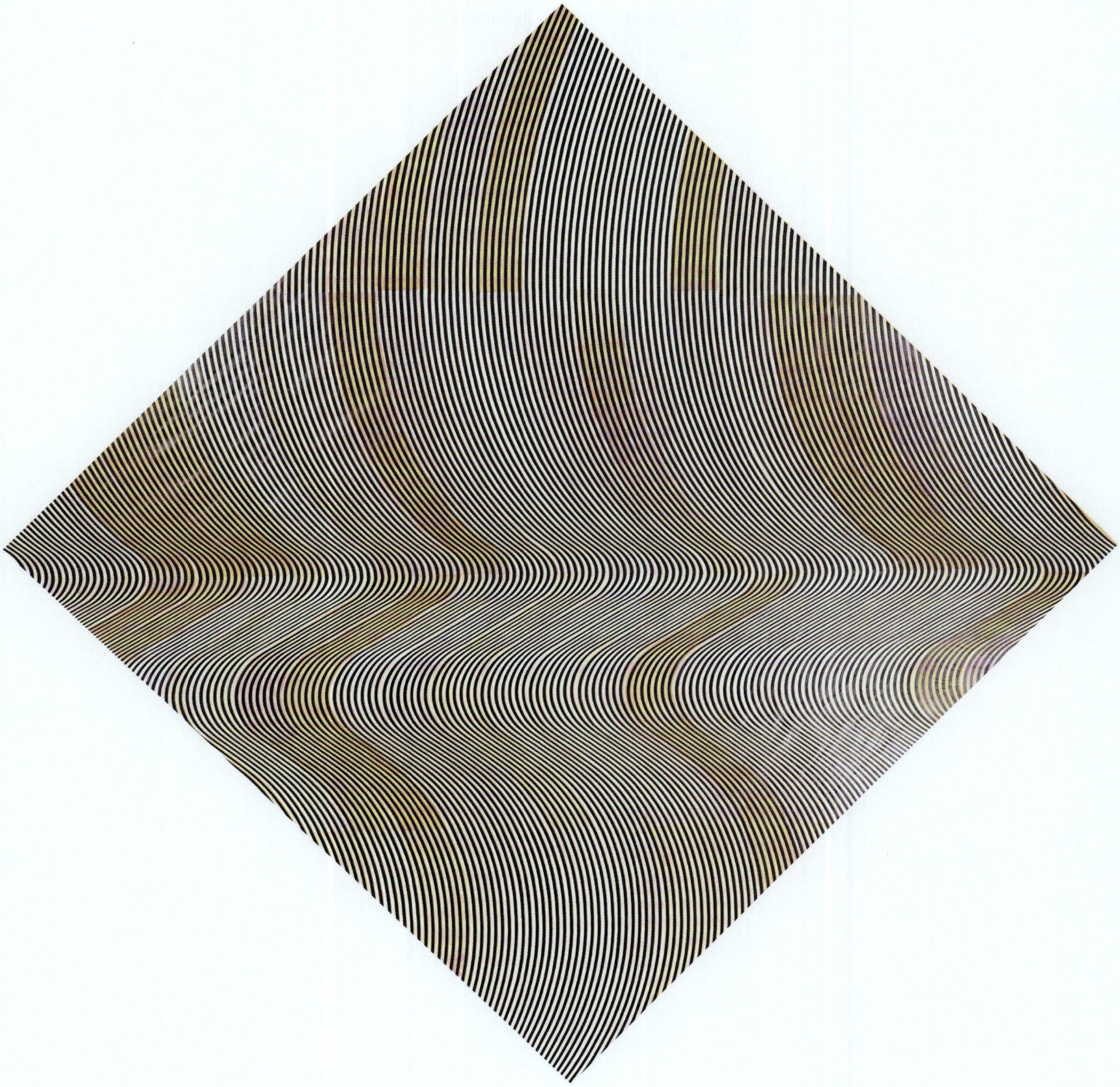

Philip Taaffe
Brest, 1985
Linoprint collage on paper mounted on canvas
78 1/4 × 78 1/2 inches
Rubell Family Collection, Miami
Image Courtesy of the Artist and Luhring Augustine, New York

Andy Warhol

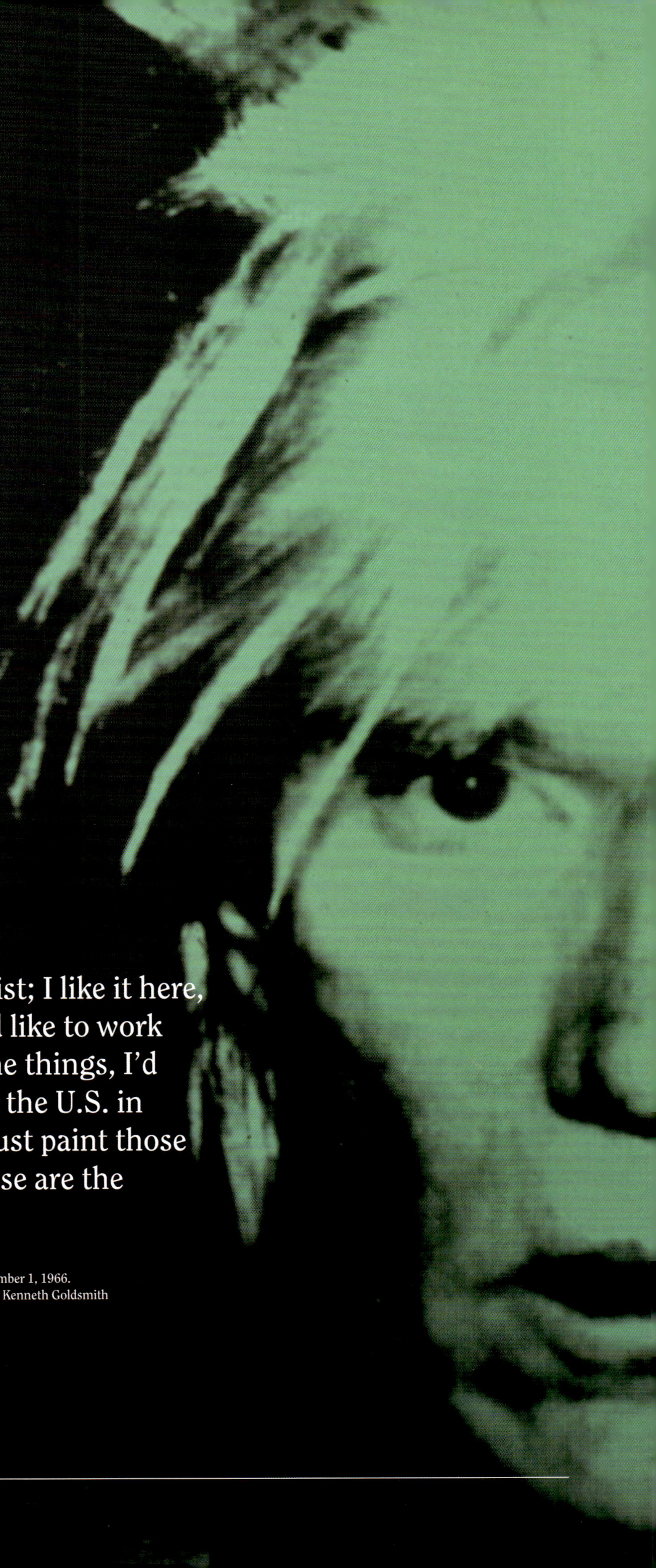

I think of myself as an American artist; I like it here, I think it's so great. It's fantastic. I'd like to work in Europe but I wouldn't do the same things, I'd do different things. I feel I represent the U.S. in my art but I'm not a social critic. I just paint those objects in my paintings because those are the things I know best.

Quoted in Gretchen Berg, "Andy Warhol: My True Story," *The East Village Other*, November 1, 1966. Reprinted in *I'll Be Your Mirror: The Selected Andy Warhol Interviews, 1962–1987*, ed. Kenneth Goldsmith (New York: Carroll & Graf Publishers, 2004), 88

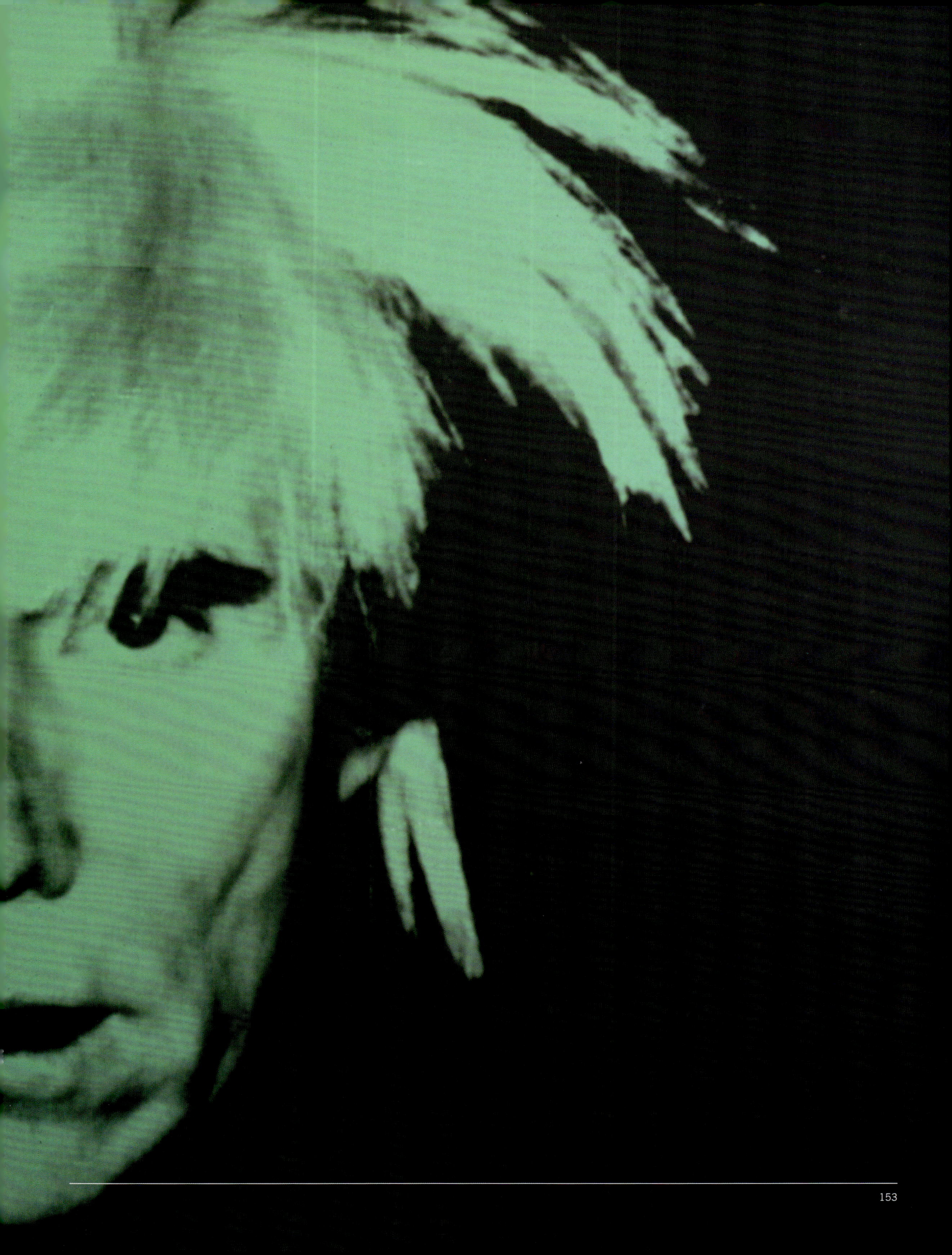

Making money is art and working is art and good business is the best art.

Andy Warhol, *The Philosophy of Andy Warhol (From A to B and Back Again)* (New York: Harcourt, 1975), 92

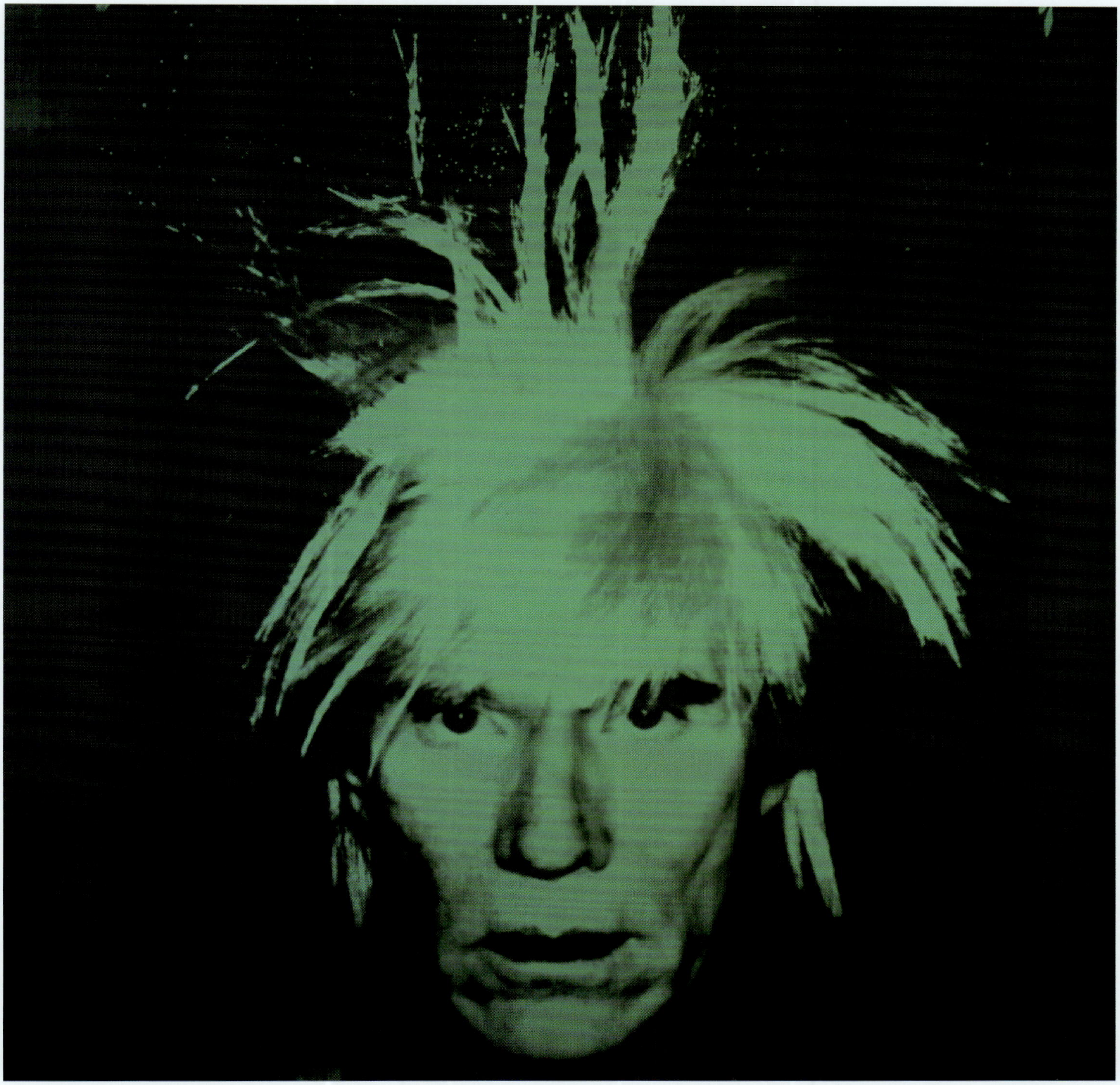

Andy Warhol
Self-Portrait, 1986
Synthetic polymer paint and silkscreen ink on canvas
108 × 108 inches
Collection of the Modern Art Museum of Fort Worth,
Museum purchase, The Friends of Art Endowment Fund

Christopher Wool

The problem is: If you take text and image and you put them together, the multiple readings that are possible in either poetry or in something visual are reduced to one specific reading.

By putting the two together, you limit the possibilities. Text and image don't always work together in the way music and song lyrics become part of each other.

Quoted in Glenn O'Brien, "Christopher Wool & Richard Hell," *Interview*, November 18, 2008.
Excerpt of article originally published in *Interview* magazine, November 2008. Courtesy BMP Media Holdings, LLC

Christopher Wool
Untitled, 1990
Alkyd and acrylic on aluminum
96 × 64 inches
Collection of Marguerite Steed Hoffman
Image Courtesy of the Artist and Luhring Augustine, New York

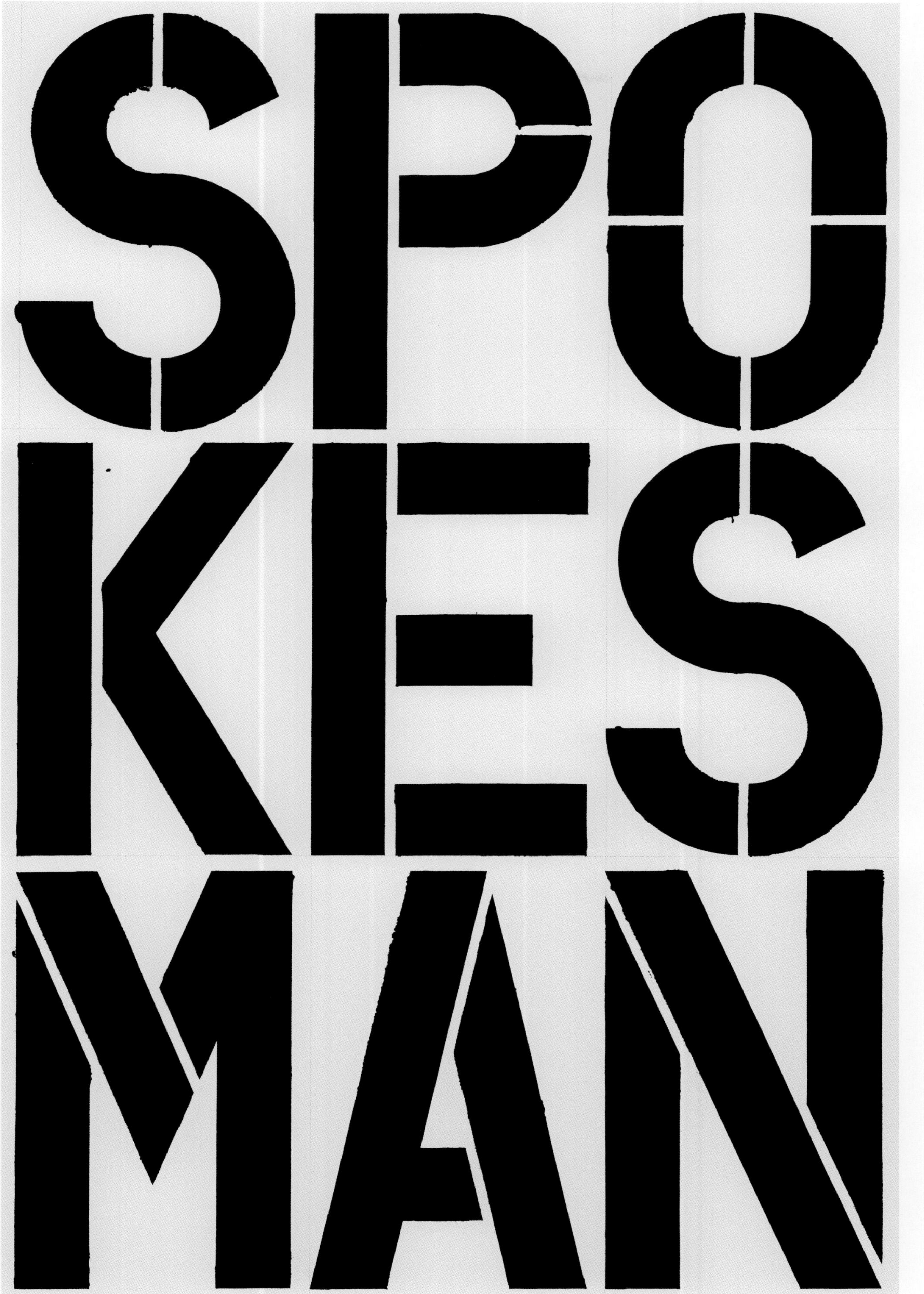
SPO
KES
MAN

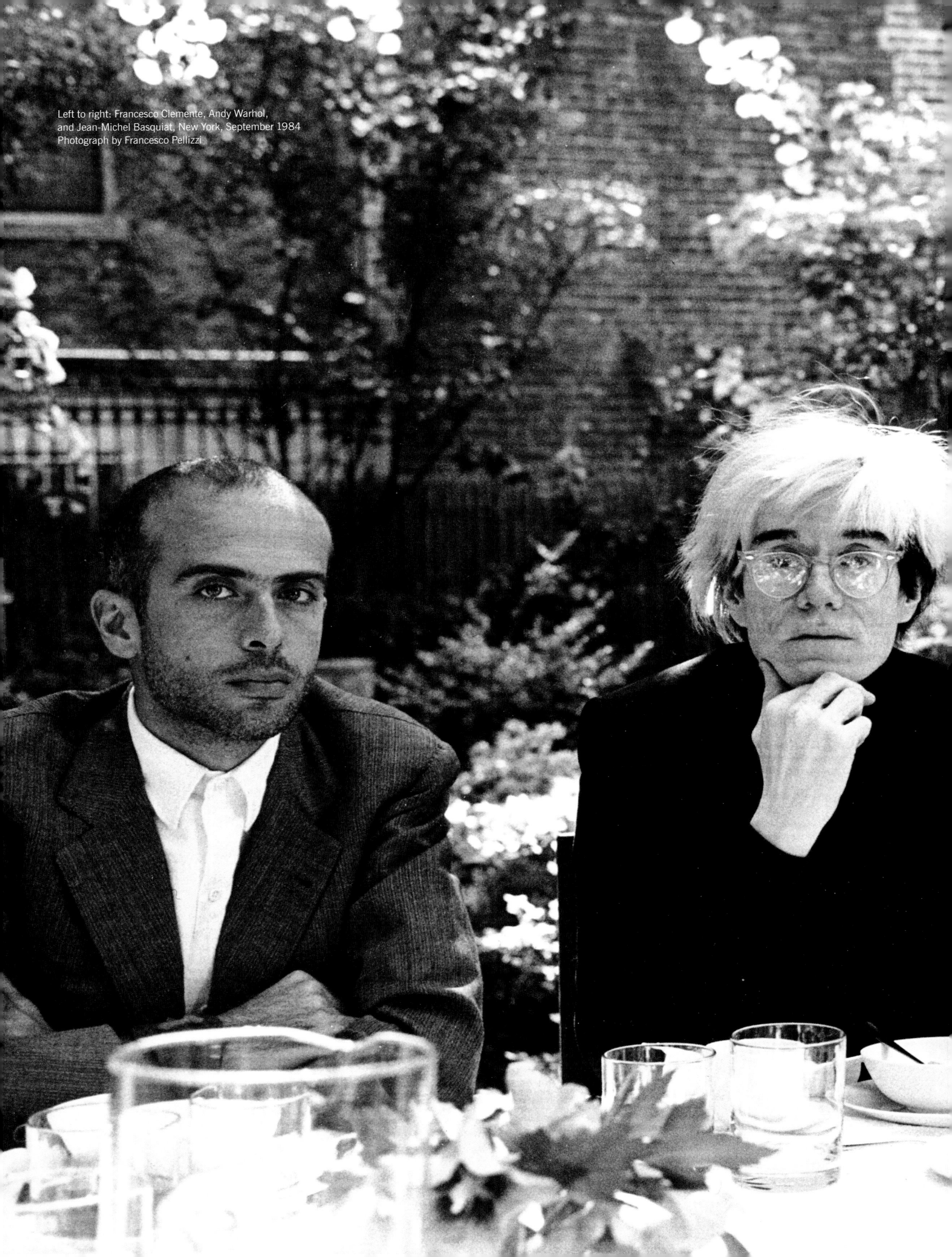

Left to right: Francesco Clemente, Andy Warhol, and Jean-Michel Basquiat, New York, September 1984
Photograph by Francesco Pellizzi

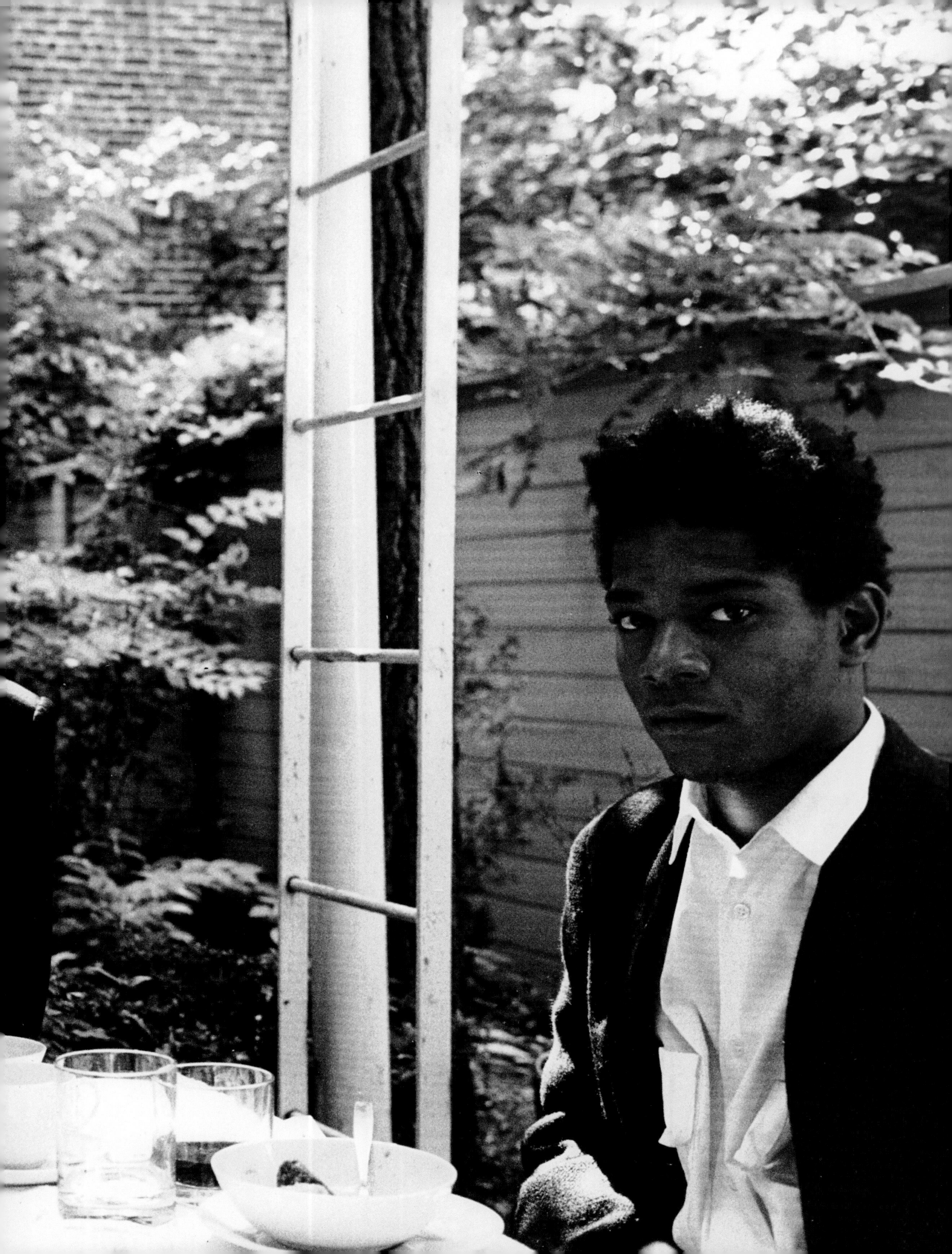

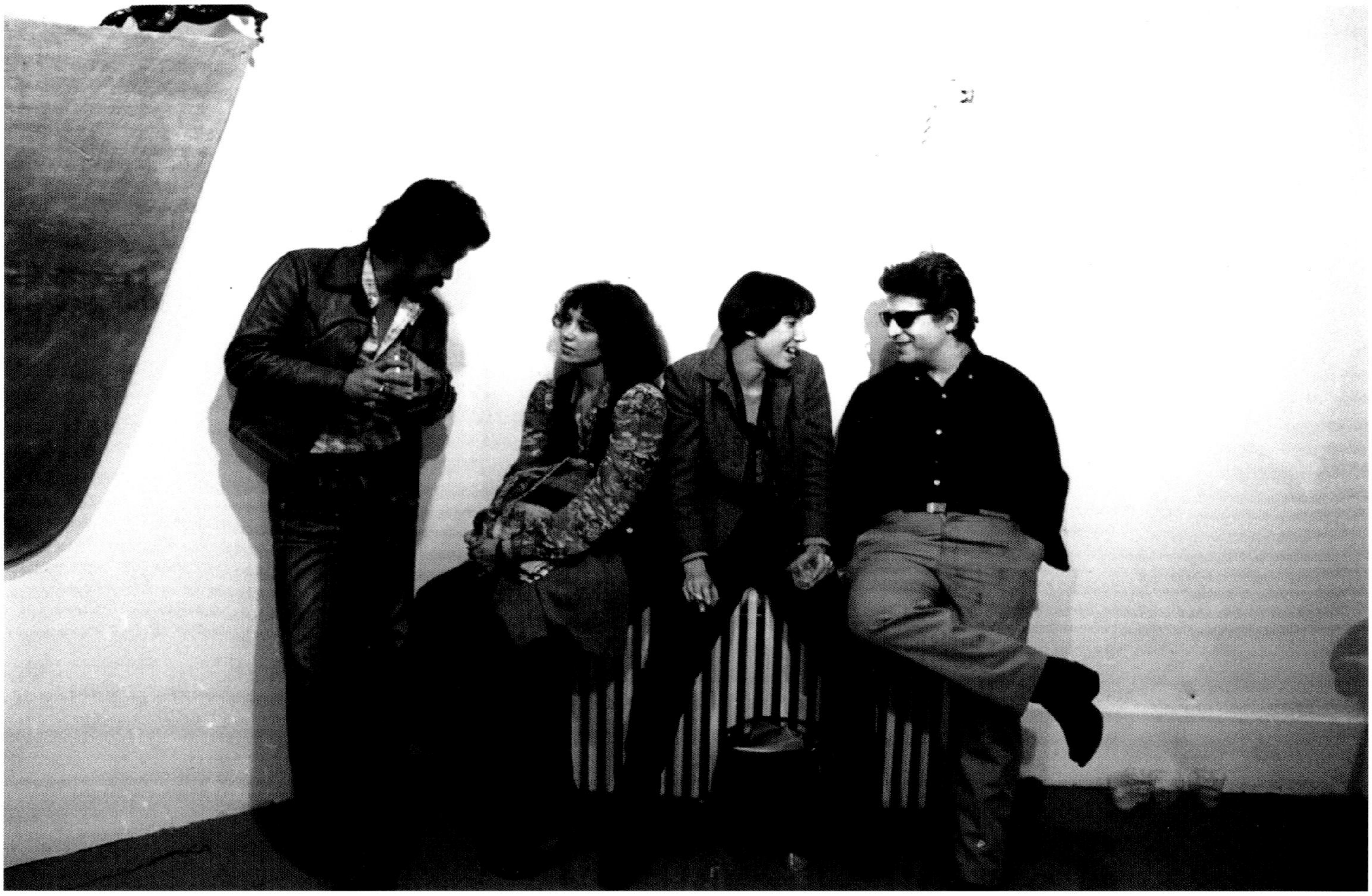

Pictures opening at Artists Space, New York, 1977
Courtesy of Artists Space

Personality Complex

Andrea Karnes

With New York City as their backdrop—a compact area filled with diversity—Nan Goldin, Jenny Holzer, Barbara Kruger, Sherrie Levine, Robert Longo, Robert Mapplethorpe, Richard Prince, and Cindy Sherman, all coming of age in the 1980s, played out life in works that communicate their artistic personalities. Through this process, they explored gender, one of the most salient social topics of the day. With numerous post-modern, feminist, and psychoanalytic texts swirling around issues of masculinity, femininity, and sexuality, these artists reflected the idea that gender is defined and interpreted through an abundance of cultural signs (images and language) that simulate and fabricate reality.[1] They also began to critique representation itself and how it elicits comparisons to the self via social mores and idealized media concepts.

Each of these artists questioned the notion of objectivity through their subversive use of subjectivity, posed as objectivity. At the center of these explorations was photography, the avant-garde medium of the decade, which manifested in distinct ways in their works—either as a primary medium, as a tool to repurpose existing imagery, or as a reference to inform their paintings, drawings, sculptures, or public projects.[2] With varying approaches to gender and to photography's influence, three main modes of artistic personality emerge in their bodies of work: the impersonal, the personal as public, and the confessional. The impersonal describes Levine, Longo, Prince, and Sherman, who address widely accepted models of gender in imagery that appears neutral, unemotional, and detached. The personal as public refers to Holzer and Kruger, who defy culturally accepted gender roles by using a personal, feminist perspective and an emotionally inflammatory tone in public settings. The confessional illustrates Goldin and Mapplethorpe, who operate on the periphery of the main tenets of postmodernism, but shed light on notions of difference, using the language of photography to reveal intimate segments of their private lives that often break with a traditional understanding of gender.

The Impersonal

Rather than imparting a personal viewpoint in their works, Levine, Longo, Prince, and Sherman offer takes on, and appropriate, public images of men and women from an impersonal perspective. Each of these "impersonal" artists is also associated with the "Pictures Generation." In 1977, art critic Douglas Crimp curated the exhibition *Pictures* at Artists Space in New York, which featured the work of Levine, Longo, Troy Brauntuch, Jack Goldstein, and Philip Smith. Though the exhibition only included these five young artists, Crimp's thesis pointed out a much larger trend in art: one in which the seduction of recognizable imagery determined a new model of artmaking that, though figurative, was as cerebral as Minimalism. These artists were subsequently referred to as

As a female artist redoing male artists' works, is Sherrie Levine revising or eulogizing the past? Is she marketing herself on the coattails of her white male predecessors, or expressing her desire to be part of art history?

the Pictures Generation, and the group expanded to include Louise Lawler, Prince, Sherman, Laurie Simmons, and others. Crimp's essay in the show's accompanying catalogue argued that the power of these artists lies in their analyses of the familiar, and that such depictions in art create a psychological resonance for the viewer.[3] In other words, in turning a mirror on the world around them, sometimes critically, other times humorously, they exaggerate life and reflect it back onto viewers in ways that ignite potent questions about how we view ourselves. Most of the Pictures Generation embraced the realms of photography and film for their presentations of "reality." Photography, with its ability to seem real even when what it depicts is manipulated by the decisions of the artist/photographer, was the perfect medium to blur these lines between fact and staged artifice.

The impersonal aptly describes the cool and contrived visual styles of Levine, who creates deadpan copies of well-known masterworks originally created by men, and of Longo, Prince, and Sherman, who riff on Hollywood and mass media images of masculinity and femininity. They evoke stereotypes and clichés, resulting in works that seemingly function without bias toward or against social norms. This look of the real creates uncertainty between parody and sincerity in what viewers see, a notion that is reinforced by the artists placing us in the power position of voyeur (the dominant role of viewer, as opposed to the passive role of subject). Whether male or female, this dynamic stimulates an internal dialogue for viewers about the nature of representation, especially when it comes to gender constructs. Voyeurism—with deep roots in the psychoanalytic theory of Jacques Lacan, especially his "mirror stage" (gazer/object of gaze); in French philosopher Michel Foucault's "panopticism" (self-regulation under systems of surveillance); and in what feminist film critic Laura Mulvey pejoratively called "to-be-looked-at-ness" of females in film—is one of the most important apparatuses for impersonal works.[4] These artists show men and women with a detachedness that allows us to peer in and evaluate established patterns of masculinity and femininity within our inherited and preserved societal systems.

Since the late 1970s, Sherrie Levine has appropriated important modernist works originally made by white male artists, such as the photographers Eliot Porter, Edward Weston, and Walker Evans; and painters Willem de Kooning, Egon Schiele, Piet Mondrian, and Henri Matisse. Carefully re-photographing their photographs, re-painting their paintings, and in some cases, transforming their most well-known images from one medium to another, Levine's career is emblematic of postmodernism and feminism. This is especially so because her remakes

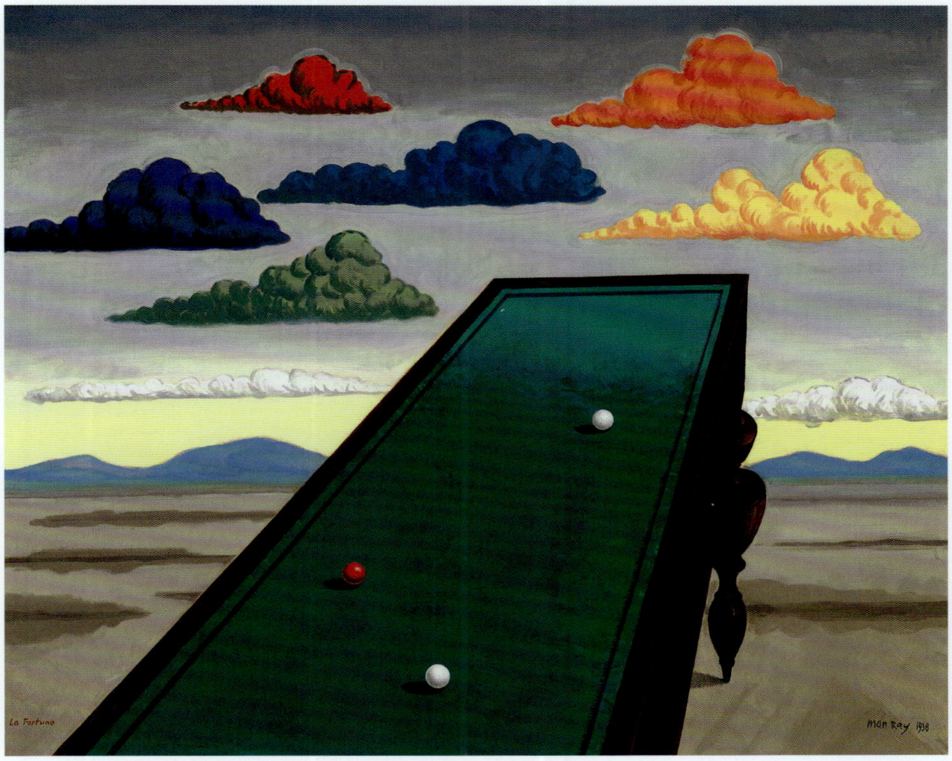

Man Ray
La Fortune, 1938
Oil on linen
$23^{11}/_{16} \times 28^{13}/_{16}$ inches
Whitney Museum of American Art, New York;
Purchase, with funds from the Simon Foundation, Inc.
72.129

call attention to the firm grip of patriarchy in the art world—and everywhere—and because they question the importance of original artworks. By using reproductions from books, for example, as source material, Levine compounds layers of distance between the primary work, the reproduced image in the book, and her copy. She assesses seminal artworks and their relationship to the past and present: Is the copy as good as seeing the original to create meaning for viewers? As a female artist redoing male artists' works, is she revising or eulogizing the past? Is she marketing herself on the coattails of her white male predecessors, or expressing her desire to be part of art history? Her oeuvre has been both praised and criticized for such possible readings.

For *La Fortune (After Man Ray): 6*, 1990, Levine replicated in sculptural form Man Ray's painted, fantasy billiard table in *La Fortune*, 1938. Man Ray's painting depicts a semblance of a billiard table with a masculine (rectilinear) playing surface and feminine (curved) legs. Other male/female attributes are noticeably absent in the original work—there are no pockets or pool sticks. And since there are just three billiard balls, it is an inoperable construction in terms of the actual game. Levine's large-scale sculptural version dimensionalizes, and therefore amplifies this impotent game. The idea that the female legs uphold the male table becomes a metaphor for women's supporting role in the art world. Man Ray's illusive image is Levine's challenge: She transforms his painting into an object that imitates the original work, and she one-ups him, making her *La Fortune* an edition of six identical tables. These multiples further question the nature of originality and reproducibility and their relevance when viewing an artwork. There is, of course, postmodern irony in this and all of Levine's visual output, but there is an even greater irony in that her re-creations, the very vehicles to address fetishized artworks of the past, have become iconic of her career.

Having several pieces in *Pictures*, Robert Longo received widespread critical and public attention, especially for *The American Soldier*, 1977. *Soldier* is an enameled, cast aluminum wall relief depicting a man in a hat, khakis, white button-down shirt, and striped tie standing with an arched back and thrust-back head, as if being hit by an unseen gust of wind or a violent force. The figure was inspired by a scene at the end of the Rainer Werner Fassbinder film *The American Soldier*, 1970, after which the sculpture was named, and it led to the artist's other explorations into Hollywood-inspired gender portrayals and to his formative series from 1979–82, *Men in the Cities*. For *Men*, Longo photographed his artist friends (including women, such as Cindy Sherman) in contorted postures and business attire, and then made larger-than-life charcoal drawings and paintings of their single silhouettes, based on the photographs he staged. Each work in the series shows a professionally dressed, isolated figure to address the branding of the urban creature, as well as corporate culture and power—the figures, recognizable from the business world, are like puppets manipulated by unseen strings.

The black-and-white imagery, in the case of the charcoal and graphite drawings, is rendered in finessed yet muscular chiaroscuro, and, in all forms, is set in high contrast against clean white backgrounds. The use of black and white suggests the reproduced images found in media and journalism, underscoring how truth and subjectivity are mediated in

Longo's choice to present lone figures gives the imagery an existential ring. Yet their anonymity suggests the corporate apparatus and subverts individual essence to instead underscore the alienated, generic everyman.

those industries. The figures read as psychologically charged (are they dancing or dying?),[5] but they are also strangely elusive in terms of the subjects' own unreadable emotions. Longo's choice to present lone figures gives the imagery an existential ring. Yet their anonymity suggests the corporate apparatus and subverts individual essence to instead underscore the alienated, generic everyman.

Like Longo, Richard Prince questions an idealized male archetype in work such as *Untitled (Cowboys) #8*, from a series of Ektacolor prints made between 1980 and 1984, for which he directly appropriated the Marlboro Man from the "Marlboro Country" campaign begun in 1963 by the Philip Morris corporation (now Altria). The cowboy, set against a dramatic sky, roping wild horses, presumably in the American West, symbolizes heroism and virility—the American icon of masculinity. Prince presents the image in a straightforward way, but omits the brand name and warning label. This lack of embellishment to the image, combined with the absence of text, highlights the predatory nature of advertising with stylized photographs that magnify machismo, but sell something harmful. The message of the glossy ads without the text—that real men command nature, real men are robust, real men smoke—is in itself ironic. That Prince makes it into art, not advertising, further parodies the Marlboro cowboy. His work poses the absurdity of such imagery: Is big corporate money copying life or defining it? In *On Photography*, Susan Sontag wrote, "Despite the presumption of

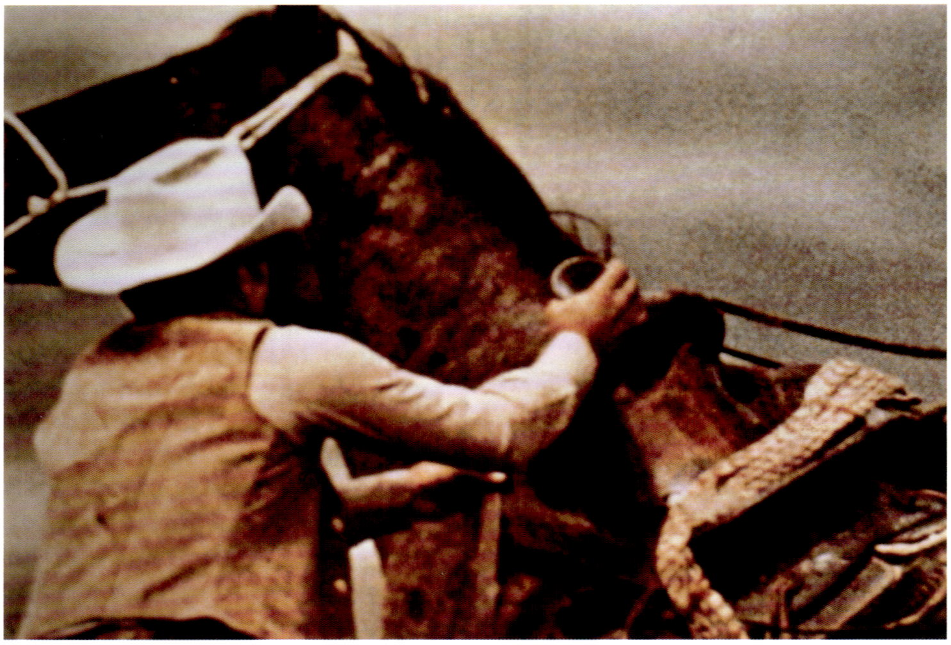

veracity that gives all photographs authority, interest, seductiveness, the work that photographers do is no generic exception to the usually shady commerce between art and truth. Even when photographers are most concerned with mirroring reality, they are still haunted by tacit imperatives of taste and conscience."[6] Prince uses photography's ability

The message of the glossy ads without the text —that real men command nature, real men are robust, real men smoke—is in itself ironic. That Prince makes it into art, not advertising, further parodies the Marlboro cowboy.

to generate desire in us to believe what we see by readily appealing to our mainstream taste and conscience, but his image also activates the idea of duplicities within it.

In 1983, Prince directly appropriated a controversial image of the prepubescent actress and model Brooke Shields, taken years earlier by commercial photographer Gary Gross in 1978 to promote the film *Pretty Baby*, directed by Louis Malle. His re-presented image came after scandal within the starlet's career and caused a stir in the art world and in the mainstream due to the depiction of Shields nude at such a tender age.[7]

Richard Prince
Untitled (Cowboys) #8, 1980–84
Ektacolor print, edition of 2
30 × 45 inches
Collection of the Modern Art Museum of Fort Worth, Museum purchase made possible by a grant from The Burnett Foundation
© Richard Prince

Prince titled the work *Spiritual America*, after a photograph with the same title taken by Alfred Stieglitz in 1923. Stieglitz's black-and-white photograph depicts a close-up view of a harnessed, castrated horse. A rare instance, at the time, of commentary through art on the state of America, Stieglitz's image of bridled energy and emasculated sexuality addresses the economically dismal years leading to the Great Depression.

For the display of his *Spiritual America*, Prince opened a makeshift gallery on Manhattan's Lower East Side. When viewers entered the space, they were faced with the single image of Shields, naked in an awkward frontal pose. Her glistening body, engulfed in a reddish-yellow glow, suggests sex appeal and womanliness, and also lack thereof. After exhibiting the work, Prince became the "purveyor of pornography, the pimp, the pedophile, the shady operator, the opportunist and the scandalmonger" for certain critics.[8] The isolation of both viewing the image without the advertising/commercial context and of seeing it as the sole work in the gallery was even too much for the ostensibly liberal art world, as it places the female child's body within the politics of gender and sexuality.

Cindy Sherman, who uses herself as a model, is always personifying someone else, usually averting her eyes away from us as viewers, in photographs that focus on female image-making. In the series *Untitled Film Stills*, 1977–80, she posed for sixty-nine black-and-white photographs to portray various Hollywood ingenues. The roles—femme fatale, "good" woman, career woman, troubled woman, housewife, damsel in

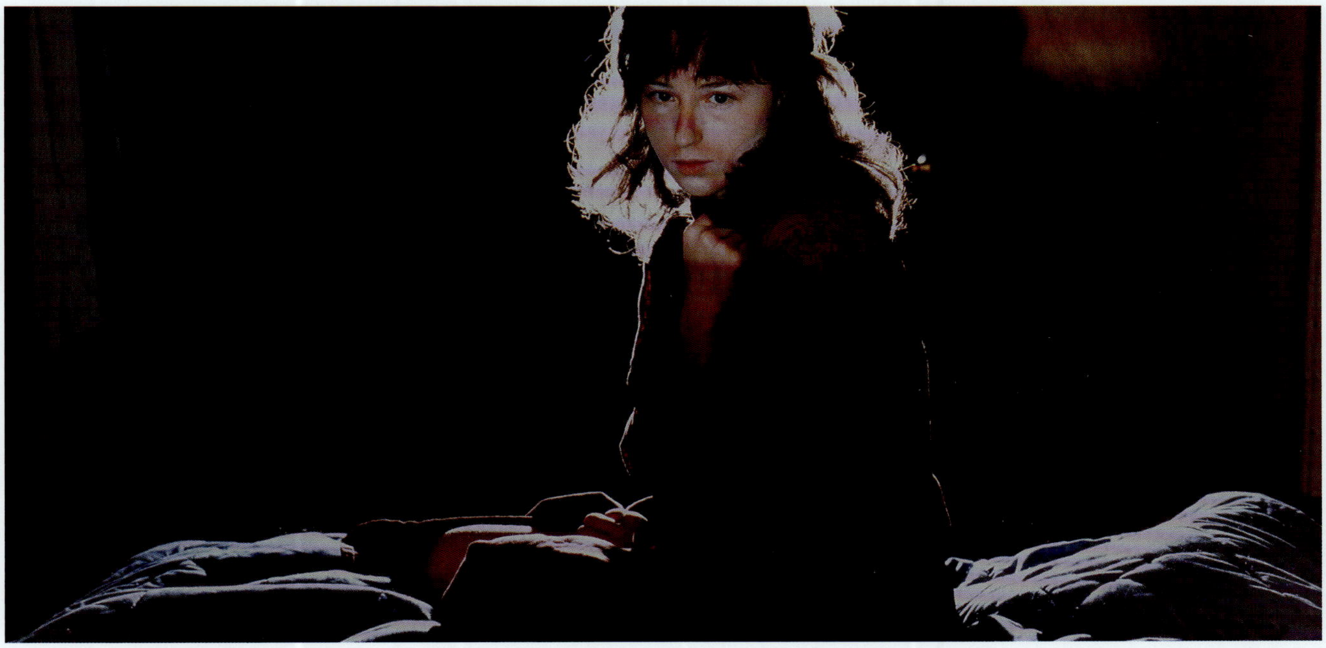

Cindy Sherman
Untitled, 1981
Cibachrome print
24 × 48 inches
Collection of the Modern Art Museum of Fort Worth,
Museum purchase made possible by a grant from
The Burnett Foundation

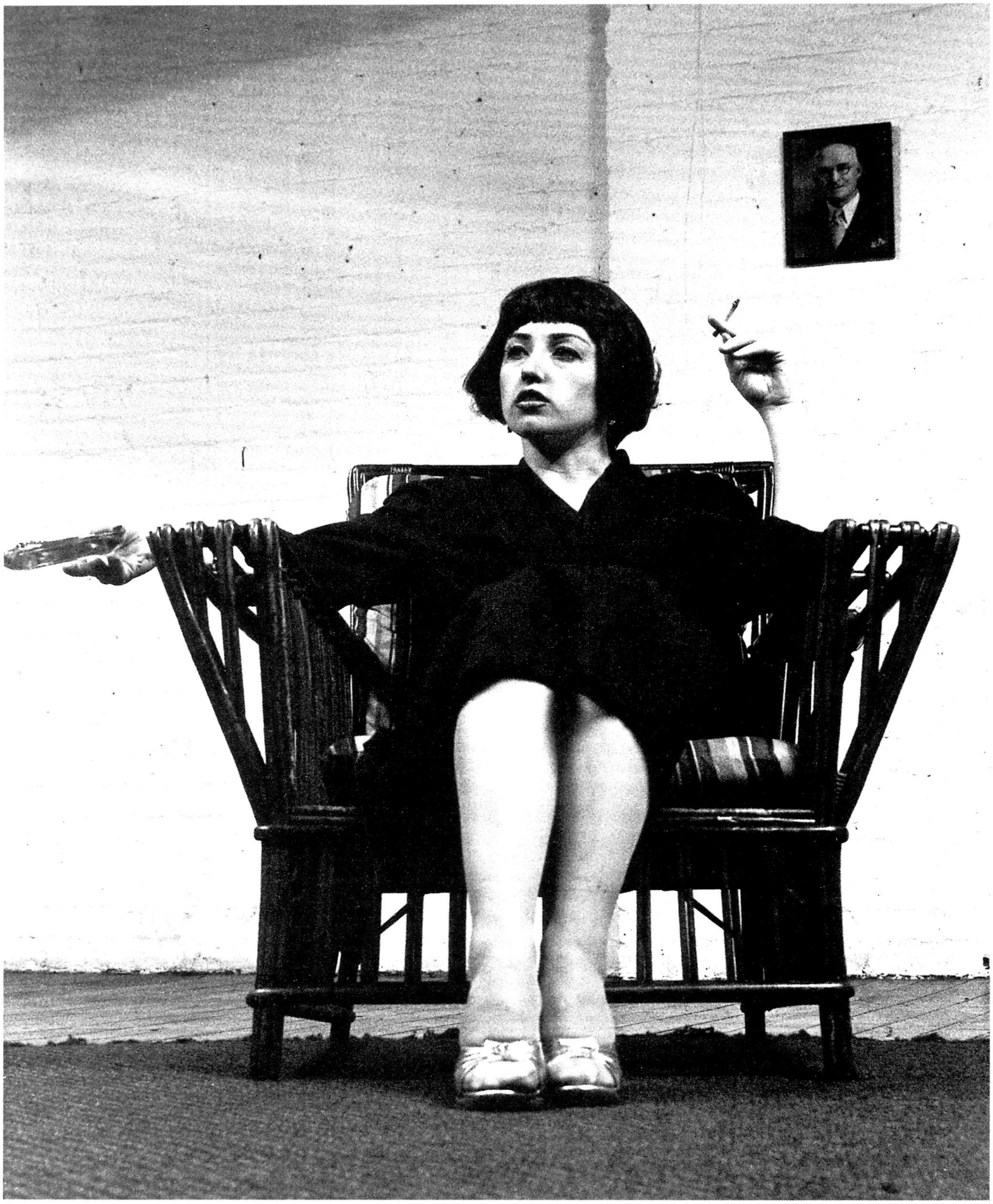

Cindy Sherman
Untitled Film Still #16, 1978
Gelatin silver print
40 × 30 inches
Aaron and Leslee Cowen, NY, NY
Image Courtesy of the Artist and Metro Pictures

distress, farm girl, rich girl, and temptress—were all inspired by 1950s and 1960s film noir, psycho-thrillers, melodramas, and B movies.

The entire series is numbered sequentially, like stills from existing movies, yet there is no reference to an actual movie frame. In this way, Sherman's *Film Stills* rouse familiarity, but with no story to back up

---

The woman's disposition in Sherman's image stirs feelings of melancholy and isolation, calling attention to internalized consequences for real women, who compare themselves to fictionalized versions of male desire.

---

the images, or as art critic Rosalind Krauss aptly described them, each is "a copy without an original."[9] The absence of narrative propels these works, at least for a moment, into the realm of reality—we cannot place the film exactly, so perhaps this is a real woman.

The question of reality signals the viewers' voyeurism: Is this something we are supposed to see, or are we intruding? Often depicting women as the object of the male gaze, the pictures go hand-in-hand with some of the most important feminist critics' works of the day. In her essay "Visual Pleasure and Narrative Cinema," 1973, Laura Mulvey wrote, "Woman stands in patriarchal culture as a signifier for the male other, bound by a symbolic order in which man can live out his fantasies and obsessions through linguistic command by imposing them on the silent image of woman still tied to her place as bearer of meaning, not maker of meaning."[10] By layering more artifice onto already contrived archetypes, Sherman presents a number of ironies, including that the pictures themselves are fakes of fakes; and she, as the female creator, puts herself in the traditional male roles of artistic maker and of Hollywood icon maker.

In *Untitled Film Still #16*, 1978, a forlorn brunette sits in a chair, smoking a cigarette and holding an ashtray. The image conflates and evokes a number of big-screen heroines, such as the tortured Joan Crawford in Robert Aldrich's film from 1962, *What Ever Happened to Baby Jane?* The scene is stark—just the woman, the chair, the cigarette, the ashtray, a rug, and a corner of a room. On the wall hangs a portrait resembling Harry S. Truman, the United States president from 1945 to 1953. This hint at Truman suggests narrative strands, even with the absence of a complete narrative: the woman is in America in the post–World War II era. This gives us as viewers context, but no resolve. Further, in this image, the woman's disposition stirs feelings of melancholy and isolation, calling attention to internalized consequences for real women, who compare themselves to fictionalized versions of male desire.

In the 1980s, Levine, Longo, Prince, and Sherman shared an impulse toward conceptual and performance art and toward the photograph, which aided in distancing them against the unique object and against modern art's heroic and elitist tendencies and preferences for painting and sculpture. Photography provided a way to merge the mechanisms of the media with fine art and to speak through a vehicle that also intertwines with each of us individually, since the camera is the primary tool used by most of us to document events, passages, and hallmarks in our personal lives. No longer consigned to the categories of "straight," traditional, or documentary in the art world, photography was the preferred medium to examine the anonymous, filmic, and commercialized images encountered in daily life by these artists in the '80s. Its slippery ability to move between reality and the contrived meant that it could speak to the social models of masculinity and femininity that sway our self-definitions.

The Personal as Public

Holzer's and Kruger's work in the 1980s adapted text and graphics from advertisements and consumer culture to replace a pervading masculine voice with a feminine viewpoint. They used the nonpersonal approach of Minimalism and conceptualism to bring social meaning to personal issues in works that are monumentally visible, legible, and publicly accessible. Their artistic endeavors, like those of Levine, Longo, Prince, and Sherman, are in line with postmodern theory, especially in their critique of the impact of culturally driven images of gender and power. Unlike the artists discussed as impersonal, however, Holzer's and Kruger's text-based works are not oblique, cool, or distant with regard to message; instead their tones are hot, provocative, and forthright.

Here photography is a springboard to go deeper into the influential offshoots within the language of advertising in the form of mass broadcasts, posters, and signage. Media-savvy Holzer and Kruger synthesize the visually packed world around them, operating within the blended languages of postmodernism, politics, psychoanalysis, feminism, consumerism, television, and pop culture to create works that "advertise" stereotypes, plain truths, mock political rhetoric, and clichés. "The age of photography," wrote Roland Barthes in 1980, "corresponds precisely to the explosion of the private into the public, or rather into the creation of a new social value, which is the publicity of the private."[11]

When Jenny Holzer was part of the Whitney Museum of American Art's prestigious Independent Study Program from 1976 to 1977, she began to write a series of one-liners that combined personal philosophy with conventional wisdom, calling the works *Truisms*. The alphabetical listings (which number more than 250), presented in an official-seeming jargon as if they were public service announcements, were placed anonymously on posters throughout New York City, made into T-shirts and stickers, and carved into public stone benches:

> A MAN CAN'T KNOW WHAT IT'S LIKE TO BE A MOTHER
> BEING JUDGMENTAL IS A SIGN OF LIFE
> CHILDREN ARE THE MOST CRUEL OF ALL
> MONEY CREATES TASTE
> POLITICS IS USED FOR PERSONAL GAIN
> SEX DIFFERENCES ARE HERE TO STAY
> YOUR OLDEST FEARS ARE THE WORST ONES

Oscillating between being disturbing, humorous, and confrontational, these works activate and engage public discourse.

Holzer was invited to present her work on the new Spectacolor board in Times Square in 1982. This was the first time she showed her statements in the form of scrolling LED signs, for which she is now best known. The texts included some of her *Truisms* and were from what she would publish as her *Survival* series, 1983–85. Reaching an enormous audience in this forum, the distilled sentences spoke to the absurdities of contemporary life with clarity and conviction. The artist's use of unconventional methods and language also challenged the aesthetic tradition of what could be considered art and where it could be shown. In other words, Holzer instigated a dialogue between the nature of art shown in institutional settings and accepted modes of operating within society and turned away from the implicit heroic and authoritative *male* pronouncement, toward a candid and overtly *female* voice. Her enterprising artistic career changed the face of art, evidenced by her winning the most prestigious honor awarded to contemporary artists, the Golden Lion at the Venice Biennale, where, in 1990, her LED signboards and marble benches were featured in the American Pavilion as the first female artist to represent the United States.

A graphic designer, art director, picture editor, then later poet, writer, curator, and professor, Barbara Kruger added serious artmaking to her

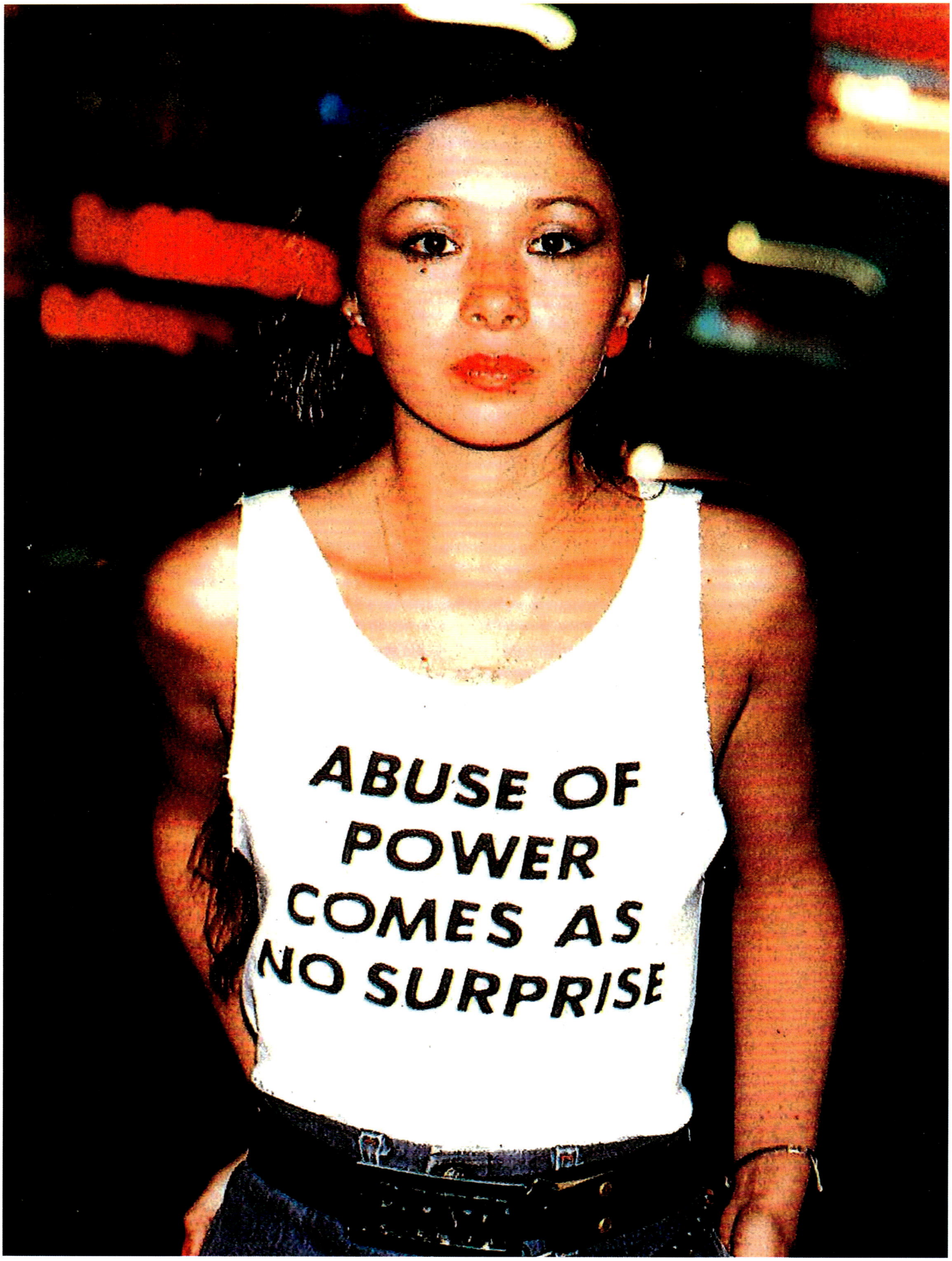
ABUSE OF
POWER
COMES AS
NO SURPRISE

multidisciplinary practice in the early 1970s, after studying art under Diane Arbus at Parsons School of Design. Introduced to the Pacific Film Archive while teaching at Berkeley in the late 1970s, Kruger

Kruger's well-known work *Untitled (I shop therefore I am)*, 1987, turns the Cartesian philosophical statement "I think therefore I am" away from humanity's essence hinging on individual intellect, to echo contemporary cultural drives toward capitalism and the vapid nature of consumerism.

returned to New York in 1979 and made experimental films and collages of appropriated images with words superimposed onto them. Later that year, she began to use existing black-and-white photographs from the 1940s and 1950s juxtaposed with her own text in Futura Bold Italic typeface. The works were framed in red lacquered wood. Eventually she began to use black-and-white images with red, black, and white text to address the public in the form of billboards, posters, merchandise, and architectural projects. Kruger was influenced by the look of journalism and skilled at editing, and her pragmatic, daring phrases speak to and challenge the public spectator with gender-centric topics. Works such as *Untitled (Your gaze hits the side of my face)*, 1981, illustrating the profile of a classical female statue with the words of the title in black blocks and white text, framed in red, became touchstones for feminist and postmodern critics and scholars. This was true especially because it, and much of her work, contests the dominant male gaze and the female as being gazed upon. That she is a woman also brings to bear the idea that female artists were historically, and are still, underrepresented in the art world.

Kruger's well-known work *Untitled (I shop therefore I am)*, 1987, turns the Cartesian philosophical statement "I think therefore I am" away from humanity's essence hinging on individual intellect, to echo contemporary cultural drives toward capitalism and the vapid nature of consumerism, with status symbols replacing thought to define the self. The "I" places self-analysis, feminism, and classism at center stage, like in her other works that use pronouns such as you, we, and they—"Your body is a battleground." Her recognizable phrases and images are often described as "slogans," though they are originated by her rather

Lady Pink photographed in Times Square,
July 1983, wearing a T-shirt by Jenny Holzer
from *Truisms* (1977–79), 1983

than being actual cultural mottoes created by political or media machines. Kruger's influence has spread (ironically) to the very thing she critiques, the consumer world, both in terms of her products being sold and her influence on commercial art in general. Her visual style and use of directives in the form of an "ad" has connected with a younger generation of artists—Shepard Fairey's "OBEY" campaign begun in 1990 comes to mind.

Using media as a vehicle as Holzer and Kruger did in the 1980s is not without precedent. In November of 1974, New York's rising art star Lynda Benglis placed a series of "ads" in the most prominent art magazine of the day, *Artforum*, to announce her upcoming exhibition at Paula Cooper Gallery. The image shows the artist, nude, with sexy tan lines, wearing nothing but cat-eye sunglasses and holding a giant dildo between her thighs. Defiant and erotic, the ads took the art world by storm. With a commercialized image, Benglis indicated that male power, authority, and aggression were alive and well in the art world in the '70s; with their works in the guise of media, Holzer and Kruger questioned power and gender constructs in culture-at-large the following decade.

The Confessional

In a parallel but contrasting approach to the mimetic and impersonal style of Levine, Longo, Prince, and Sherman, or the mock-ad-campaign framework of Holzer and Kruger, is the more ad-libbed imagery of Goldin and the work of Mapplethorpe, which often walks the line between real and idealized. Beginning in the late 1970s, these two artists assumed diaristic tones that offered intensely private and often taboo glimpses of themselves and their friends. The images are "confessional" in that the artists are implicated in them, each boldly autobiographical to explore gender roles, sexuality, and life in general.

Goldin's and Mapplethorpe's works adapt, albeit in divergent styles, elements of a "street" aesthetic, famously explored first by Henri Cartier-Bresson, and others who came after him. The artists also migrated toward what is often described as the marginalized within society, though the people depicted in their pictures were part of their inner circles and, therefore, not on the periphery to them. Diane Arbus, before them, had taken up people on the fringe as subject matter, and while she influenced Goldin and Mapplethorpe, she documented people from an outsider's perspective, not as a participant, as they did. Because they operated in the zone of reality, and they were part of the street scene they recorded, to varying degrees their pictures became sensationalized both for what they portrayed and for their coming from a personal viewpoint.

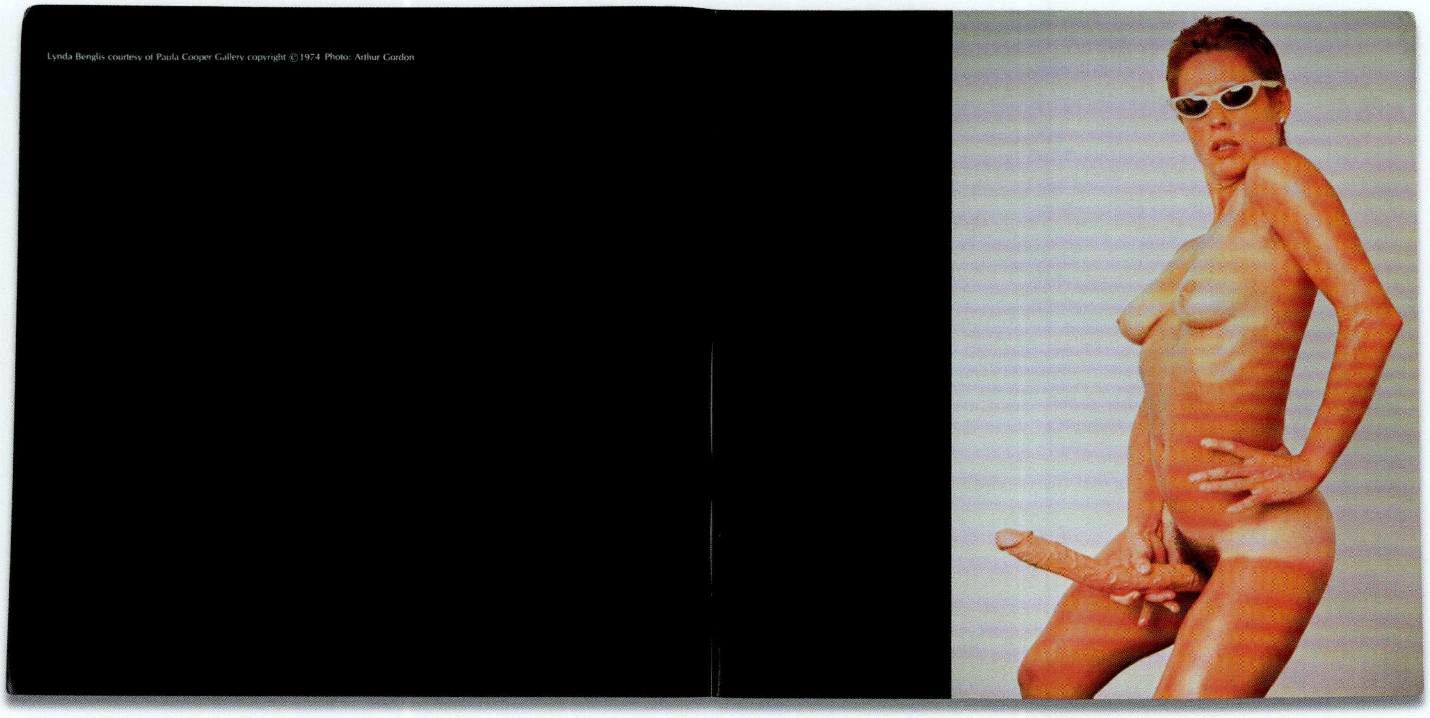

Though they represent slices of reality, their works are framed, in a sense: Goldin's in that she actively shaped a view of herself and her world by documenting, publishing, and exhibiting her life with frankness, but also with narration, to tell the tales of bittersweet love stories, junkies (Goldin was an addict herself until the late 1980s), drag queens (in her early work), domestic quarreling, and sleazy goings-on in hundreds of photographs that are now remembrances of her world at the time; Mapplethorpe's in that he choreographed and controlled the printing of his most important pictures. Goldin employed a "snapshot" aesthetic, whereas Mapplethorpe looked to classic black-and-white photography as inspiration for his visual style. Each artist created poignant pictures that document an era and a place. In their works, narrative is derived by their decisions behind and in front of the camera, and the power of the images lies in their bluntness in exposing unconventional paths to self-exploration and discovery.

Upon finishing art school in Boston, Nan Goldin moved to New York in the late 1970s. Shortly after relocating, she began chronicling her social scene—the post-punk, gay, transgender, and hard-core drug users of the Bowery. This style of taking pictures would eventually lead to her pivotal work, *The Ballad of Sexual Dependency*, 1973–86. The portfolio, exhibited in slide or print form, takes its title from a song in Bertolt Brecht's 1928 *The Threepenny Opera*, an adaptation of *The Beggar's*

Lynda Benglis
Ad in *Artforum*, November 1974
Art © Lynda Benglis/Licensed by VAGA, New York, NY
Photograph Courtesy Cheim & Read, New York

Opera of 1728, which is a socialist critique of a capitalist world. Like the opera, the works in *Ballad* are melancholic. They are also unflinching in their presentations of the artist and her extended family, or her "tribe," as

There is a compassionate and intimate side to the images in *Ballad*—they express a basic need for human dependency, even if dysfunctional, and they reveal the struggles of relationships, coming of age, and nonconformity.

she has called them. The informal vignettes that make up *Ballad* depict her, her lovers, friends, and other couples in states ranging from distress, ecstasy, or the mundane, through travels, partying, home life, abuse, sex, and addiction. There is a compassionate and intimate side to these images—they express a basic need for human dependency, even if dysfunctional, and they reveal the struggles of relationships, coming of age, and nonconformity. By the time it was published as a book in

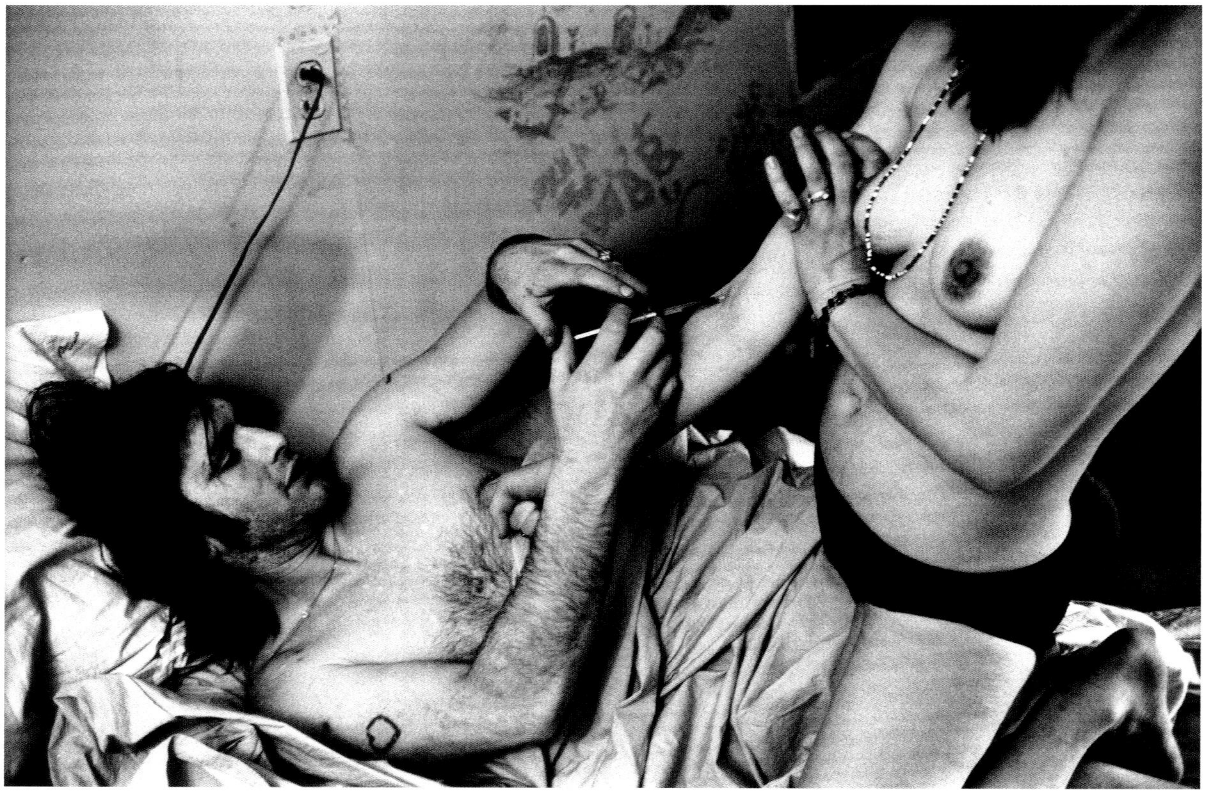

Larry Clark
Untitled, 1971
Black-and-white photograph
11 × 14 inches
Courtesy of the Artist and Luhring Augustine, New York

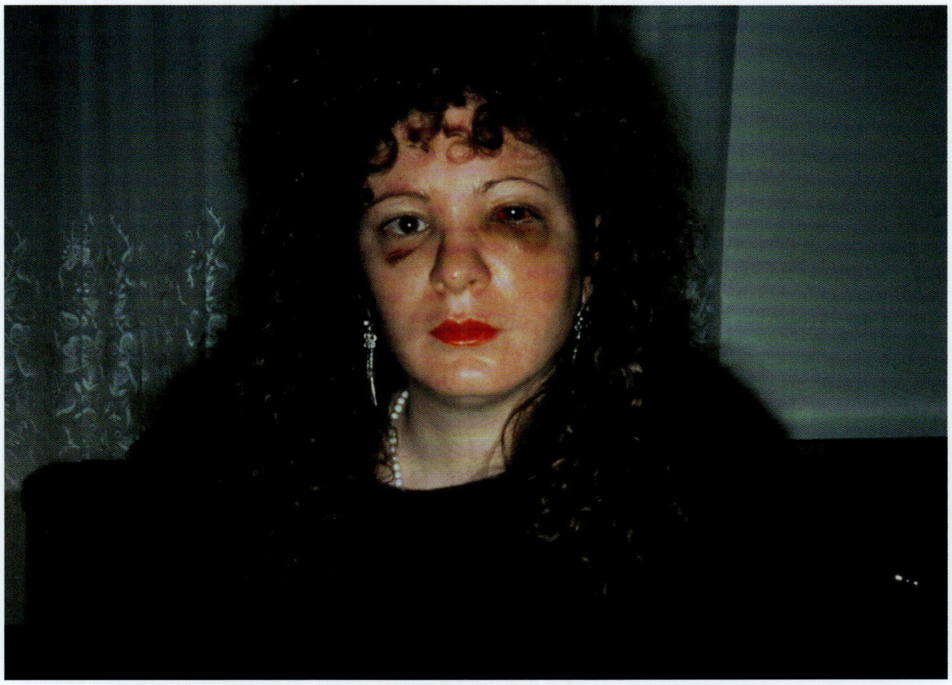

1986, *Ballad* was a sort of epilogue to the many people depicted in the photographs who died mostly from AIDS, which was an epidemic by then. It was also the culmination of, and tribute to, a generation. "I still believe pictures can preserve life," Goldin wrote in 1996 in the afterword for a reprinting of the images in *Ballad*, a decade after it was first published. "The pictures in the *Ballad* haven't changed. But Cookie is dead, Kenny is dead, Mark is dead, Max is dead, Vittorio is dead. So for me, the book is now a volume of loss, while still a ballad of love."[12]

Goldin's work extends the documentary aesthetic of Arbus and others who convey a street style, especially Larry Clark. Clark's black-and-white photo-essay published in 1971, *Tulsa*, in which he chronicled his hometown friends in Tulsa, Oklahoma, engaged in sexual acts, gunplay, violence, and drug abuse, creates a direct lineage to Goldin. Both Clark and Goldin have been criticized for glamorizing drug use and, even as insiders as they both were, accused of exploiting their friends. Both have also been praised for their groundbreaking influence and daring presentations. Goldin's work, in particular, might be seen as a direct influence on a young generation of artists, such as Dash Snow, known for photographing his social circle of New York City artists by portraying sex, drugs, violence, and art world pretense. Snow sadly died in 2009, succumbing to drug overdose. His friend, Ryan McGinley, whose work also traces to Goldin's, continues to explore notions of identity through portrayals of his friends' gay and straight encounters and by showing their moments

Nan Goldin
Nan after being battered
(from *The Ballad of Sexual Dependency*), 1984
Cibachrome
Image 9⅞ × 13½ inches; Sheet 11 × 14 inches
© Nan Goldin, Courtesy Matthew Marks Gallery

of self-discovery through photographs in works such as the self-published *The Kids Are Alright*, 2000, that catapulted him into the art world.

Robert Mapplethorpe studied art (mostly painting and drawing) at Pratt Institute in Brooklyn in 1963. In 1970, he began to use a Polaroid camera to take pictures of his cohorts, which included fellow artists, musicians, socialites, gay porn stars, and S&M practitioners. "Somebody gave me a Polaroid camera," Mapplethorpe explained in an interview

---

Goldin, Levine, Longo, Holzer, Kruger, Mapplethorpe, Prince, and Sherman each personify gender in varying ways to speak to its complexities and reflect the contradictory ethos of the 1980s—feminism, gay pride, otherness or difference, the conservatism of the Reagan/Thatcher years, and persistent patriarchal authority.

---

conducted by artist Robert Indiana for *Bomb Magazine* in 1988. "For years I worked solely with the Polaroid. Which is how I developed my whole style: instant playback."[13] The extent of "instant playback" in his imagery morphed during his career, from life unfolding before the camera to flawless black-and-white gelatin silver prints, inspired by life, but set up behind the viewfinder and in the darkroom. His most important series include self-portraits, male and female nudes, portraits, still-life flowers, and statuary. The explicit nature of the gay scene and S&M underbelly of New York City's Lower East Side—though masterfully executed as photographs—reached beyond sexual "norms" politically and socially at the time they were made, sparking scandal and later becoming a battle cry for conservatives in the culture wars of 1989.[14] In these pictures, Mapplethorpe applied traditional aesthetics to raw subject matter, which (though Clark and Goldin did a similar thing with more casually shot imagery) had never before been offered in the mode of serious, classical portraiture.

Like Goldin's work, Mapplethorpe's pictures flesh out self-exploration. In his case, a long-term series of self-portraits showing various good-guy/bad-guy scenarios, sometimes in drag, other times projecting a butch image or donning devil horns, reveals multiple personae, often linked to his sexual explorations. The artist even made a haunting late image of himself, *Self Portrait*, 1988, one year before his death from complications with AIDS. His handsome visage appears gaunt in the image, his eyes

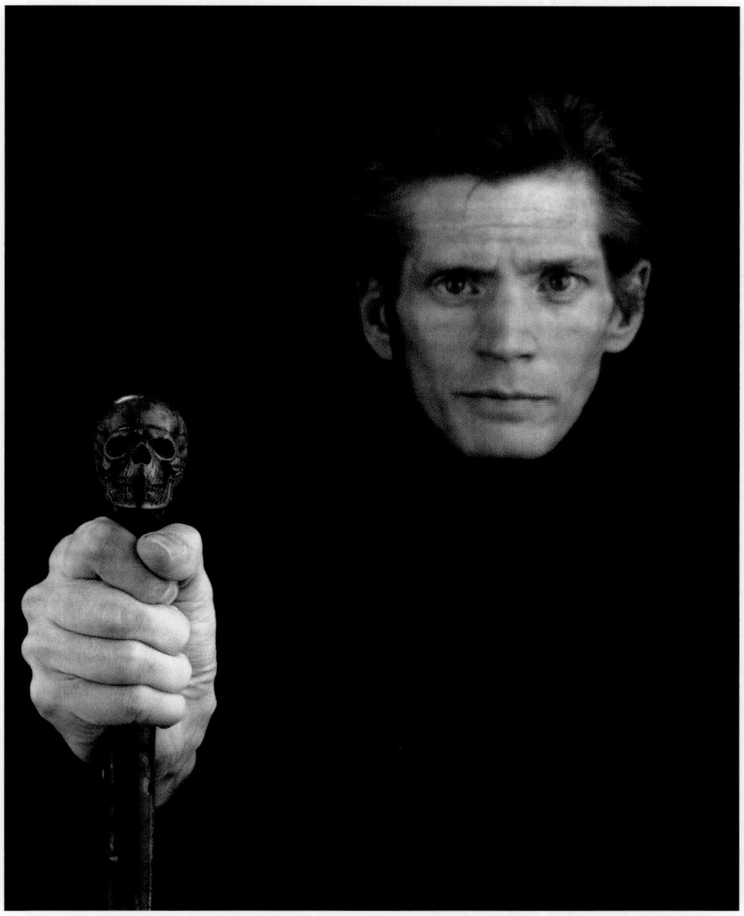

weary. His head is in the background and appears disembodied as his black turtleneck blends into the surrounding darkness. In sharp focus in the foreground is his hand, clutching a cane topped by a skull—the picture makes a striking comparison between the two heads. Echoing Susan Sontag's words, "All photographs are memento mori. To take a photograph is to participate in another person's (or thing's) mortality, vulnerability, mutability,"[15] Mapplethorpe's image relies on photography's ability to signal this transience by its very nature of capturing a fleeting moment, and, in this case, documenting his own impending death. His body of work takes us through his journey of exploring not only sexuality, but also the cycle of life.

Goldin, Levine, Longo, Holzer, Kruger, Mapplethorpe, Prince, and Sherman each personify gender in varying ways to speak to its complexities and reflect the contradictory ethos of the 1980s—feminism, gay pride, otherness or difference, the conservatism of the Reagan/Thatcher years, and persistent patriarchal authority. In the process, they define the art of a generation as photograph-based and pluralistic in its view

Robert Mapplethorpe
Self Portrait, 1988
Silver gelatin print
24 × 20 inches

of what constitutes art. They were publicly minded in their portrayals and critiques of gender constructs and in those constructs' symbiotic relationship to the nature of representation, whether from the standpoint of the impersonal, the personal as public, or the confessional.

These ideas of artistic personality, infiltrated with references to advertisement, media, and photography used as a means to explore representation, were handed down largely from the life and work of Andy Warhol. Warhol carefully crafted a public persona, in part to make fashionable his own effeminate and asexual gender attributes in ways that were fluctuating and oblique in contrast to the masculine, heroic personalities of the Abstract Expressionists. Further, Warhol replicated aspects of commercial and celebrity worlds in photo-based, off-register silkscreens that propelled him and the New York art world into rock-star status. According to critic Robert Hughes in his essay "The Rise of Andy Warhol," Warhol's only subject "was detachment: The condition of being a spectator, dealing hands-off with the world through the filter of photography."[16] This detachment through photography surely manifests in the works of Longo, Prince, Sherman, and Levine. In an interview for *Arts Magazine* in the summer of 1985, Levine explained, "There's an emptiness in Warhol's work that's always been very interesting to me. There are three spaces: the original image, his image, and then a space in between, a sort of Zen emptiness."[17] That Zen emptiness goes back to what Crimp called "psychological resonance" in the catalogue for *Pictures*. And like Warhol, media tools are used, but turned on their heads in the works of Kruger and Holzer. Mapplethorpe and Sherman share Warhol's affinity for exploring personae in their pictures; and Warhol's family of factory kids in the 1960s, made up mostly of societal misfits (transvestites, drug addicts, etc.) is similar to the subjects in Goldin's and Mapplethorpe's New York City subculture photography.

In 1968, Warhol famously coined the phrase, "In the future, everyone will be world-famous for fifteen minutes,"[18] a statement that proved truer in the 1980s, the age of MTV, the inception of the information era (the first Personal Computer was introduced by IBM in 1981), and the dawning of globalization. The generation of artists after Warhol, including each artist discussed in this essay, brings to light multiple personalities, broadening the notion of fame and its pervasive impact on how we define ourselves. Today Warhol's statement is true beyond his wildest dreams, with smartphones, social media, and YouTube making it possible for anyone to post or view the formerly private moments of life. The camera in the 1980s and its branches into the world of advertising, though outmoded now, could be seen as the launch of this tendency, with Goldin, Levine, Longo, Mapplethorpe, Prince, and Sherman forging truths and deceptions out of images, and with Holzer and Kruger shaping mental pictures of our world out of words.

1 For further reading, see texts by Roland Barthes, Jean Baudrillard, Benjamin Buchloh, Hal Foster, Michel Foucault, Fredric Jameson, Rosalind Krauss, Lucy Lippard, Laura Mulvey, Craig Owens, Abigail Solomon-Godeau, and others in *Art After Modernism: Rethinking Representation*, ed. Brian Wallis (New York: The New Museum of Contemporary Art, 1984).

2 Another inroad for photography in the works of many of these artists—Kruger, Prince, and Mapplethorpe, for example—was that they had worked in the field of commercial photography.

3 For further reading on the Pictures Generation, see Douglas Crimp, *Pictures: An Exhibition of the Work of Troy Brauntuch, Jack Goldstein, Sherrie Levine, Robert Longo, Philip Smith* (New York: Committee for the Visual Arts, 1977); and a follow-up article in *October*, vol. 8 (Spring 1979), and reprinted in *Art After Modernism: Rethinking Representation*, 1984, 175–188. Crimp takes Michael Fried's seminal article "Art and Objecthood," 1967, which criticized Minimalism for its theatricality, as a starting point to argue that, just as Fried had predicted in relationship to Minimalism, theatricality, or the staged, had infiltrated Minimalism and had moved through it and into the works of the Pictures Generation. These shifts sealed the end of late Modernism and created a new paradigm, according to Crimp, in which transcendence through high art is usurped by the repurposed, representational image.

4 For further reading, see: Jacques Lacan, *Écrits: The First Complete Edition in English* (New York: W. W. Norton & Co., 2006); Michel Foucault, *Discipline and Punish: The Birth of the Prison* (New York: Pantheon Books, 1977); and Laura Mulvey, "Visual Pleasure and Narrative Cinema," *Screen* 16.3 (Autumn 1975): 6–18.

5 Robert Longo in a video interview, "Robert Longo: Man in the City," *Nowness*, June 18, 2013, accessed March 2014, http://www.nowness.com/day/2013/6/18/3111/robert-longo-man-in-the-city.

6 Susan Sontag, *On Photography* (New York: Anchor Books Doubleday, 1973), 6.

7 In the late 1970s and early 1980s, Shields was featured in a provocative television commercial for Calvin Klein jeans. In the commercial, the thirteen-year-old Shields, wearing tight jeans and lying on her back with her legs reaching upward, suggestively asks, "You know what comes between me and my Calvin's? Nothing." The ad generated a range of interpretations, from youth empowerment to obscenity. Nevertheless, Klein, capitalizing on the controversy swirling around Louis Malle's 1978 film *Pretty Baby*, which featured Shields and addressed the taboo subject of child prostitution, created one of the most controversial—and successful—ad campaigns in Madison Avenue history.

8 Rosetta Brooks, "Spiritual America: No Holds Barred," in *Richard Prince*, ed. Lisa Phillips (New York: Whitney Museum of American Art and Harry N. Abrams, 1992), 90.

9 Rosalind Krauss, *Cindy Sherman 1975–1993* (New York: Rizzoli International Publications, Inc., 1993), 17.

10 Mulvey, "Visual Pleasure and Narrative Cinema," in *Art After Modernism*, 362

11 Roland Barthes, *Camera Lucida: Reflections on Photography* (London: Fontana, 1982), 98.

12 Nan Goldin, "Afterword," in *The Ballad of Sexual Dependency* (New York: Aperture Foundation, Inc., 1996), 146.

13 Robert Mapplethorpe in an interview with Gary Indiana, *Bomb Magazine* 22 (Winter 1988), accessed March 2014, http://bombmagazine.org/article/1003/robert-mapplethorpe.

14 Along with other artists, such as Andres Serrano, who were protested against during the culture wars of the late 1980s, Robert Mapplethorpe was targeted, especially for his imagery of explicit representations of homosexuality and underground bondage. This was particularly so because his postmortem retrospective *Robert Mapplethorpe: The Perfect Moment* was funded, in part, by the government's National Endowment for the Arts. The highly publicized argument between the religious and conservative right and left-wing citizens and politicians instigated anger and protest on both sides, on a national level. Issues of obscenity, censorship, first-amendment rights, and how taxpayers' dollars are spent were at the heart of this debate.

15 Sontag, *On Photography*, 15.

16 Robert Hughes, "The Rise of Andy Warhol," in *Art After Modernism: Rethinking Representation*, 49.

17 Sherrie Levine, quoted in Jeanne Siegel, "After Sherrie Levine," *Arts Magazine* 59 (June 1985): 141–44.

18 Andy Warhol, quoted in Pontus Hultén, *Andy Warhol* (Stockholm: Moderna Museet, 1968).

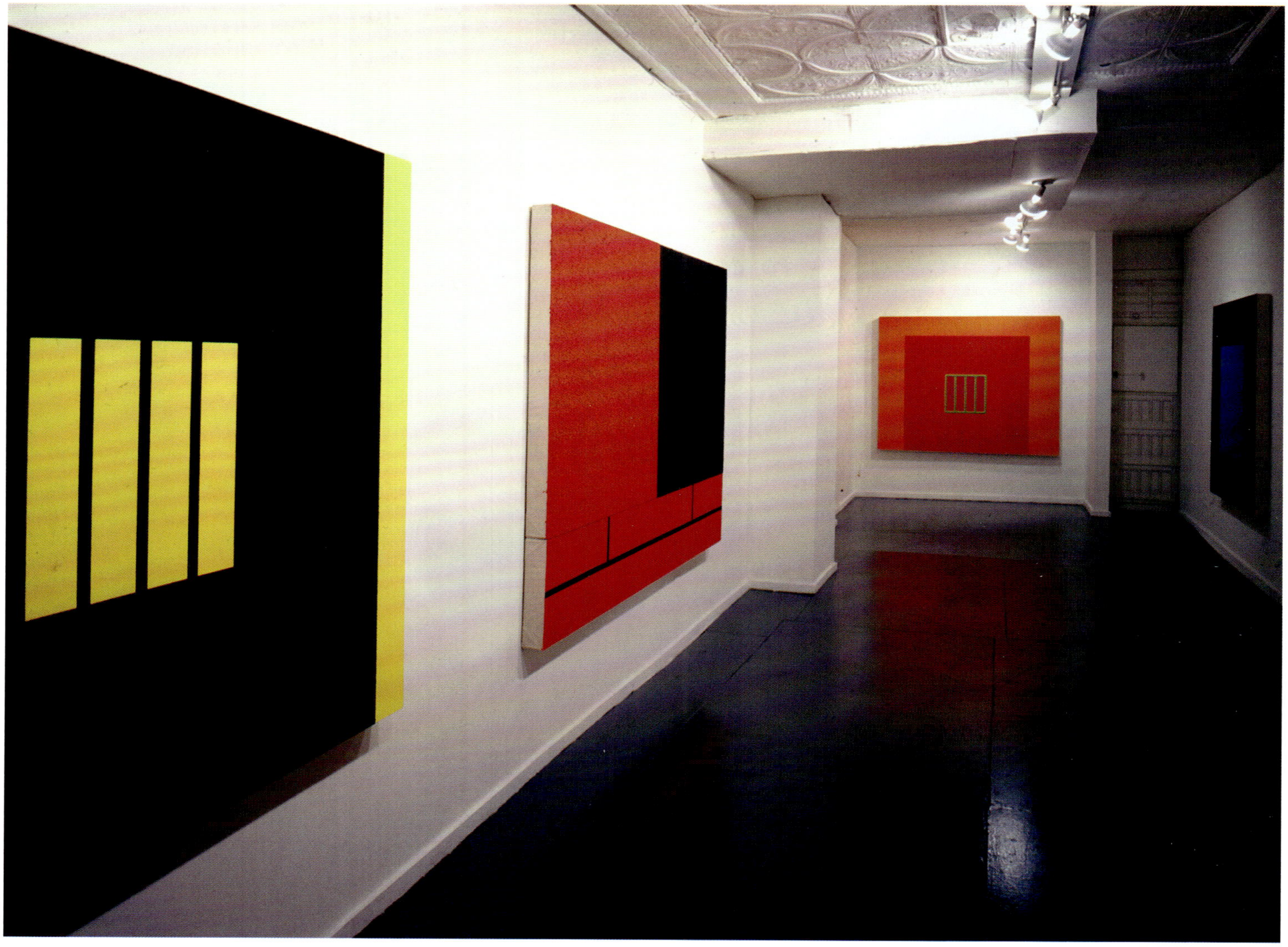

Peter Halley's first solo exhibition
at International with Monument
in New York's East Village
April 1985
Courtesy of the Artist

Keeping It Real: The Impure Abstractions of Ross Bleckner, Troy Brauntuch, Peter Halley, Donald Sultan, Philip Taaffe, and Christopher Wool

Alison Hearst

There is something ridiculous and miserly in the myth we inherit from abstract art. That painting is autonomous, pure and for itself, therefore we habitually analyze its ingredients and define its limits. But painting is "impure." It is the adjustment of "impurities" which forces its continuity. We are image-makers and image-ridden.—Philip Guston[1]

The '80s Began with Guston

In 1980, the artist Philip Guston died. His influence loomed large in New York throughout the following decade, and as the painter Terry Winters aptly stated, "The '80s began with Guston."[2] Guston, like his contemporaries Willem de Kooning and Jackson Pollock, was a member of the New York School and an Abstract Expressionist painter in the mid-twentieth century. Yet, as the epigraph attests, the artist questioned abstraction's established philosophies and set parameters,[3] and he eventually withdrew from the practice around 1968. For the next decade, until his death, Guston returned to "image-making," creating some of his best-known works. These works are noted for their characteristic blocky, cartoonlike figures and representations of quotidian objects, such as shoes, albeit in an abstracted manner. Countering modernist abstraction's requisites for pureness and autonomy, Guston's last period of art production favored impurity in painting as he saw the need to connect to broader contexts beyond himself and the frame, often through figuration. Guston's attitude toward the impure set the tone for the 1980s, specifically in regard to the reinvestigation of painting by emerging and mid-career artists alike. He became a strong influence on both the abstract and Neo-Expressionist movements in New York.

In investigating the abstract—and abstracted—paintings of six New York–based artists in the 1980s, Ross Bleckner, Troy Brauntuch, Peter Halley, Donald Sultan, Philip Taaffe, and Christopher Wool, it becomes clear how these artists continued Guston's critical break with the aesthetic pedigree of late-modernist abstraction in favor of a hybrid, impure approach to abstract painting. Refuting formalist purity and the visualization of emotion, these artists pushed the prior parameters of abstraction by infusing their works with images, language, or signs that specifically denote the 1980s cultural milieu. It is important to note that Guston's attitude toward what he saw as an impasse in modernist abstraction reverberates throughout these varied works. Moreover, these artists are, in many cases, only related by preconditions and shared ideas and not by a unified practice. As postmodern painters in the '80s, they also followed Frank Stella's disavowal of the emotional "inner self" in painting, arguably one of Stella's most significant contributions toward postmodernism.[4] Considerably closely tied to appropriation art, these artists sometimes also emulated abstraction and used prior iterations of the style as ready-made citations in order to critique abstraction from within.[5] Furthermore, they also bucked the fiercely emotional Neo-Expressionist approach to painting (exemplified by the work of Julian Schnabel, David Salle, and Eric Fischl), which was making a more visible mark on the New York art world and market at the time.

As Guston's rejection of abstraction resounds throughout the 1980s in the work of these six artists, it is important to briefly explain what Guston and these New York painters were up against: the essentializing character of formalist abstraction. At its inception in the early twentieth century, abstraction—such as the European avant-garde work of Wassily Kandinsky and Piet Mondrian—was energetic, utopian, and often motivated by natural and man-made forms. Aligned with the opinions of many historians, artists, and critics, artist Peter Halley stated that abstraction shifted in the mid-twentieth century when the essentialist formalism of postwar art critics Alfred Barr and Clement Greenberg "relocated abstraction in a tightly-locked garden of Kantian design where cultural power has been all too content to keep it for all these years."[6] The tenets of the highly influential Barr and Greenberg argued that abstraction, particularly Abstract Expressionism in the United States, was purely formal and self-sufficient—not tied to anything beyond the artist and the frame of the canvas. Barr's view that an artwork was best appreciated for its color, line, and composition,[7] demonstrates that

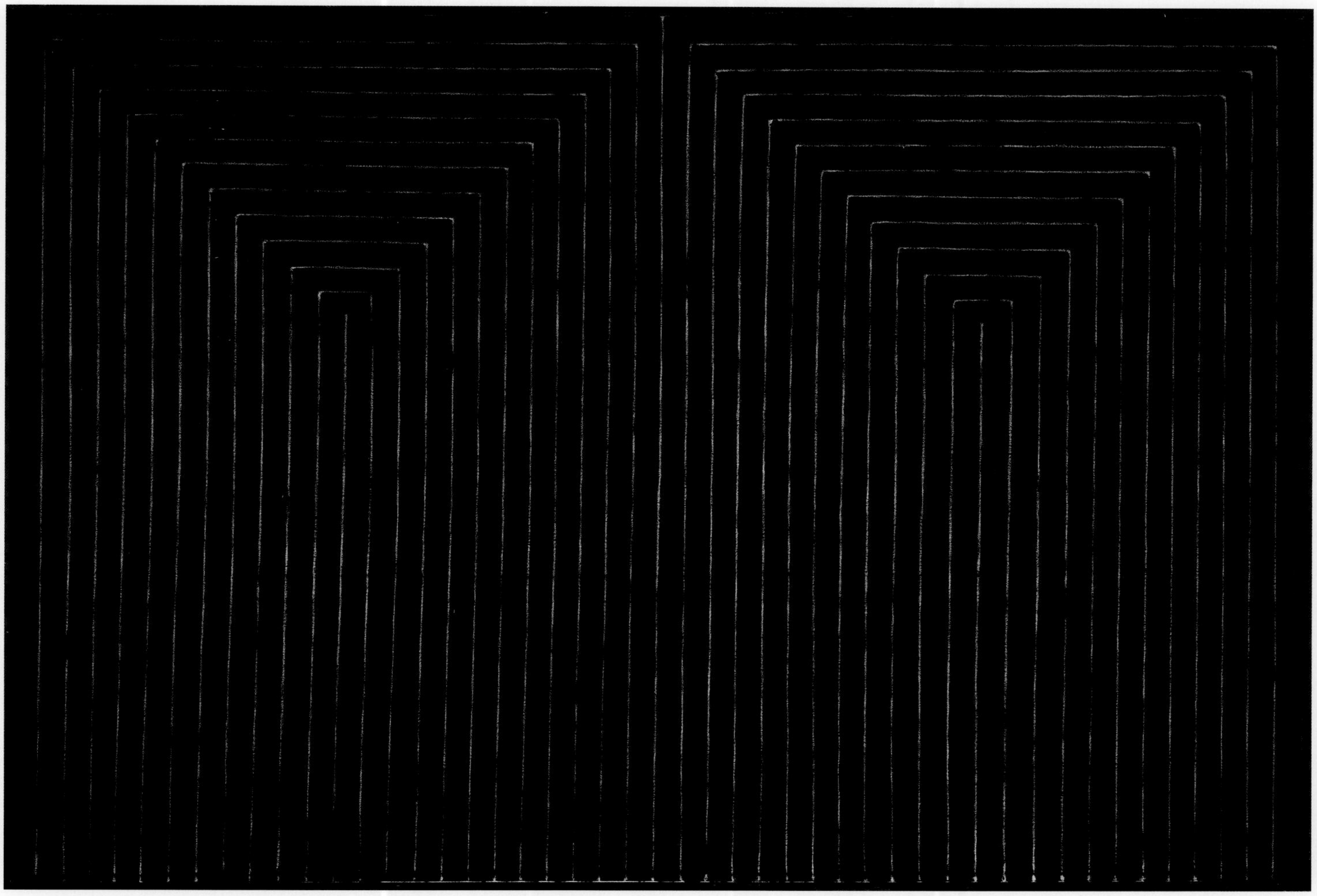

subject matter was no longer viewed as a viable ingredient in abstract painting.[8] New York Abstract Expressionism set forth to exemplify absolute feeling and the metaphysical, and it was large in scale, performative in execution, emphatically nonrepresentational, and often considered to be "high-strung" compared to the earlier abstract styles in avant-garde Europe.[9] Stella extended abstraction further in the late 1950s and 1960s with a push toward minimalism. While he adhered to the Greenbergian sense of medium specificity—where the unique physical characteristics of paint are emphasized rather than illusionistic space—his often-quoted "what you see is what you see" approach to abstract painting promoted the canvas as more of an impersonal, literal object rather than a window onto the metaphysical realm or self.

Many art historians believe that Greenbergian formalism was so successful at rationalizing the gradual elimination of illusionism and space that it continues to be the primary history.[10] As the foremost

Frank Stella
The Marriage of Reason and Squalor, II, 1959
Enamel on canvas
90¾ × 132¾ inches
The Museum of Modern Art, New York, Larry Aldrich Foundation Fund

philosophy, Greenberg's and Barr's rigid principles had a weighty, dogmatic effect on both criticism and painting after 1940.[11] According to this formalist ideology, the nearly century-long history of modernism was merely a path leading up to medium self-sufficiency, with the monochrome field or the grid acting as painting's grand finales.[12] With his black-on-black paintings in the 1960s, Ad Reinhardt claimed he was

Working against the mainstream, these abstract painters set forth to critically engage and relocate abstraction to a broader cultural context and aimed to prove that the reductive history of abstraction and its subsequent endgame, the grid or monochrome, was null and void.

"making the last paintings which anyone can make,"[13] and with this, like many other artists, he attempted to usher in the death of painting. Formalist abstraction's essentializing story line seemed to have reached its predicted conclusion, and many artists in the 1960s began turning to other media and practices.[14] For the next two decades, painterly abstraction was mostly disregarded in favor of Pop, conceptual art, and minimalist objects, yet it never really ceased to exist.[15]

While abstract painting was mostly marginalized in the second half of the twentieth century, artists like Bleckner, Brauntuch, Halley, Sultan, Taaffe, and Wool, although distinctly varied, challenged abstraction in the 1980s by breaking its presumed rules and rigidity—the same conventions that Guston denounced. Working against the mainstream, these abstract painters set forth to critically engage and relocate abstraction to a broader cultural context and aimed to prove that the reductive history of abstraction and its subsequent endgame, the grid or monochrome, was null and void. As Hal Foster said of the Neo-Geo artists in particular, their work can be considered for its "ambiguous relationship to both representation and abstraction"[16]—yet this statement is applicable to all of the '80s artists discussed in this essay. Moreover, 1980s abstraction distanced itself from the formalist myth in favor of the impure, often incorporating biomorphic imagery and representational allusions to figures, landscapes, everyday objects, text, current events, culture, and technology. Bleckner, Brauntuch, Halley, Sultan, Taaffe, and Wool intersect through various "impurities," as their work seeks to represent the cultural signs and events specific to the larger 1980s context in which they lived. Moreover, their work reaches outward beyond the canvas and points toward, as Halley put it, abstraction's connection "between culture and other histories and between the artist and the world," such as developing technologies, art commerce, the economy, environmental concerns, and the AIDS epidemic.[17]

Neo-Geo/Simulationism

Halley, Bleckner, and Taaffe were key figures in the '80s movement deemed Simulationism or "Neo-Geo" (short for Neo-Geometry), which also included artists Sherrie Levine, Ashley Bickerton, and Jeff Koons, among others. For the Neo-Geo artists discussed in this essay, appropriations of earlier geometric and Op art abstraction in particular were used in a critical manner to poke fun at abstraction's ambitions of transcendence and inventiveness, and to underline its flaws.[18] The Neo-Geo artists accepted abstraction's demise and were therefore recycling it in order to critique the style and infuse it with more global and concrete themes. This attitude counters the notion of the unique self as perpetuated by prior abstract artists, but parallels the postmodern theory of Fredric Jameson that claims that individuality ceases to exist.[19]

Because of this presumably pessimistic approach to abstraction by Neo-Geo artists, some critics, such as Donald Kuspit, stated that the movement was "secretly dead on arrival."[20] Many critics also believed Neo-Geo works were reduced to sheer commodities, as they were mainly marketable for their familiarity of style; however, it can be argued that this was purposefully strategic to illustrate and deconstruct the art market's proclivity for tradition. Grace Glueck's 1987 article explaining Neo-Geo in the *New York Times* clearly articulated the movement:

> One generalization that can be made about the new work is that it deals—as did some of the work in its predecessor movements, Pop and Conceptual—with images rather than primary sources. ... It is preoccupied with the barrage of reproductions purveyed by television, film, advertising and print mediums. It also exhibits a concern with the threats—glamorous in their danger—posed by the technological advances of Western society.[21]

Whether it be technological advances, the bombardment of media images, or a booming capitalist economy, the 1980s existence itself was being experienced through increasingly simulated means as these new realities grew harder to define.

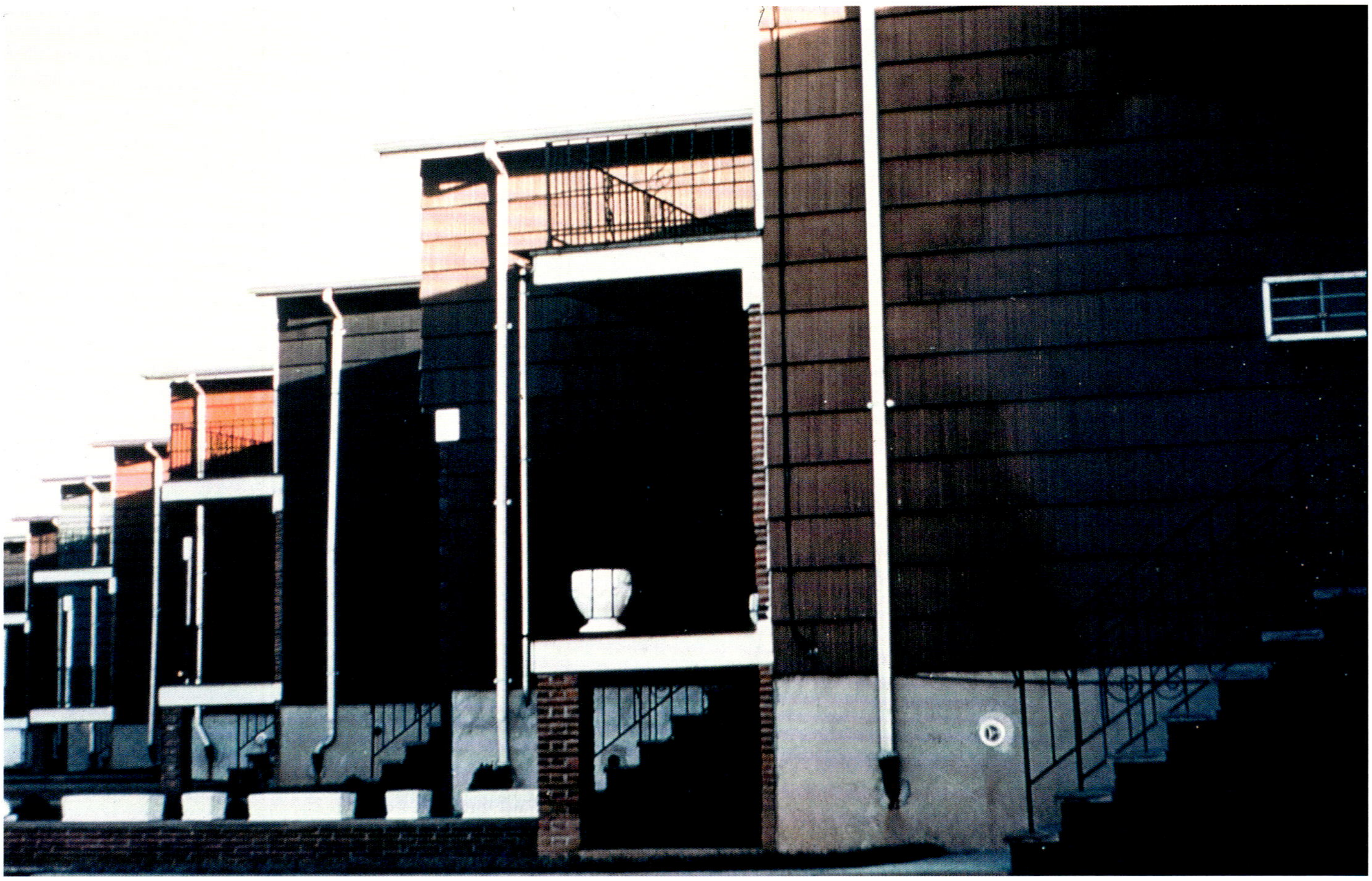

Peter Halley's writings concur that Neo-Geo work makes reference to these broader themes and illustrates the pluralist and increasingly abstract existence we occupy.[22] In Halley's paintings, such as *Glowing and Burnt-Out Cells with Conduit*, 1982, geometric abstraction is the primary motif used to convey "the increasing geometricization of social space in the world in which we live."[23] With a limited palette and only a few geometric forms in each work, Halley's paintings are hard-edged and reductive. Like the systematic color coding of electronic wires, Halley color codes squares or rectangles and often paints narrow black bands that connect the larger shapes. This represents a network of gridded "cells" and "conduits" on his canvases, but also implies an aerial view of an orderly urban or suburban complex connected by sidewalks. The demonstration of the geometricization of social space was earlier exemplified in Dan Graham's series of photographs *Homes for America*, 1966–67.

Halley's *Glowing and Burnt-Out Cells with Conduit* is a large, symmetrical composition with two color-coded squares situated horizontally

Dan Graham
Homes for America (detail), 1966–67
Slide projection, 20 color 35mm slides
Courtesy of the Artist and
Marian Goodman Gallery, New York/Paris

next to each other; the left square is a roughly textured red, and the right square is black. Thin, black strips connect the two squares on the bottom of the canvas. Halley's technological geo-abstractions counter the transcendental or mystical properties often associated with geometry and geometric abstraction as he relates the spaces in his work to those of the "video game, the microchip, and of the office tower."[24] The paintings depict spaces that resist representation and demonstrate how the world is coded and how abstraction underpins almost every aspect of modern life.

In Halley's paintings, such as *Glowing and Burnt-Out Cells with Conduit*, 1982, geometric abstraction is the primary motif used to convey "the increasing geometricization of social space in the world in which we live."[23]

Halley was an outspoken writer for the painters of this time period, and his writings and works are influenced by the 1980s resurgence of theories on semiotics and post-structuralism.[25] His essays, including "Abstraction and Culture" of 1991, related the standpoint of how and why such artists at the time turned toward this new form of abstraction. Halley described a great disconnect between Greenbergian abstraction and historical events, as mid-century abstraction was primarily guided by spirituality, alienation, and phenomenology. He asserted that abstraction is a popular form of communication in our society (for example, signs directing travelers to baggage, toilets, and tobacco shops are ubiquitous and recognizable symbols that are by no means truthfully representative), and that it should no longer be reserved for high art. Curator Dan Cameron bolstered this point of view, stating, "What we call abstraction is so well understood as a system of signs and symbols and modes of representation that it's really just another kind of representation."[26]

In the 1980s, Ross Bleckner also appropriated abstraction to critique the utter lack of meaning of 1960s Op art, recycling the style to communicate the social condition in New York in regard to death, loss, and the AIDS epidemic. Bleckner is often credited as the first artist to make work about the AIDS crisis. In an interview, he said, "AIDS, and fear, made me make the images a little more representational, and at the same time personal and more political."[27] In such early paintings as *The Arrangement of Things*, 1982–85, black vertical bars, akin to the retinally pulsating visual effects of '60s Op art, lie atop an overall white painting infused with sparse clouds of color. To Bleckner, these bands connote jail bars and signal death as the ideas in the work are eternally locked in. The artist also stated that these bars deny access for the viewer to the background image.[28]

As suggested by Neville Wakefield, Bleckner's paintings express two losses: that of his peers to AIDS, but also painting's capacity to fully articulate that loss.[29] Bleckner's memorial paintings, such as *Hospital Room* and *8,122+ as of January 1986*, evoke content through their titles alone and poeticize the AIDS epidemic, death, and loss as much as possible within abstract painting. Often dark and ambiguous, paintings such as *Sanctuary*, 1989, which is composed of numerous yellow-hued painterly dots arranged in concentric, incomplete circles over a black background, suggest illumination or flickers of light within an otherwise

> "AIDS, and fear, made me make the images a little more representational, and at the same time personal and more political," said Bleckner.[27]

darkened space. *Sanctuary*'s polka dots are imperfect, expressive, roughly painted, and evoke individualism, but en masse. Bleckner is also known for taking materials such as DNA structures and blood cells, and magnifying them under a microscope in order to fragment and transform them in his paintings. On this process, Bleckner said, "Sometimes the paintings show a fragment. Sometimes they blur the object . . . sometimes they need to go very close, as they did in the mid-'80s. . . . You need to . . . in the vernacular, 'to keep it real.'"[30]

Like Halley and Bleckner, Philip Taaffe also used the mechanics of abstraction—1960s Op art in particular—as it was considered a futile style by the eighties that was free to be coded with new meanings and signs. The artist explained that he is not a formalist, although his paintings have formalist qualities. In *Brest*, 1985, hypnotic, black, hairpin lines curve and undulate on a tilted square canvas that gives the appearance of a street sign in its orientation. The work is nearly identical to Bridget Riley's *Crest*, 1964, and raises questions about originality and authorship. While Riley's canvas is solely black and white, Taaffe's incorporates patches of yellow that imply discoloration and age, especially in comparison to Riley's work. As Pepe Karmel stated, the Op art devices used by Taaffe, while "usually seen as demonstrations of purely optical phenomena, might also be read as representations of the hypnotic power of the mass media."[31] For Taaffe and many other artists in the 1980s, the

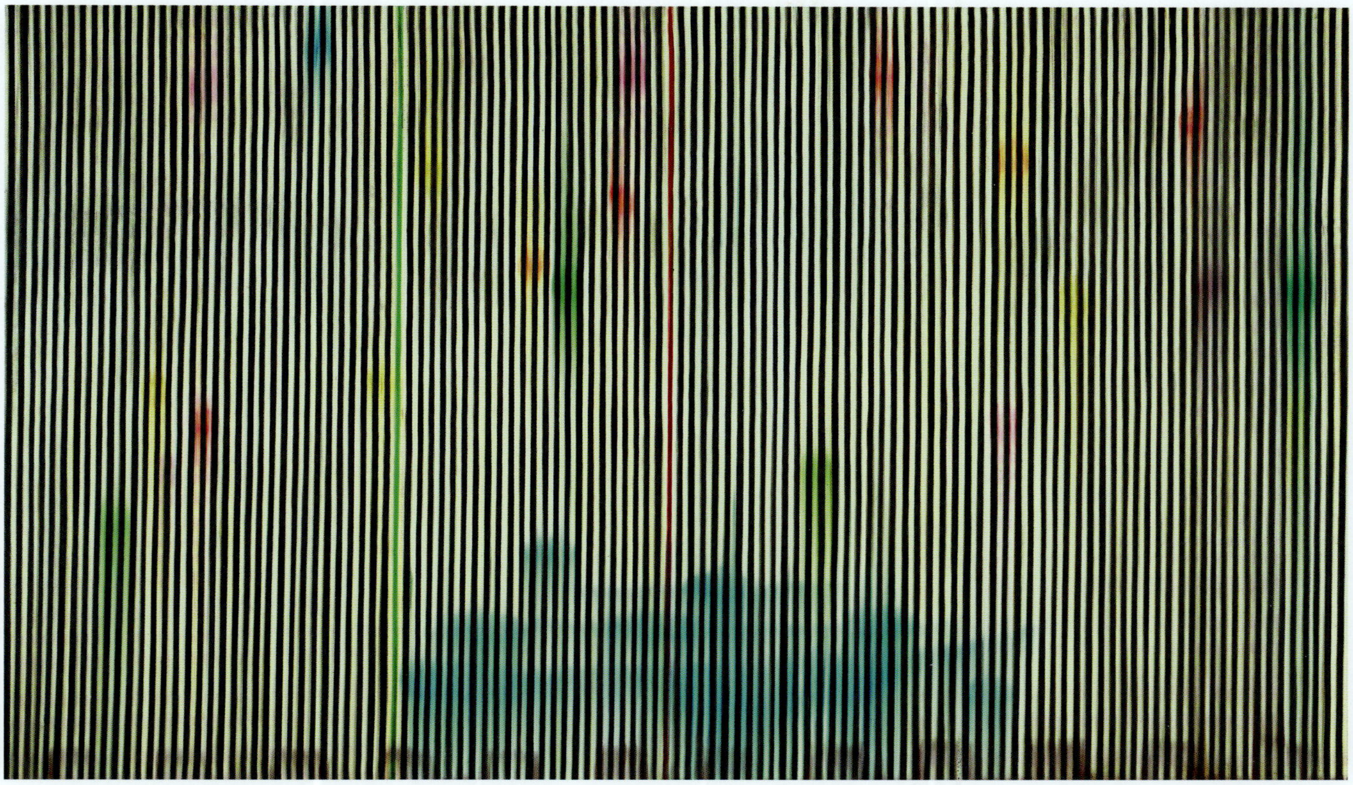

daily blasts of media and print images induced a trancelike state, which is suggested in the rhythmic patterns, fragmentation, and appropriated images in his paintings.

While using formal elements of Op art, Taaffe's works also combine a wealth of other multicultural appropriations, from fine art to decor, such as architecture, mosaics, and natural history illustrations. In this sense, his practice operates within the guise of abstraction, but is rather following a trajectory of collage as he unites disparate formal elements from various sources. By merging repetitive forms from both geometry and craft, Taaffe's work destabilizes the established hierarchies of power in regard to these allegedly high and low visual referents. Additionally, these collaged elements express the innovations and genuineness of historical and current cultures; this implies globalism, a growing reality within the postmodern context of the 1980s as people and cultures were becoming better connected. On his work in general, Taaffe explained that it is "one way of pushing the dimensions of what an abstract image can contain."[32]

Ross Bleckner
The Arrangement of Things, 1982–85
Oil on canvas
96 × 162 inches
Museum of Fine Arts, Boston.
M. Theresa B. Hopkins Fund, 1986.21

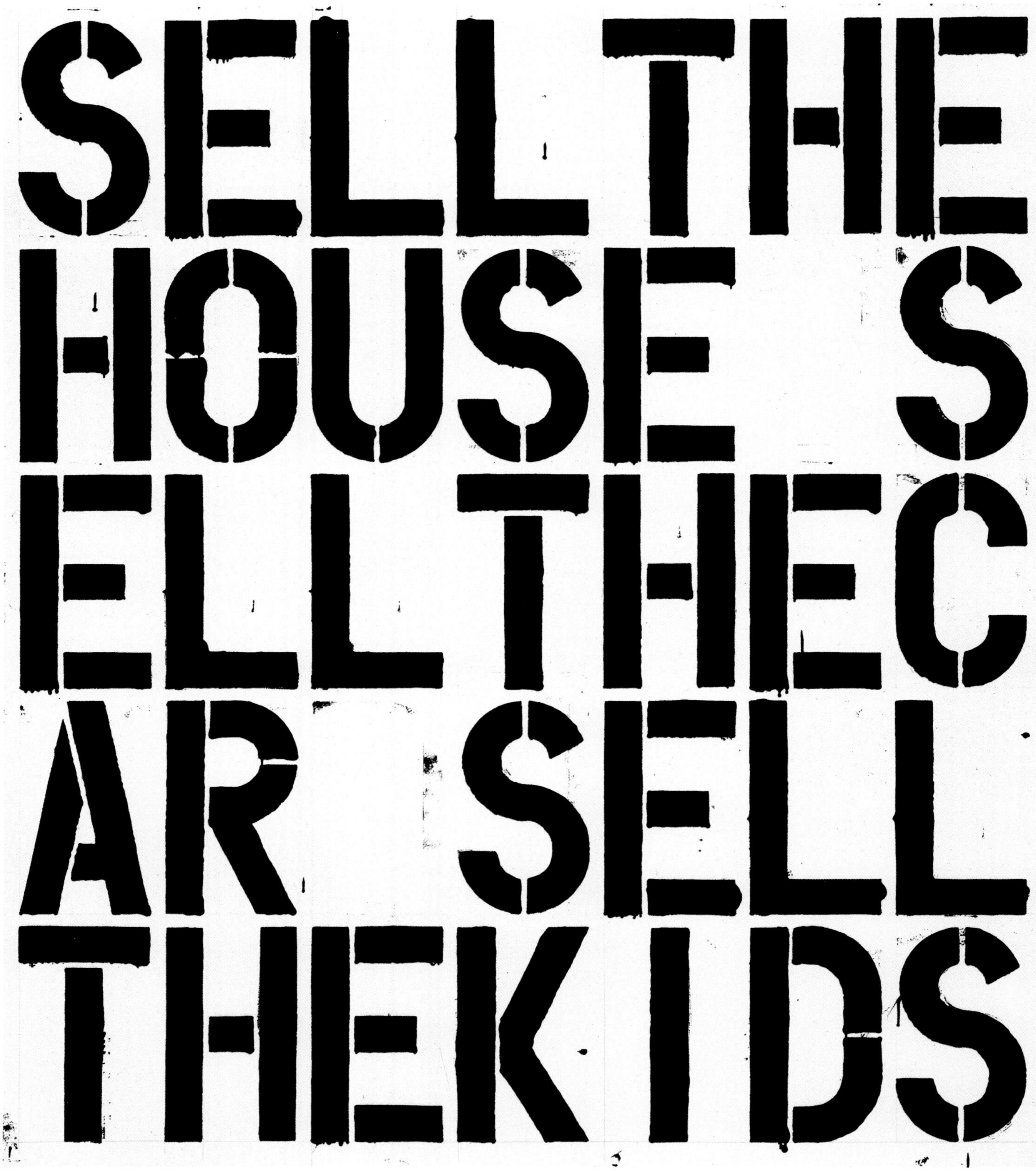

Christopher Wool
Apocalypse Now, 1988
Alkyd and Flashe on aluminum
84 × 72 inches
Courtesy of the Artist and Luhring Augustine, New York

Urban Abstraction

While Christopher Wool's paintings are not Neo-Geo, his work explores similar canons of abstraction. Wool often incorporates photography, stencil, spray paint, stamps, and everyday painting techniques into his practice. Moreover, the artist investigates abstract painting while working as an abstract painter. For example, a series of Wool's paintings, including *Untitled*, 1987, feature repetitive, allover floral or botanical designs painted with the same incised paint rollers typically used by tenement landlords that, for very little money, print a wallpaper-like ornamental motif when rolled on a wall and that often only demonstrate variety

---

Wool's word paintings not only speak to theories on semiotics and the limitations and abilities of linguistics and art, but present "text as image" and exhibit new ways to look at both language and abstraction.[33]

---

via flaws in their application. Wool's varied techniques run the gamut of high and low sources—from the street to the fine-art studio. His gritty sources and gestural, bold techniques lend the work a characteristic punk aesthetic typical of the downtown New York scene he was living and working in.

While straddling the divide of nonrepresentation and representation, Wool's paintings incorporate the urban vernacular—whether it be through street-inspired techniques, visual appropriation, or language. At the same time, he tests the conceptual limits of abstraction. In the late 1980s, the artist began creating his iconic, signlike word paintings. In these works, Wool often appropriates text and language from films and historical events; his 1988 painting *Apocalypse Now* quotes the movie of the same title with "SELL THE HOUSE SELL THE CAR SELL THE KIDS." The letters in these paintings are always capitalized and in a ubiquitous stencil font. Wool's textual appropriations interlace popular culture and history, while fragmenting the original source in that each painting only presents a tight selection of words. The artist often breaks up the words in a progression that is at times difficult to read. In his iconic and visually strong painting *Untitled*, 1990, "SPO" fills the top third of the work and is stacked above the middle line "KES," while "MAN" is on the bottom line. The stenciled letters are black on a white background. By breaking up the letters and by presenting text as form, the word's meaning becomes dry and isolated. Wool's word paintings challenge the connotative authorities of both text and abstraction, and also the ability to decipher the text through the fragmented and disjunctive presentation. The word paintings not only speak to theories on semiotics and the limitations and abilities of linguistics and art, but present "text as image" and exhibit new ways to look at both language and abstraction.[33]

Bordering Abstraction

Donald Sultan's works are situated within the tradition of painting, yet rather than using abstraction as the main device to infuse meaning, they employ reductive compositions that border on abstraction. His paintings often make reference to landscapes or still lifes, but they are flattened, generalized, and contain no shading or color gradations. In the case of his industrial landscape paintings, Sultan challenges the confines of painting and confronts the viewer with the sheer physicality of the works' scale, materials, and subject matter. In *Dead Plant November 1 1988*, 1988, the artist presents a silhouette of a highly abstracted form—an abandoned industrial warehouse. Sultan reduces such images to the breaking point of indistinguishability, yet they retain their value as subjects through their titles and subtle visual cues. For *Dead Plant,* Sultan covered the surface of the canvas with molten tar and worked out the image using a knife and blowtorch in a subtractive process somewhat akin to sculpture. The artist smeared plaster and pigment onto the canvas with a rag to build up the negative space and reveal the painting's main structure, the plant. The result is a roughly textured surface and a muddled and hazy articulation of the central subject.

Dead Plant uses the form of an obsolete industrial plant to reflect the transient, and, as the artist explained, "the unseen impact of emotional and economic distress."[34] The themes of anguish and loss parallel the work of Ross Bleckner, as well as the general sentiment of the 1980s during the AIDS crisis and mounting environmental concerns. In Sultan's interview with Barbara Rose in 1988, Rose stated that

> Almost all the landscapes he calls "events" are about disasters. They warn of the toxic poison floating in the haze of our ignorance of what creates chaos and breakdown in postindustrial civilization. A fuller reading of Sultan's iconography ... would focus on the slippage between subject matter, content and form that takes place in a work of fine art created within the context of mass culture.[35]

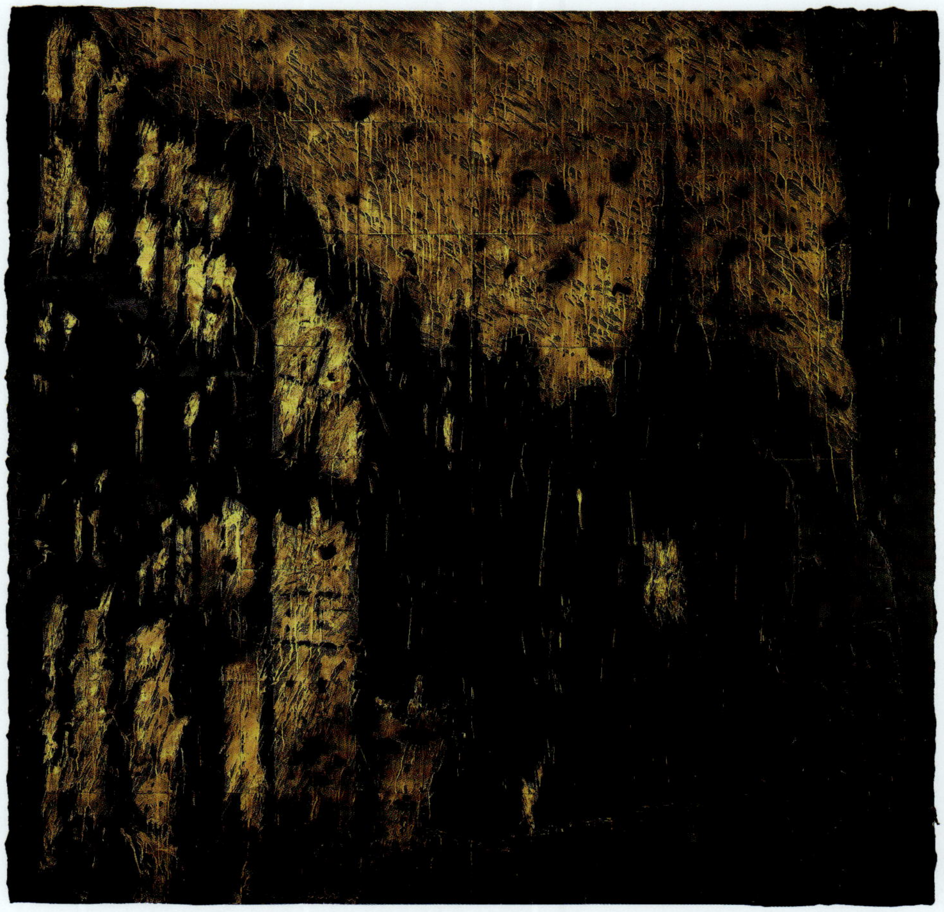

Also of importance, according to Rose, is that Sultan arrived in New York during Guston's last decade.[36] Though he does not fully operate within abstraction, the general attitude of denouncing abstraction in the 1980s reverberates throughout Sultan's oeuvre as he simultaneously suggests it, while also inhibiting it with the inclusion of somewhat discernible images such as fruit, flowers, buildings, and landscapes. On abstraction, Sultan said,

> I'd like to go on the record as saying purely abstract painting is a relatively small block in the history of art. Pure abstract painting without imagery is a very small period in art history and it's about to come to a close. It will reappear but in a different guise.... They are going to have to go back through us, through abstract image painting in order to make another abstraction.[37]

The work of Troy Brauntuch is often tied to that of the Pictures Generation, a group of artists in the 1970s and 1980s that included

Donald Sultan
Double Church Nov 8 1990, 1990
96 × 96 inches
Tar and latex on tile over Masonite

Robert Longo, Cindy Sherman, and Sherrie Levine, among others. These artists appropriated images from the media, film, and television, and re-photographed and re-presented them in order to reveal and deconstruct the seductive and manipulative devices inherent in such images, as well as to explore broader theories of representation and authenticity. Unlike many of his peers in the Pictures Generation, Brauntuch fragmented and cut up images and re-presented them as paintings. Often monochromatic and highly ambiguous in what they depict, as in *Untitled*, 1984, his paintings are simultaneously familiar and mysterious. Brauntuch's works also often explore the dark underside of modernism in their subject matter, as with his Nazi-related paintings and loaded Fascist documentary photographs;[38] however, his sources are widely varied and include his own personal snapshots. As fellow Pictures Generation artists often demonstrated with photography, Brauntuch's paintings reveal the inadequacies of both photography and painting for presenting a unified whole with regard to a narrative, history, or connotation. Brauntuch's paintings simulate abstraction as they are reductive, fragmented, monochromatic, and often unclear, yet he arrives at this abstraction through the lens of photography and its inability to communicate a clear message. His work also reaffirms that, on a general level, the images that the 1980s generation were increasingly bombarded with, via the media and popular culture, were too ubiquitous to ignore within any artistic practice, including painting.

As Guston opened the 1980s with a renunciation of abstraction in favor of a return to the real in painting, these six artists dealt with analogous concerns throughout the decade and illustrated that the endgame of abstract painting, as proposed by modernism, was a failed concept. While Bleckner, Brauntuch, Halley, Sultan, Taaffe, and Wool are diverse in their ideologies and styles, they all tested the prior parameters in abstraction and revived the practice in new and innovative ways. The preconditions set forth by abstraction's Greenbergian narrative were abandoned by them in favor of pluralist amalgamations of images, cultural signifiers, and contemporary anxieties within their works, reconnecting the abstract artist with the world at large. Moreover, these artists reevaluated and reconfigured abstraction by incorporating the "impure," which, as Guston stated on painting, ultimately "forces its continuity."

1 Philip Guston, quoted in Musa Mayer, *Night Studio: A Memoir of Philip Guston* (New York: Alfred A. Knopf, 1988), 141.
2 Terry Winters, quoted in "Thick and Thin," a roundtable discussion on painting, *Artforum* 41, no. 8 (April 2003): 240.
3 Andrew Graham-Dixon, "Impure Thoughts: On Guston's Abstractions," in *Philip Guston Retrospective*, ed. Michael Auping (Fort Worth: Modern Art Museum of Fort Worth in association with Thames & Hudson, 2003), 37.
4 Hal Foster, quoted in Frances Colpitt, "Systems of Opinion: Abstract Painting Since 1959," in *Abstract Art in the Late Twentieth Century*, ed. Frances Colpitt (Cambridge, UK: Cambridge University Press, 2002), 167.
5 Hal Foster, *The Return of the Real: The Avant-Garde at the End of the Century* (Cambridge, MA: The MIT Press, 1996), 120.
6 Peter Halley, "Abstraction and Culture," in *Abstraction: Documents of Contemporary Art*, ed. Maria Lind (London: Whitechapel Gallery in association with the MIT Press, 2013), 137. First published in *Tema Celeste* (Autumn 1991): 56–60.
7 Alfred H. Barr, Jr., *Cubism and Abstract Art* (New York: The Museum of Modern Art, 1936), 13.
8 Colpitt, "Systems of Opinion: Abstract Painting Since 1959," 158.
9 Lind, "Introduction," in *Abstraction: Documents of Contemporary Art*, 13.
10 Colpitt, "Systems of Opinion: Abstract Painting Since 1959," 158.
11 Johanna Drucker, *Theorizing Modernism: Visual Art and the Critical Tradition* (New York: Columbia University Press, 1996), 62–63.
12 Ibid., 61.
13 Ad Reinhardt, 1966, quoted in Lucy Lippard, *Ad Reinhardt* (New York: Harry N. Abrams, 1981), 158.
14 Douglas Crimp, "The End of Painting," in *Abstract Art in the Late Twentieth Century*, ed. Colpitt, 96. First published in *October* 16 (Spring 1981): 69–86.
15 For more information, see Mark Rosenthal, *Abstraction in the Twentieth Century: Total Risk, Freedom, Discipline* (New York: Solomon R. Guggenheim Museum in association with Harry N. Abrams, 1996).
16 Hal Foster, "Signs Taken for Wonders," in *Abstract Art in the Late Twentieth Century*, ed. Colpitt, 115. First published in *Art in America* 74, no. 6 (June 1986): 80–91, 139.
17 Halley, "Abstraction and Culture," 137.
18 Foster, *The Return of the Real*, 101.
19 Fredric Jameson, "Postmodern and Consumer Society," in *The Anti-Aesthetic*, ed. Hal Foster (New York: The New Press, 2002), 151.
20 Donald Kuspit, "The Abstract Self-Object," in *Abstract Art in the Late Twentieth Century*, ed. Colpitt, 181.
21 Grace Glueck, "What Do You Call Art's Newest Trend: 'Neo-Geo' … Maybe," *The New York Times*, July 6, 1987, accessed February 7, 2014, http://www.nytimes.com/1987/07/06/arts/what-d-you-call-art-s-newest-trend-neo-geo-maybe.html.
22 Lind, "Introduction," 18.
23 "Peter Halley Biographical Summary," accessed January 20, 2014, http://www.peterhalley.com.
24 Jeanne Siegel, "Geometric Desurfacing: Ross Bleckner, Alan Belcher, Ellen Carey, Peter Halley, Sherrie Levine, Philip Taaffe, James Welling," *Arts Magazine* 60 (March 1986): 29.
25 In brief, semiotics is the study of etymological, graphic, and gestural signs and how and why such signs communicate meaning. Post-structuralism is a label given to philosophical theories from such French authors of the 1970s as Michel Foucault, Jacques Derrida, and Jacques Lacan that discuss power dynamics within various social constructions. Post-structuralism deciphers how power is expressed in society by asserting that power is relational and therefore acts according to political, financial, and public tendencies. For example, an author (or artist) has presumed power over the text or work; post-structuralism sets forth to evaluate and destabilize such power in order to garner meaning from various other readings, such as the reader's interpretation, other texts, cultural standards, etc. Post-structuralism thus favors pluralism, and in this way relates to postmodernism; it also counters mid-twentieth-century writings on structuralism, which maintains that human culture is shaped and can be understood by set structures and traditions. For more information, see Julia Kristeva, *Desire in Language: A Semiotic Approach to Literature and Art* (New York: Columbia University Press, 1982).
26 Dan Cameron, "'80s Then: Ross Bleckner Talks to Dan Cameron," *Artforum* 41, no. 7 (March 2003): 231.
27 Ross Bleckner, quoted in "Ross Bleckner Talks to Dan Cameron," 230.
28 Ross Bleckner, quoted in Jeanne Siegel, "Geometric Desurfacing," 28.
29 Neville Wakefield, "Mourning Glory: Ross Bleckner in Retrospect," *Artforum* 33, no. 6 (February 1995): 74.
30 Ross Bleckner, quoted in "Ross Bleckner Talks to Dan Cameron," 231.
31 Pepe Karmel, "Still Conceptual After All These Years," in *Conceptual Abstraction*, Pepe Karmel and Joaquin Pissaro (New York: Hunter College, 2012), 15.
32 Philip Taaffe in an interview with Shirley Kaneda, *Bomb Magazine* 35 (Spring 1991), accessed February 6, 2014, http://bombsite.com/issues/35/articles/1411.
33 Katherine Brinson, "Trouble Is My Business," in *Christopher Wool*, ed. Katherine Brinson (New York: Solomon R. Guggenheim Museum, 2013), 39–40.
34 Donald Sultan, quoted in Andrea Karnes, "Donald Sultan," in *Modern Art Museum of Fort Worth 110*, ed. Michael Auping (Fort Worth: Modern Art Museum of Fort Worth in association with Third Millennium Publishing, 2002), 306.
35 Barbara Rose, "Introduction," in *Sultan: An Interview with Donald Sultan by Barbara Rose* (New York: Vintage Books, 1988), 8–9.
36 Ibid., 4.
37 Donald Sultan, quoted in *Sultan: An Interview with Donald Sultan by Barbara Rose*, 62.
38 For more information, see Douglas Eklund, *The Pictures Generation, 1974–1984* (New York: The Metropolitan Museum of Art, 2009).

Works in the Exhibition

Laurie Anderson

Drum Dance, Home of the Brave, 1986
Courtesy of the Artist
(pages 51–53)

Jean-Michel Basquiat

Six Crimee, 1982
Acrylic and oil paintstick on Masonite
Overall, 72 × 144 × 1 inches
Each panel, 72 × 48 × 1 inches
The Museum of Contemporary Art,
Los Angeles, The Scott D. F. Spiegel Collection
(pages 54–55)

Untitled, 1982
Oilstick on paper
42¾ × 30⅜ inches
Collection of the Modern Art Museum
of Fort Worth, Museum purchase
(page 57)

Ross Bleckner

Sanctuary, 1989
Oil on canvas
84 × 60 inches
The Doris and Donald Fisher Collection
(page 61)

Troy Brauntuch

Untitled, 1984
Inks and pigment on linen
60 × 60 inches
The Rachofsky Collection
(page 63)

Francesco Clemente

Perseverance, 1981
Oil on canvas
78 × 93 inches
The Museum of Modern Art, New York, NY, USA;
Partial and promised gift of UBS
(page 67)

Eric Fischl

Bad Boy, 1981
Oil on canvas
66 × 96 inches
Private Collection, Courtesy
Thomas Ammann Fine Art AG, Zurich
(page 71)

Nan Goldin

The Ballad of Sexual Dependency, 1973–86
Portfolio of 126 Cibachrome prints
Each sheet, 11 × 14 inches
Courtesy Matthew Marks Gallery
(pages 73–75)

Jack Goldstein

Untitled (Fireworks Exploding), 1984
Acrylic on canvas
96 × 96 inches
Collection of B.Z. + Michael Schwartz, New York
(page 77)

Peter Halley

Glowing and Burnt-Out Cells with Conduit, 1982
Acrylic, Day-Glo acrylic, and Roll-a-Tex on canvas
64 × 96 inches
Collection of B.Z. + Michael Schwartz, New York
(page 79)

Keith Haring

Untitled, 1981
Enamel on fiberboard
48 × 48 inches
Rubell Family Collection, Miami
(page 84)

Untitled, 1981
Enamel on fiberboard
48 × 48 inches
Rubell Family Collection, Miami
(page 85)

Untitled, 1982
Sumi ink on paper
107 × 160 inches
Courtesy Collection of Scott and Yael Braun
(page 83)

Red, 1982–84
Gouache and ink on paper
106¾ × 274 inches
Courtesy Gladstone Gallery, New York and Brussels
(pages 80–81)

Untitled, 1984
Acrylic on canvas tarp
120 × 120 inches
Courtesy Keith Haring Foundation and
Gladstone Gallery, New York and Brussels

Jenny Holzer

Inflammatory Essays, 1979–82
Sheets of paper with printed text
Each, 11 × 8½ inches
Courtesy of the Artist
(page 87)

Kind of Blue, 2012
9 LED signs with blue diodes
9⁄10 × 120 × 576 inches
Text: *Truisms*, 1977–79; *Inflammatory Essays*, 1979–82; *Living*, 1980–82; *Survival*, 1983–85; *Under a Rock*, 1986; *Laments*, 1989; *Mother and Child*, 1990; *Erlauf*, 1995; *Arno*, 1996
Collection of the Modern Art Museum
of Fort Worth, Museum purchase
(pages 88–91)

Jeff Koons

New Hoover Convertibles, Green, Red, Brown, New Hoover Deluxe Shampoo Polishers, Yellow, Brown Doubledecker, 1981–87
Three vacuum cleaners, two shampoo polishers, and fluorescent lights in Plexiglas casing
82⅜ × 54 × 28 inches
Glenstone
(page 95)

One Ball Total Equilibrium Tank (Spalding Dr. J Silver Series), 1985
Glass, steel, sodium chloride reagent, distilled water, and basketball
64¾ × 30¾ × 13¼ inches
Collection of Jeffrey Deitch
(page 93)

Buster Keaton, 1988
Polychromed wood, edition 1/3 + 1 AP
66 × 47⅞ × 27⅛ inches
Courtesy David Zwirner Gallery, New York
and London

Art Magazine Ads, 1988–89
Portfolio of 4 lithographs, edition of 50
plus 10 artist proofs
45 × 37¼ inches
Collection of the Modern Art Museum of Fort Worth,
Anonymous Gift
(pages 96–99)

Barbara Kruger

Untitled (I shop therefore I am), 1987
Photographic silkscreen on vinyl
111⅝ × 113¼ × 2½ inches
Glenstone
(page 101)

Sherrie Levine

La Fortune (After Man Ray): 6, 1990
Felt, mahogany, and resin
33 × 110 × 60 inches
Dallas Museum of Art, anonymous gift
(pages 102–103)

Robert Longo

Untitled, 1981
Charcoal, graphite, and dye on paper
98 × 48 inches
Courtesy of the Artist
(page 105)

Untitled, 1981
Charcoal and graphite on paper
96 × 60 inches
Collection Metro Pictures
(page 106)

Untitled, 1981
Charcoal and graphite on paper
96 × 60 inches
UBS Art Collection
(page 107)

Robert Mapplethorpe

Joe/Rubberman, 1978
Silver gelatin print
20 × 16 inches
(page 112)

Brian Ridley and Lyle Heeter, 1979
Silver gelatin print
20 × 16 inches
(page 113)

Patti Smith, 1979
Silver gelatin print
20 × 16 inches
(page 111)

Self Portrait, 1980
Silver gelatin print
20 × 16 inches
(page 116)

Self Portrait, 1980
Silver gelatin print
20 × 16 inches
(page 117)

Ajitto, 1981
Silver gelatin print
20 × 16 inches
(page 118)

Lisa Lyon, 1982
Silver gelatin print
20 × 16 inches
(page 115)

Self Portrait, 1985
Silver gelatin print
20 × 16 inches
(page 109)

Self Portrait, 1988
Silver gelatin print
24 × 20 inches
(page 119)

Allan McCollum

Collection of Two Hundred Plaster Surrogates, 1982/1983–85
Enamel on cast Hydrostone
Dimensions variable
The Rachofsky Collection
(pages 121–123)

Richard Prince

Spiritual America, 1983
Cibachrome print
24 × 20 inches
Courtesy of the Artist
(page 125)

Creative Evolution, 1985
Ektacolor photograph, edition 2/2
86 × 47 $\frac{1}{4}$ inches
Courtesy David Zwirner Gallery, New York and London

Untitled (Cowboy), 1995
Ektacolor print, edition 1 of 2
48 × 72 inches
Collection of the Modern Art Museum of Fort Worth, Museum purchase made possible by a grant from The Burnett Foundation
(pages 126–127)

David Salle

Clean Glasses, 1985
Acrylic and oil on two canvas panels
105 × 100 inches
The Broad Art Foundation, Santa Monica
(page 129)

Kenny Scharf

Agua Pollination, 1983
Oil and spray paint on canvas
91 $\frac{1}{2}$ × 103 $\frac{1}{2}$ inches
Courtesy of Paul Kasmin Gallery, New York and Honor Fraser Gallery, Los Angeles
(page 131)

Julian Schnabel

The Jute Grower, 1980
Oil, plates, and Bondo on wood
90 × 120 inches
Ara Arslanian
(page 133)

Cortes, 1988
Oil and velvet on drab tarpaulin
132 × 228 inches
Collection the Artist
(pages 136–137)

Zum Solitaire, 1988
Oil on carpet
138 × 104 inches
Collection of Joseph Mizzi
(page 135)

Cindy Sherman

Untitled Film Still #5, 1977
Gelatin silver print
30 × 40 inches
Gayle and Paul Stoffel
(page 141)

Untitled Film Still #16, 1978
Gelatin silver print
40 × 30 inches
Aaron and Leslee Cowen, NY, NY
(page 140)

Untitled Film Still #41, 1979
Gelatin silver print
30 × 40 inches
Barbara and Michael Gamson
(page 139)

Untitled Film Still #55, 1980
Gelatin silver print
30 × 40 inches
Collection of the Modern Art Museum of Fort Worth, Museum purchase made possible by a grant from The Burnett Foundation
(page 144)

Untitled Film Still #65, 1980
Gelatin silver print
40 × 30 inches
Collection of the Modern Art Museum of Fort Worth, Museum purchase made possible by a grant from The Burnett Foundation
(page 145)

Untitled, 1981
Cibachrome print
24 × 48 inches
Collection of the Modern Art Museum of Fort Worth, Museum purchase made possible by a grant from The Burnett Foundation
(page 143)

Donald Sultan

Dead Plant November 1 1988, 1988
Tar and latex paint on canvas
108 $\frac{1}{8}$ × 144 $\frac{1}{4}$ × 6 $\frac{3}{8}$ inches
Collection of the Modern Art Museum of Fort Worth, Museum purchase made possible by a grant from The Burnett Foundation
(page 149)

Philip Taaffe

Brest, 1985
Linoprint collage on paper mounted on canvas
78 $\frac{1}{4}$ × 78 $\frac{1}{2}$ inches
Rubell Family Collection, Miami
(page 151)

Andy Warhol

Self-Portrait, 1986
Synthetic polymer paint and silkscreen ink on canvas
108 × 108 inches
Collection of the Modern Art Museum of Fort Worth, Museum purchase, The Friends of Art Endowment Fund
(page 155)

Christopher Wool

Untitled, 1990
Alkyd and acrylic on aluminum
96 × 64 inches
Collection of Marguerite Steed Hoffman
(page 157)

Biographies

Laurie Anderson was born in Chicago in 1947. In 1969, she graduated from Barnard College in New York, and she received an MFA in sculpture from Columbia University in 1972. Anderson is a performance and visual artist, writer, director, vocalist, and musician who is best known for her groundbreaking uses of technology in multimedia presentations. She creates pioneering works that straddle the worlds of theater, art, and experimental music. In 1981, Anderson's music career was propelled into the mainstream with her track "O Superman," which rose to number two on the UK pop charts. The song was part of her seminal stage work *United States I–IV*, 1981, and appears on her album *Big Science*, the first of seven records released on the Warner Brothers label. She currently lives in New York.

Anderson has extensively toured the United States and abroad, with shows vacillating from spoken word performances to complex multimedia events. Among her many solo exhibitions are *Jukebox*, Holly Solomon Gallery, New York, 1977; *Projects: Laurie Anderson*, The Museum of Modern Art, New York, 1978; *Laurie Anderson: Works from 1969–1983*, Institute of Contemporary Art, University of Pennsylvania, Philadelphia, 1983; *Whirlwind*, Artists Space, New York, 1998; *Laurie Anderson*, Fondazione Prada, Milan, 1998; and *The Record of the Time: Sound in the Work of Laurie Anderson*, Musée d'art contemporain de Lyon, France, 2003. Anderson also served as NASA's first artist-in-residence, 2003–05.

Jean-Michel Basquiat was born in Brooklyn, New York, in 1960 and died in New York in 1988. As a teenager, Basquiat gained recognition as a musician and a graffiti artist in the informal group SAMO. By the age of twenty, in 1981, Basquiat was showing and selling his Neo-Expressionist paintings in galleries and museums, quickly becoming one of the most acclaimed artists of his time. In 1985, he was on the cover of the *New York Times Magazine* as the archetype of the young, popular artist in a thriving art market. Basquiat starred in *Downtown 81*, a verité movie written by Glenn O'Brien, filmed by Edo Bertoglio, and produced by Maripol in 1981, but released in 2000.

Major solo exhibitions of Basquiat's work include shows at the Fruitmarket Gallery, Edinburgh, 1984 (traveled to the Institute of Contemporary Arts, London; and Museum Boijmans Van Beuningen, Rotterdam); Kestnergesellschaft, Hannover, 1986–87; Whitney Museum of American Art, New York, 1993 (traveled to the Menil Collection, Houston; Des Moines Art Center, Iowa; and Montgomery Museum of Fine Arts, Alabama); Brooklyn Museum, New York, 2005 (traveled to The Museum of Contemporary Art, Los Angeles; and Museum of Fine Arts, Houston); and Fondation Beyeler, Basel, 2010 (traveled to Musée d'Art Moderne de la Ville de Paris).

Ross Bleckner was born in New York in 1949, where he lives today. Bleckner graduated with a BA in 1971 from New York University, then earned an MFA from the California Institute of the Arts in Valencia in 1973. Bleckner is best known for his large-scale paintings that deal with memory and loss, operating as remembrances to those lost to catastrophe through such events as the AIDS epidemic. Bleckner served as president of the AIDS Community Research Initiative of America (ACRIA), and more recently has been working with the United Nations Office on Drugs and Crime in Northern Uganda. In May 2009, he was awarded the title of Goodwill Ambassador by the United Nations.

Bleckner's first solo museum exhibition was organized by the San Francisco Museum of Modern Art in 1988. His work has since been the subject of numerous solo exhibitions, including a mid-career retrospective organized by the Solomon R. Guggenheim Museum in New York in 1995. He has been represented in many group exhibitions, such as the Whitney Biennial, Whitney Museum of American Art, New York, 1975, 1987, and 1989; Biennale of Sydney, 1988; and *Carnegie International*, Carnegie Museum of Art, Pittsburgh, 1988.

Troy Brauntuch was born in 1954 in Jersey City, New Jersey. In 1975, he received a BFA from the California Institute of the Arts in Valencia. After many years in New York, he now lives in Austin, Texas, and teaches at the University of Texas. Brauntuch was in the important 1977 *Pictures* exhibition at Artists Space and is known for his large, enigmatic paintings that often appropriate historic and personal images.

Brauntuch was a recipient of the Joan Mitchell Foundation Grant in 1999 and was awarded a Guggenheim Fellowship in 2010. In addition to solo exhibitions around the world, his major group shows include Documenta 7, Kassel, 1982; Venice Biennale, 1982; *Modern Art Despite Modernism*, The Museum of Modern Art, New York, 2000; and the Whitney Biennial, Whitney Museum of American Art, New York, 2006.

Francesco Clemente was born in 1952 in Naples, Italy. With a background in classical languages and literature, he attended the University of Rome in 1970 to study architecture. He currently divides his time between New York, Madras, and Rome. Clemente's work is a hybrid mix of cultures and concepts, and he often engages in collaborations with a wide range of people, from local craftsmen in India, to artists such as Jean-Michel Basquiat and Andy Warhol, and poets including John Wieners, Allen Ginsberg, Robert Creeley, and René Ricard.

Clemente's work has been the subject of numerous exhibitions, including several traveling retrospectives: *Francesco Clemente*, John and Mable Ringling Museum of Art, Sarasota, Florida, 1985 (traveled to the Walker Art Center, Minneapolis; Dallas Museum of Art; University Art Museum, University of California, Berkeley; Albright-Knox Art Gallery, Buffalo, New York; and The Museum of Contemporary Art, Los Angeles); *Francesco Clemente: Three Worlds*, Philadelphia Museum of Art, 1990 (traveled to the Wadsworth Atheneum Museum of Art, Hartford, Connecticut; San Francisco Museum of Modern Art; and Royal Academy of Arts, London); and *Clemente*, Solomon R. Guggenheim Museum, New York, 1999–2000 (traveled to the Guggenheim Museum Bilbao).

Eric Fischl was born in 1948 in New York City; he currently lives in Sag Harbor, New York. He attended Phoenix College, then went on to earn a BFA from the California Institute of the Arts in Valencia in 1972. Fischl is a Fellow at the American Academy of Arts and Letters and at the American Academy of Arts and Science. His paintings exploring the darker aspects of suburban, middle-class America propelled him to acclaim in the 1980s. His autobiography *Bad Boy: My Life On and Off the Canvas* was published by Crown Publishers and Random House, Inc., in 2013.

Fischl's work has been featured in numerous solo exhibitions, including *Eric Fischl: Paintings*, 1985, Mendel Art Gallery, Saskatoon, Saskatchewan (traveled to the Institute of Contemporary Art, Boston; Institute of Contemporary Arts, London; Art Gallery of Ontario, Toronto; Museum of Contemporary Art Chicago; and the Whitney Museum of American Art, New York). Select group exhibitions include the Whitney Biennial, Whitney Museum of American Art, New York, 1983, 1985, and 1991; Venice Biennale, 1984; *An International Survey of Recent Painting and Sculpture*, The Museum of Modern Art, New York, 1984; Documenta 8, Kassel, 1987; *Avant-Garde in the Eighties*, Los Angeles County Museum of Art, 1987; *Hypermental: Rampant Reality 1950–2000, from Salvador Dali to Jeff Koons*, Kunsthaus Zurich, 2000–01; and *This Will Have Been: Art, Love & Politics in the 1980s*, Museum of Contemporary Art Chicago, 2012 (traveled to the Walker Art Center, Minneapolis; and Institute of Contemporary Art, Boston).

Nan Goldin was born in Washington, DC, in 1953. She spent her formative years in Boston and attended the School of the Museum of Fine Arts, Boston / Tufts University, graduating in 1977. Shortly after, Goldin moved to New York where she continued to build her career as a photographer by creating transgressive images of personal, spontaneous, and sexual subjects that have since become iconic of her oeuvre. In 1979, Goldin presented her first slide show in a New York nightclub, an evolving group of images that would eventually become her seminal work, *The Ballad of Sexual Dependency*, 1973–86. Her candid, snapshotlike photographs are praised for their groundbreaking contributions to fine art photography. Goldin currently lives between Paris and New York.

Goldin's work has been the subject of two major touring retrospectives, the first organized by the Whitney Museum of American Art, New York, 1996 (traveled to Kunstmuseum Wolfsburg; Stedelijk Museum Amsterdam; Fotomuseum Winterthur, Switzerland; Kunsthalle Wien, Vienna; and the National Museum, Prague); and the second arranged by the Centre national d'art et de culture Georges Pompidou, Paris, 2001 (traveled to Whitechapel Gallery, London; Museo Nacional Centro de Arte Reina Sofía, Madrid; Museu de Arte Contemporanea de Serralves, Porto, Portugal; Castello di Rivoli Museo d'Arte Contemporanea, Turin; and the Centre for Contemporary Art Ujazdowski Castle, Warsaw). Goldin's work has been exhibited across the globe, and she has won numerous honors and awards for her enduring vision and creativity, including being admitted to the French Legion of Honor in 2006 and receiving the Hasselblad Foundation International Award in 2007. In 2012, the MacDowell Colony awarded her the Edward MacDowell Medal.

Jack Goldstein was born in Montreal, Canada, in 1945 and died in 2003 in San Bernardino, California. He received a BFA from Chouinard Art Institute in Los Angeles in 1969 and was one of the first graduates of the California Institute of the Arts in

Valencia in 1972. Included in the seminal *Pictures* exhibition of 1977, his work spans multiple media, including performance, painting, sound recordings, and film. He was awarded two National Endowment for the Arts grants, as well as a Pollock-Krasner Foundation grant.

Goldstein's work was featured in many solo exhibitions, including presentations at One Times Square, Spectacolor lightboard, New York, 1984; The Power Plant, Toronto, 1991; Whitney Museum of American Art, New York, 2002; MMK Museum für Moderne Kunst Frankfurt am Main, 2009; The Museum of Contemporary Art, Los Angeles, 2012; and the Orange County Museum of Art, Newport Beach, California, 2012. Major group exhibitions include *Avant-Garde Film (Jack Goldstein, Babette Mangolte and Yvonne Rainer)*, Art Institute of Chicago, 1975; *Pictures*, Artists Space, New York, 1977; *The Record as Artwork from Futurism to Conceptual Art*, Fort Worth Art Museum, 1977; Documenta 7, Kassel, 1982; *New York Painting Today*, Carnegie Institute, Pittsburgh, 1983; and the Whitney Biennial, Whitney Museum of American Art, New York, 1985 and 2004.

Peter Halley was born in New York in 1953. He received his BA from Yale University and his MFA from the University of New Orleans in 1978. Since 1980, Halley has lived in New York. For more than twenty-five years, his geometric paintings have been engaged in a play of relationships between what he calls "prisons" and "cells"—icons that reflect the increasing geometricization of social spaces in our world. Halley has also written on art and culture throughout his career. His early essays, which address post-structuralism, postmodernism, and the digital revolution of the 1980s, have been anthologized in two books of collected writings. In 2001, he received the Frank Jewett Mather Award from the College Art Association for his critical writing.

Halley has had solo museum exhibitions at the CAPC musée d'art contemporain, Bordeaux, 1991; Museo Nacional Centro de Arte Reina Sofía, Madrid, 1992; Stedelijk Museum Amsterdam, 1992; Des Moines Art Center, 1992; Dallas Museum of Art, 1995; The Museum of Modern Art, New York, 1997; Kitakyushu Municipal Museum of Art, 1998; Museum Folkwang, Essen, 1998; and the Butler Institute of American Art, Youngstown, Ohio, 1999. His work has also been exhibited in galleries in Chicago, London, Madrid, Moscow, New York, Paris, Rome, Seoul, and Tokyo. Since the mid-1990s, Halley has produced site-specific installations for exhibitions and as permanent public works. These projects have been realized at the State University of New York, Buffalo, 1998; the city library in Usera, Spain, 2002; Banco Suisso d'Italia Art Collection, Turin, 2003; and the Dallas/Fort Worth International Airport, Texas, 2005.

Keith Haring was born in Reading, Pennsylvania, in 1958. He enrolled at the School of Visual Arts in New York in 1978. Throughout the decade of the 1980s, Haring became well known for his quickly executed, unsanctioned drawings throughout the New York subway system as he sought a truly public artform. His start in the alternative art community, where he both organized and participated in shows at spaces such as Mudd Club, Palladium, and Club 57, thrust him to fame and led to numerous gallery and museum exhibitions around the world before his death in 1990 of complications related to AIDS.

During Haring's lifetime, his work was featured in solo exhibitions at the CAPC musée d'art contemporain, Bordeaux, 1985; Stedelijk Museum Amsterdam, 1986; and the Whitney Museum of American Art, New York, 1986. His work has been the subject of numerous international retrospectives since his death. Group exhibitions include the *Times Square Show*, New York, 1980; Documenta 7, Kassel, 1982; *Urban Kisses*, Institute of Contemporary Arts, London, 1982; Whitney Biennial, Whitney Museum of American Art, New York, 1983; Bienal de São Paulo, 1983; Aperto 84, Venice Biennale, 1984; Havana Biennial, 1986; and *Avant-Garde in the Eighties*, Los Angeles County Museum of Art, 1987, among many others.

Jenny Holzer was born in Gallipolis, Ohio, in 1950 and currently lives in New York. She graduated from Ohio University with a BFA in 1972 and from the Rhode Island School of Design with an MFA in 1977. She holds honorary degrees from Williams College, the New School, and Smith College. In 1977, she participated in the Whitney Museum of American Art's Independent Study Program in New York. For more than thirty years, Holzer has evolved her style of using language as art, presenting works with frank texts to address contemporary society in public places and in international exhibitions. Her writings are the key component in her artistic career, whether seen on T-shirts, benches, plaques, or LED signs, and they rely on the public dimension as an integral part of their delivery. Starting in the 1970s with her posters placed around New York, and up to her recent light projections on landscape and architecture, Holzer continues to challenge audiences with humor, bluntness, and courage.

Holzer received the Golden Lion at the Venice Biennale, 1990; the Crystal Award from the World Economic Forum, 1996; and the Barnard Medal of Distinction in 2011. The artist has had major solo exhibitions at such institutions as Dia Art Foundation, New York, 1989; Solomon R. Guggenheim Museum, New York, 1989; Whitney Museum of American Art, New York, 1990; Walker Art Center, Minneapolis, 1991; and Museum of Contemporary Art Chicago, 2008 (traveled to the Whitney Museum of American Art, New York).

Jeff Koons was born in 1955 in York, Pennsylvania, and currently lives in New York. He studied at the School of the Art Institute of Chicago and earned a BFA from the Maryland Institute College of Art in 1976. His first solo exhibition, *The New* at the New Museum of Contemporary Art in New York in 1980, famously presented vacuum cleaners in exhibition display cases, a unique take on ubiquitous pop culture commodities juxtaposed with fine art aesthetics, which he continues to investigate today. His forty-foot-tall *Puppy* features live, flowering plants, an edition of which is permanently installed at the Guggenheim Museum Bilbao. Among his numerous awards are the US State Department's Medal of Arts, the John Singleton Copley Award from the American Associates of the Royal Academy Trust in New York, and officer of the French Legion of Honor.

Koons has had many solo exhibitions at major institutions, such as the Stedelijk Museum Amsterdam, 1992; San Francisco Museum of Modern Art, 1992; Walker Art Center, Minneapolis, 1993; Solomon R. Guggenheim Museum, New York, 2002; Victoria and Albert Museum, London, 2006; The Metropolitan Museum of Art, New York, 2008; and the Whitney Museum of American Art, New York, 2014. Select group exhibitions include the Whitney Biennial, Whitney Museum of American Art, New York, 1987 and 1989; *Carnegie International*, Carnegie Museum of Art, Pittsburgh, 1988–89; Venice Biennale, 1990 and 1997; *Innocence and Experience*, The Museum of Modern Art, New York, 2000; *Happiness: A Survival Guide for Art and Life*, Mori Art Museum, Tokyo, 2003; *Translation*, Palais de Tokyo, Paris, 2005; *Common Objects: Pop Art from the Collection*, The Museum of Contemporary Art, Los Angeles, 2011; and the Lyon Biennale, 2013.

Barbara Kruger was born in Newark, New Jersey, in 1945. After attending Syracuse University, the School of Visual Arts, and studying with Diane Arbus at Parsons School of Design in New York, Kruger took a design job at Condé Nast Publications and became head designer for *Mademoiselle* magazine. Later she worked as a graphic designer, art director, and picture editor in the art departments at *House & Garden* and *Aperture*, among other publications. Kruger's professional background is evident in the work for which she is now internationally known. The artist layers found photographs from existing sources with forthright and aggressive phrases. Some of her most famous expressions include "I shop, therefore I am" and "Your body is a battleground." Like these examples, much of her text-based works question and confront the viewer on topics such as feminism, classism, and consumerism made with images culled from the mainstream magazines that sell the ideas she is disputing. She currently lives between New York and Los Angeles.

Kruger's work has been shown in galleries and museums worldwide, including P.S.1 Contemporary Art Center, Long Island City, New York, 1980; Contemporary Arts Museum, Houston, 1985 (traveled to Wadsworth Atheneum Museum of Art, Hartford, Connecticut; and Los Angeles County Museum of Art); The Museum of Contemporary Art, Los Angeles, 1999; Whitney Museum of American Art, New York, 2000; Moderna Museet, Stockholm, 2008; and Hirshhorn Museum and Sculpture Garden, Smithsonian Institution, Washington, DC, 2012. Her work has also appeared on billboards, bus cards, and posters, and in parks, train station platforms, and other public places. Kruger has taught at the California Institute of the Arts, School of the Art Institute of Chicago, and the University of California, Berkeley.

Sherrie Levine was born in 1947 in Hazleton, Pennsylvania, and earned her BFA in 1969 and MFA in 1973 from the University of Wisconsin, Madison. She currently lives in New York. Associated with the Pictures Generation, Levine is an American photographer and conceptual artist who explored appropriation art as it gained momentum in the early 1980s. Although she is most known for re-photographing famous photographs, Levine is also known for her paintings and sculpture, which are appropriated from significant artists of the past, such as Piet Mondrian, El Lissitzky, and Marcel Duchamp. As a female artist redoing male artists' works, Levine is closely aligned with feminism.

Levine has exhibited widely throughout the United States and Europe, including solo exhibitions organized by the San Francisco Museum of Modern Art, 1991; Philadelphia Museum of Art, 1993; Kunstverein in Hamburg, 1999; and the Whitney

Museum of American Art, New York, 2011. Select group exhibitions include Documenta 7, Kassel, 1982; Whitney Biennial, Whitney Museum of American Art, New York, 1985, 1989, and 2008; and *Carnegie International*, Carnegie Museum of Art, Pittsburgh, 1988.

Robert Longo was born in 1953 in Brooklyn, New York, and currently lives in New York City. He earned a BFA at New York State University College, Buffalo, in 1975. For more than thirty years Longo has been a prominent figure in New York's art and cultural scene. His work includes drawings, paintings, sculpture, performance pieces, music performances, films, and videos. Much of his visual lexicon is culled and recycled from a wealth of existing cultural imagery, which he uses to address the power of pictures and their production and circulation. He was among the five artists included in the seminal 1977 Artists Space exhibition *Pictures*, and he is a key figure in the Pictures Generation.

Longo has had one-person exhibitions at museums and galleries across the globe, including the Brooklyn Museum, New York, 1985; Stedelijk Museum Amsterdam, 1985; Menil Collection, Houston, 1988; Los Angeles County Museum of Art, 1989 (traveled to the Museum of Contemporary Art Chicago; and Wadsworth Atheneum Museum of Art, Hartford, Connecticut); Hamburger Kunstverein and Deichtorhallen, Hamburg, 1991; Isetan Museum of Art, Tokyo, 1995 (traveled to Ashikaga City Museum; and Kirin Plaza Art Space, Osaka); Musée d'Art Moderne et d'Art Contemporain, Nice, 2009; and the Aldrich Contemporary Art Museum, Ridgefield, Connecticut, 2013. The artist has participated in Documenta 7 and 8, Kassel, 1982 and 1987; Whitney Biennial, Whitney Museum of American Art, New York, 1983 and 2004; and the Venice Biennale, 1997.

Robert Mapplethorpe was born in Floral Park, Queens, New York, in 1946. In 1963, he enrolled at Pratt Institute in nearby Brooklyn, where he studied drawing, painting, and sculpture. He acquired a Polaroid camera in 1970 and began to focus on photography as his primary medium. In his early career, he worked on a number of commercial projects, creating album cover art for Patti Smith (whom he met in 1967 and lived with in the early 1970s) and the band Television, as well as a series of portraits and party pictures for *Interview* magazine. In 1973, Light Gallery in New York mounted his first solo gallery exhibition, titled *Polaroids*. Two years later, Mapplethorpe acquired a Hasselblad medium-format camera and began making self-portraits and shooting his circle of friends and acquaintances, including artists, musicians, socialites, porn film stars, and members of the S&M community. By the 1980s, he added statuesque male and female nudes, delicate flower still lifes, and highly formal portraits of artists and celebrities to his body of work.

In 1986, Mapplethorpe was diagnosed with AIDS. A year before his death in 1989, the Whitney Museum of American Art in New York mounted the artist's first major retrospective in an American museum. Since that time, Mapplethorpe's work has been the focus of solo exhibitions in museums worldwide, including the recent *Robert Mapplethorpe: XYZ*, Los Angeles County Museum of Art, 2012–13; *In Focus: Robert Mapplethorpe*, J. Paul Getty Museum at the Getty Center, Los Angeles, 2012–13; *Robert Mapplethorpe*, Musée Rodin, Paris, 2014; and *Artist Rooms: Robert Mapplethorpe*, Tate Modern, London, 2014.

Allan McCollum was born in 1944 in Los Angeles; he now lives in New York. His *Surrogate* paintings were first shown in 1979 in New York and led to a long career exploring the nature of a mass of objects, each with unique features; such series as *Plaster Surrogates*, *Perfect Vehicles*, *Individual Works*, *Natural Copies*, and *The Shapes Project* exemplify this ongoing investigation.

McCollum has had solo exhibitions at Artists Space, New York, 1979–80; Institute of Contemporary Art, University of Pennsylvania, Philadelphia, 1986; Stedelijk Van Abbemuseum, Eindhoven, Netherlands, 1989–90; and the Denver Art Museum, 1990, among many others. Select group exhibitions include the Whitney Biennial, Whitney Museum of American Art, New York, 1975, 1985, and 1989; *Damaged Goods: Desire and the Economy of the Object*, New Museum of Contemporary Art, New York, 1986; Venice Biennale, 1988 and 2013; *A Forest of Signs: Art in the Crisis of Representation*, The Museum of Contemporary Art, Los Angeles, 1989; *Carnegie International*, Carnegie Museum of Art, Pittsburgh, 1991; *Repetition/Transformation*, Museo Nacional Centro de Arte Reina Sofía, Madrid, 1992; *The Museum as Muse*, The Museum of Modern Art, New York, 1999; and *Singular Forms (Sometimes Repeated): Art from 1951 to the Present*, Solomon R. Guggenheim Museum, New York, 2004.

Richard Prince was born in 1949 in the Panama Canal Zone. For twenty-five years he lived in New York City and currently resides in upstate New York. Prince has spent his career mining images from mass media, advertising, and entertainment to investigate and redefine issues of authorship, ownership, and the aura of originality. He began appropriating existing images in 1975 with his photograph *Untitled (Cowboy)* taken from a Marlboro cigarette advertisement. Within his varied bodies of work, Prince has explored the mythic status of cowboys, bikers, customized cars, and celebrities, probed the depths of racism and sexism in his joke paintings and other works, and examined the push/pull allure of pulp fiction and soft porn through his nurse paintings.

Prince's work has been shown extensively in solo exhibitions across the United States and Europe, including Artists Space, New York, 1980; Institute of Contemporary Arts, London, 1983; One Times Square, Spectacolor lightboard, New York, 1988; Whitney Museum of American Art, New York, 1992; San Francisco Museum of Modern Art, 1993; and Haus der Kunst, Munich, 1996. More recently, his work was the subject of a major exhibition organized by the Solomon R. Guggenheim Museum in New York in 2007, which traveled to the Walker Art Center in Minneapolis.

David Salle was born in Norman, Oklahoma, in 1952. He earned a BFA in 1973 and an MFA in 1975, both from the California Institute of the Arts in Valencia. He has a multidisciplinary practice of painting, sculpture, set and costume design, photography, and filmmaking. Salle currently lives in Brooklyn.

Salle has been featured in two major traveling solo exhibitions. The first was organized by the Institute of Contemporary Art, University of Pennsylvania, Philadelphia, 1986 (traveled to the Whitney Museum of American Art, New York; The Museum of Contemporary Art, Los Angeles; Art Gallery of Ontario, Toronto; and Museum of Contemporary Art Chicago); and the second was organized by the Stedelijk Museum Amsterdam, 1999 (traveled to Museum Moderner Kunst Stiftung Ludwig Wien, Vienna; Castello di Rivoli Museo d'Arte Contemporanea, Turin; and Guggenheim Museum Bilbao). Major group exhibitions include the Venice Biennale, 1982 and 1993; Documenta 7, Kassel, 1982; Whitney Biennial, Whitney Museum of American Art, New York, 1983, 1985, and 1991; Bienal de São Paulo, 1983; *Carnegie International*, Carnegie Museum, Pittsburgh, 1985; and *High and Low: Modern and Popular Culture*, The Museum of Modern Art, New York, 1990.

Kenny Scharf was born in 1958 in Los Angeles, where he lives today. He earned a BFA from the School of Visual Arts in New York in 1980. Roommates with Keith Haring in the 1980s, Scharf participated in many alternative exhibitions, such as those at Mudd Club, Club 57, and the *Times Square Show*. His psychedelic paintings merge cartoon animation aesthetics with sharp detail and bright color. In addition to an established career as a painter, Scharf created the television special *The Groovenians* and paints murals in a variety of locations, including Kings County Children's Hospital in Brooklyn, Cedars-Sinai Children's Wing in Los Angeles, and a public library in West Hollywood.

Scharf has been featured in solo exhibitions at many institutions, including *Kenny Scharf: Scharf-O-Rama 1978–1995*, Museum of Art, Nova Southeastern University, Fort Lauderdale, Florida, 1995; *Kenny Scharf: Pop Surrealist*, Salvador Dalí Museum, St. Petersburg, Florida, 1997; *Kenny Scharf: New Sculpture*, The Portland Institute for Contemporary Art, 1999; *Kenny Scharf: California Grown*, Pasadena Museum of California Art, 2004; and *Kenny Scharf : El Mundo de Kenny Scharf*, Museo de Arte Contemporáneo de Monterrey, Mexico, 2006. Group exhibitions include the Whitney Biennial, Whitney Museum of American Art, New York, 1984; Venice Biennale, 1984; *Comic Iconoclasm*, Institute of Contemporary Arts, London, 1987; *Animations*, P.S.1 Contemporary Art Center, Long Island City, New York, 2001; *Splat, Boom, Pow*, Contemporary Arts Museum, Houston, 2003; *East Village USA*, New Museum of Contemporary Art, New York, 2004; and *Art in the Streets*, The Museum of Contemporary Art, Los Angeles, 2011.

Julian Schnabel was born in Brooklyn, New York, in 1951. He currently lives between New York City; Montauk, Long Island, New York; and San Sebastian, Spain. After earning a BFA from the University of Houston in 1972, he attended the Whitney Museum of American Art's Independent Study Program. A major Neo-Expressionist figure in New York in the 1980s known for his large-scale plate paintings, Schnabel's practice also includes sculpture, installation, writing, furniture design, and filmmaking. His films include the acclaimed *Basquiat*, 1996, and *The Diving Bell and the Butterfly*, 2007, for which Schnabel won Best Director at both the Golden Globes and the Cannes Film Festival.

Schnabel has been featured in many solo exhibitions, including presentations at the Contemporary

Arts Museum, Houston, 1975; a mid-career retrospective organized by Whitechapel Gallery, London, 1986 (traveled to the Whitney Museum of American Art, New York; San Francisco Museum of Modern Art; and the Museum of Fine Arts, Boston); and Museo Nacional Centro de Arte Reina Sofía, Madrid, 2004. Select group exhibitions include the Venice Biennale, 1982, 1997, and 2003; Whitney Biennial, Whitney Museum of American Art, New York, 1983; *Allegories of Modernism*, The Museum of Modern Art, New York, 1992; Bienal de São Paulo, 1994; *Lights, Camera, Action: Artists' Films for the Cinema*, Whitney Museum of American Art, New York, 2007; and *MMK 1991–2011: 20 Jahre Gegenwart*, MMK Museum für Moderne Kunst Frankfurt am Main, 2011.

Cindy Sherman was born in 1954 in Glen Ridge, New Jersey. A conceptual photographer, Sherman has been counted among the most influential American artists since her career launched in the late 1970s. Upon graduating from the State University of New York at Buffalo in 1976, Sherman relocated to New York City, where she currently lives and where she began making her seminal series *Untitled Film Stills*. With that series, and in most of her ongoing work, she has cast herself in various roles through her masterful use of costume, setting, and pose. The depersonalization and ambiguity, even with Sherman's strong presence in the imagery, is part of her works' allure; Sherman's true nature is undiscernible, yet the images address idealized women, while also relating to every woman.

Widespread acclaim for Sherman's work has led to numerous solo exhibitions across the globe, including shows at the Contemporary Arts Museum, Houston, 1980; Stedelijk Museum Amsterdam, 1982; Musée d'Art et d'Industrie, Saint Etienne, France, 1983; Saint Louis Art Museum, 1983; Whitney Museum of American Art, New York, 1987; Kunsthalle Basel, 1991; Tel Aviv Museum of Art, 1993; Hirshhorn Museum and Sculpture Garden, Smithsonian Institution, Washington, DC, 1995; The Museum of Modern Art, Shiga, Japan, 1996 (traveled to Marugame Genichiro-Inokuma Museum of Contemporary Art, Marugame, Japan; and Museum of Contemporary Art Tokyo); The Museum of Modern Art, New York, 1997; The Museum of Contemporary Art, Los Angeles, 1997 (traveled to the Museum of Contemporary Art Chicago); Scottish National Gallery of Modern Art, Edinburgh, 2003; and the National Gallery of Iceland, Reykjavik, 2010. A major retrospective of Sherman's work was organized in 2012 by The Museum of Modern Art, New York, and traveled to the San Francisco Museum of Modern Art; Walker Art Center, Minneapolis; and Dallas Museum of Art.

Donald Sultan was born in 1951 in Asheville, North Carolina. Sultan earned a BFA from the University of North Carolina at Chapel Hill in 1973 and an MFA from the School of the Art Institute of Chicago in 1975. In 1975, he moved to New York, where he currently lives. Sultan is well known for his reductively abstract large-scale paintings of still lifes and industrial plants.

Sultan's work has been exhibited extensively, including several major traveling solo exhibitions: *Donald Sultan*, Museum of Contemporary Art Chicago, 1987 (traveled to The Museum of Contemporary Art, Los Angeles; Fort Worth Art Museum; and Brooklyn Museum, New York); *Donald Sultan: A Print Retrospective*, American Federation of Arts, New York, 1992 (traveled to Lowe Art Museum, University of Miami, Coral Gables, Florida; The Butler Institute of American Art, Youngstown, Ohio; Museum of Fine Arts, Houston; Sheldon Memorial Art Gallery, University of Nebraska, Lincoln; Madison Art Center, Wisconsin; Orlando Museum of Art; and Memphis Brooks Museum of Art); and *Donald Sultan: In the Still-Life Tradition*, Memphis Brooks Museum of Art, 2000 (traveled to the Corcoran Gallery of Art, Washington, DC; and the Kemper Museum of Contemporary Art, Kansas City, Missouri).

Philip Taaffe was born in Elizabeth, New Jersey, in 1955 and studied at Cooper Union in New York. He now lives in New York and West Cornwall, Connecticut. Taaffe is associated with the Neo-Geo artists of the 1980s, who are known for appropriating historic abstract paintings in their own work. Taaffe has traveled extensively and often adopts multicultural motifs in his abstract paintings.

Taaffe's first solo exhibition was in New York in 1982. Since then, his work has been the subject of several solo museum surveys, including those organized by IVAM Centro del Carmen, Valencia, 2000; Galleria Civica, Trento, Italy, 2001; Kunstmuseum Wolfsburg, 2008; and the Irish Museum of Modern Art, Dublin, 2011. He has also exhibited widely in solo and group exhibitions in galleries across the globe, including numerous important museum exhibitions, such as the Biennale of Sydney, 1986 and 1996; Whitney Biennial, Whitney Museum of American Art, New York, 1987, 1991, and 1995; and *Carnegie International*, Carnegie Museum of Art, Pittsburgh, 1991.

Andy Warhol, born Andrew Warhola in 1928 in Pittsburgh, is one of the most influential artists from the latter half of the twentieth century. Warhol attended Carnegie Institute of Technology (now Carnegie Mellon University) in Pittsburgh from 1945 to 1949. He earned a BFA in pictorial design, with the goal of becoming a commercial illustrator. During these early years, he worked in the display department at Horne's department store. After graduating, Warhol moved to New York to pursue a career in commercial arts and became one of the most successful illustrators of the 1950s, winning numerous awards for his whimsical style of drawing, traced photographs, and other unique imagery. In 1961, Warhol made his first Pop paintings, based on comics and advertisements. The following year marked the beginning of his celebrity status when he debuted his *Campbell's Soup Cans* series, causing a sensation in the art world. Shortly thereafter, he began a large series of movie star portraits, including Marilyn Monroe, Elvis Presley, and Elizabeth Taylor. Between 1963 and 1968, Warhol worked with his Factory "superstars" and various performers to created hundreds of films, including *Empire*, 1964, *The Chelsea Girls*, 1966, and *Screen Tests*, 1964–66. In 1969, he cofounded *Interview*, a magazine that is still in circulation today. Warhol died in 1987 in New York.

Warhol was a prolific artist who produced numerous paintings, prints, photographs, drawings, sculptures, time capsules, and fashion throughout the 1960s, 1970s, and 1980s, in addition to writing books and hosting two popular television shows. Also in the 1980s, Warhol began to collaborate with young, up-and-coming artists on the New York scene, including Jean-Michel Basquiat, Francesco Clemente, and Keith Haring. Warhol has shown extensively around the world in both solo and group exhibitions. The Andy Warhol Museum opened in Pittsburgh in 1994, a collaborative project between the Dia Art Foundation, the Carnegie Institute, and the Andy Warhol Foundation for the Visual Arts.

Christopher Wool was born in Chicago in 1955. He now lives in New York and Marfa, Texas. The artist is best known for his "word" paintings, which are composed of large, black, stenciled letters on white canvases. He also explores abstraction through a variety of painterly techniques, including spray paint, silkscreen, hand painting, and stamps.

Wool has exhibited widely across the globe, including *Carnegie International*, Carnegie Art Museum, Pittsburgh, 1991; Documenta 9, Kassel, 1992; 6th International Istanbul Biennial, 1999; and *The 54th International Art Exhibition: ILLUMInations*, Venice Biennale, 2011. His solo exhibitions include *Christopher Wool: New Work*, San Francisco Museum of Modern Art, 1989; *Christopher Wool*, Museum Boijmans Van Beuningen, Rotterdam, 1991 (traveled to Kunsthalle Bern; and Kölnischer Kunstverein, Cologne); *Christopher Wool*, The Museum of Contemporary Art, Los Angeles, 1998 (traveled to the Carnegie Museum of Art, Pittsburgh; and Kunsthalle Basel); *Crosstown Crosstown*, Le Consortium, Dijon, 2002 (traveled to Dundee Contemporary Arts, Scotland); *Porto-Köln*, Museu de Arte Contemporanea de Serralves, Porto, Portugal, 2009 (traveled to Museum Ludwig, Cologne); and *Christopher Wool*, Solomon R. Guggenheim Museum, New York, 2013–14.